Design of Fire-Resisting Structures

Design of Fire-Resisting Structures

H. L. Malhotra

B.Sc. (Eng.), C.Eng., M.I.C.E., F.I. Fire E.

Head of Buildings and Structures Division
Fire Research Station
Borehamwood, Herts., U.K.

Surrey University Press

Distributed in the United States by
Chapman and Hall
New York

Published by Surrey University Press
A member of the Blackie Group
Bishopbriggs, Glasgow G64 2NZ and
Furnival House, 14–18 High Holborn, London WC1V 6BX

Distributed in the USA by
Chapman and Hall, 733 Third Avenue
New York, N.Y. 10017
in association with Methuen, Inc.

British Library Cataloguing in Publication Data

Malhotra, H. L.
Design of fire-resisting structures.
1. Fire resistant materials
I. Title
693.8′2   TH1065

ISBN 0-903384-28-0

For the USA, International Standard Book Number is
0-412-00121-7

Printed in Great Britain by Thomson Litho Ltd., East Kilbride, Scotland.

Preface

Provision of fire resistance for building elements is required for most buildings under statutory provisions or in connection with the insurance requirements. Various authorities issue guidance by listing deemed-to-satisfy constructions which satisfy their needs. Designers, when considering the adequacy of their design construction, refer to these to judge the suitability of a proposed structural solution. This approach has tended to stifle the provision of optimum engineering solutions and has separated designing for fire resistance from the rest of the design process.

Over the last two decades, research bodies in many countries have studied the behaviour of structural elements in fires and fire resistance tests, obtained data on the effect of high temperatures on properties of constructional materials and developed concepts to analyse structural behaviour under fire conditions. This has led to the possibility of computing fire resistance from a knowledge of fire severity and the structural design, and has consequently paved the way for considering designing for fire resistance as part of the normal design process. Many national and international committees are currently engaged on refining procedures which can be adopted by professional bodies, code preparing organizations and regulatory authorities.

This book has been written to acquaint the reader with the essential background to fire resistance needs and requirements, methods of denoting fire severity and determining fire resistance, design concepts and currently available techniques for assessing the fire resistance of structural elements. Data are provided on material properties so that appropriate values can be introduced in the design system. Individual chapters deal with the design of concrete, steel, masonry and timber constructions. The detailed treatment is not the same in all cases and is a reflection of unequal progress made by different material interests. Attention is drawn to the need to consider the fire behaviour of a total system, and this should include ensuring not only that a building will stand up to a fire if one were to take place, but, in many cases where the damage is not excessive, that it can be repaired and re-used.

The book should be of assistance to practising engineers in the design

v

office, to advanced students, and to those in local authorities who have to accept and approve designs. A number of educational institutions already include structural design for fire resistance in their curriculum or attempt to organize specialist courses. It is expected that they will benefit by the contents of the book and that it will provide a common basis on which to introduce the subject.

The author owes a great deal to his many colleagues in international and national technical committees with whom many discussions have been held and advice obtained. I am particularly grateful to friends and colleagues of the Fire Research Station who have helped with the preparation of the book at all stages.

H. L. MALHOTRA

Contents

Notations and Units

A	area (mm^2 or m^2)
A_c	area of the concrete section
A_s	area of the steel section or reinforcement
A_w	area of the wood section
B	breadth or width (mm or m)
C	compressive force (N or kN)
D	depth (mm or m)
E	modulus of elasticity
F	force (N or kN)
F'	revised value of force
F_c	compressive force
F_T	tensile force
F_{TU}	maximum force or ultimate strength in tension
G_K	dead load (N or kN)
H	height
I	moment of inertia (mm^4 or m^4)
K	a constant or ratio
L	length or span (m)
M	moment (kNm)
M_a	applied moment
M_u	ultimate moment
N	fire load
P	perimeter (m)
P_s	perimeter of steel section

P_i perimeter of the inner surface of insulation

P_s/A_s

or   shape factor (m^{-1})

P_i/A_s

Q heat energy

R rate of burning

S surface exposed to fire (m^2)

T temperature (°C or °K)

T_0 ambient temperature

T_s, T_c temperature of steel on concrete section

T_f temperature of fire gases, furnace temperature

U relationship between applied and ultimate load

V shear force

W external load on a beam, floor or column

Z lever arm (mm or m)

a a ratio or variable

b breadth (effective or reduced)

c specific heat (J/kg °C)

c_s specific heat of steel

d depth (effective or reduced)

d_c depth of compression zone

f stress $(\text{N/mm}^2 \text{ or kN/mm}^2)$

f_y yield strength of steel

f_{cu} cube strength of concrete

f_p extreme fibre stress

k thermal conductivity (W/m °C)

l effective length or span (m)

m mass

q_0 rate of heat transfer

t time (min or h)

α coefficient of heat transfer $(\text{W/m}^2 \text{ °C})$

α_c convective heat transfer

α_r radiative heat transfer

β rate of charring of wood (mm/min)

γ partial safety factor

γ_m, γ_f partial safety factor for material properties, loads, etc.

ε strain

θ heat energy

λ slenderness ratio

μ moisture content (volumetric or by weight)

ρ density (kg/m^3)

ρ_s, ρ_c density of steel, concrete

σ strength or strength reduction factor

ϕ thermal expansion coefficient

ψ thermal diffusivity (m^2/h)

ω emissivity

δ, Δ interval of time, temperature or deflection

Subscripts

c concrete or conductive

e equivalent

i insulation

m material strength/properties

0 at ambient temperature

r radiative or residual

s steel

T at high temperature

t total

u ultimate

v shear

w wood or windows

y yield

Special notations

t_e equivalent fire resistance (chapter 6)

A_v area of a window opening (m^2)

A_t total surface area of the inside of a room (m^2)

q_f fire load density (MJ/m^2 or $MCal/m^2$)

f_{yT} yield strength at $T°C$

M_{uT} ultimate moment capacity at high temperature

l_v shear span $= M/V$

K_v $= l_v/d$

1 Structural fire protection needs in buildings

1.1 Historical background

Considerable progress has been made in the understanding of structural fire protection since the earliest attempts to implement fire safety, although many modern approaches have their origins in this early concern. In a short history of the subject, Hamilton[1] shows that a fire in London as early as 1136 was soon followed, in 1189, by a London Building Act. Modern and contemporary references[2-6] illustrate the progress of fire protection activity after the Great Fire of London (1666) which dramatically drew attention to the need for building control as a means of fire containment. Building inspection for fire insurance dates from 1668, but structural fire protection first began to be investigated seriously in the second half of the 18th century.[4] The considerable advances in materials technology of the 19th century, making available substances such as gypsum plaster, concrete and rolled steel, enabled the first 'fireproof' structures to be built.[6] The accompanying refinement in building control regulations is exemplified by the Metropolitan Borough Act (1844) and the London Building Act (1894) which emphasized not only the fire-resistant construction of buildings, but also the provision of adequate space between them and of firefighting facilities.

The establishment of the British Fire Protection Committee (BFPC) at the end of the 19th century marks the beginning of a scientific approach to research into structural fire resistance. A considerable contribution to knowledge, particularly in the testing field, was made by the BFPC under the chairmanship of Edwin Sachs[8-10] whose original small experimental testing huts[7] were later replaced by the larger design shown in Figure 1.1. The BFPC was responsible for an international congress (London, 1903) and also for the first attempts at international harmonization of fire resistance testing, not to be attempted again until nearly 60 years later.

The BFPC ceased to operate after Sachs' death in 1920, but in 1923 a Royal

1

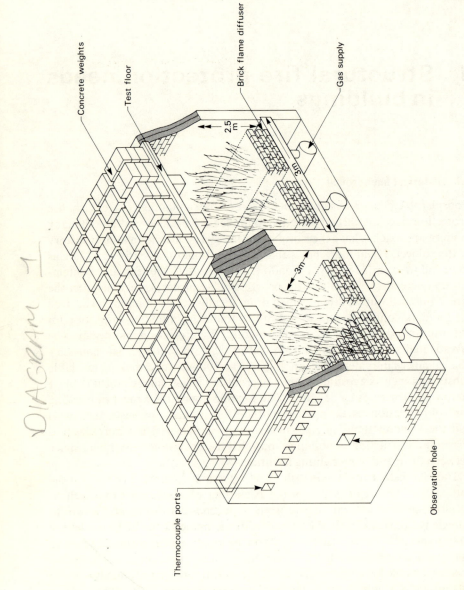

Figure 1.1 British Fire Prevention Committee fire test (1901).

Table 1.1 Some landmarks in the history of structural fire protection

Year	Event
1666	The Great Fire of London
1790	First fire test by the 'Associated Architects'
1844	Metropolitan Building Act
1890	Fire tests on floors in Denver, Colorado
1897	The Cripplegate fire—British Fire Prevention Committee (BFPC) started by Edwin O. Sachs
1901	BFPC test station at Westbourn Park
1902	Fire test facility in the USA by Prof. Ira Woolson at Brooklyn
1903	First International Fire Prevention Congress in London
1910/20	Fire test facilities in the USA and Germany
1917	ASTM—C19 (later altered to E119) issued with the Standard Curve
1932	BS 476 issued on fire resistance tests
1935	Fire Offices' Committee testing laboratory at Borehamwood
1946	Report on Fire Grading of Buildings (PWBS No. 20)
1947	Joint Fire Research Organization came into existence
1948	CP 114 issued with data on fire resistance of concrete structures
1961	ISO Committee TC92 formed on fire test specifications
1962–5	Building Regulations for Scotland and for England and Wales issued
1972	CP 110 issued with a section on fire resistance
1975–8	Joint Committee of the Institute of Structural Engineers and Concrete Society issued guidance on design of concrete structures for fire resistance
1976	Fire test facilities at Borehamwood reverted to an insurance-backed testing organization
1978	FIP* issued recommendations for the design of concrete structures
1979	BS 5268: Part 4: Section 4.2 on design of wood structural elements
1981	ECCS* issued recommendations for the design of steel structures

* FIP—International Federation of Prestressed Concrete; ECCS—European Commission on Steel Construction.

Commission reported[11] on fire prevention, and this was followed in 1932 by the publication of a standard (BS 476)[12] defining tests for fire resistance and based on research findings from the United States, Germany, and Sweden, as well as Britain. The report of a committee on fire grading of buildings set up in 1938 did not appear until 1946,[13] and in 1947 the Fire Research Station was established at Borehamwood, to become part in 1976 of the Building Research Establishment.

Table 1.1 lists some landmarks in the history of structural fire protection, mainly in Britain; however, other countries, particularly Germany, Sweden and the United States[14] have been active in fire protection studies, while international standards bodies have more recently encouraged other countries to develop an interest.

In the United States, as elsewhere, early studies[15] were given impetus by disastrous fires[16,17] and by 1905 the American Society for Testing and Materials (ASTM) had set up a committee to prepare fire test standards. In 1917 it issued standard specification C19 for a standard heating curve (Figure

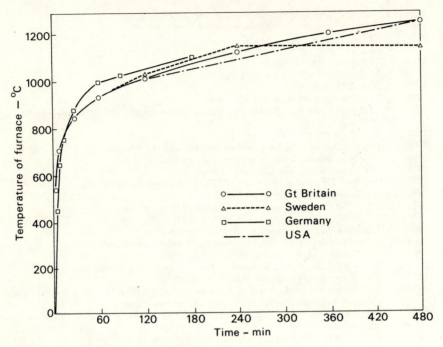

Figure 1.2   Standard time/temperature curves.

1.2). The similarity between this curve and those adopted by Britain, Germany and Sweden can be seen from the figure; refinements have since been made in the testing procedures but no alternatives have yet been proposed. The fire-testing and research community therefore owes a great deal to the early workers in the field whose initial concepts of fire resistance are still in use after almost a century.

1.2 The fire problem and fire statistics

Historically, concern with fire protection has tended to follow the occurrence of disasters, and the main objectives of fire prevention were seen as the protection of life and property.[18] Before 1946, however, there was no regular collection of statistics and hence no means of estimating damage and loss of life resulting from fires. This became one function of the Fire Research Station. Representative data (for 1979)[19] are shown in Table 1.2, and Figure 1.3 illustrates the increase in number of fires since 1946. A breakdown of data according to types of building (Table 1.3) shows that the greatest increase has been in dwellings.

Table 1.2 General fire statistics for 1979

Total number of fires	355 500
Fires in buildings	100 000
Fires in dwellings	58 600
Casualties—total	9 979
fatal	1 096
non-fatal	8 883
Fatal casualties in dwellings	865 (79 per cent of total fatalities)

Accompanying fire losses have shown a steady increase, due both to inflation and to the greater cost of replacing the contents and equipment in modern industrial buildings. Although the number of fires in buildings decreased slightly between 1974 and 1979, the direct losses increased from £194m. to £353.5m. Large fires in industrial and commercial occupancies are responsible for most of the monetary loss.

Of nearly 100 000 building fires reported in the 1979 statistics, 95 % started

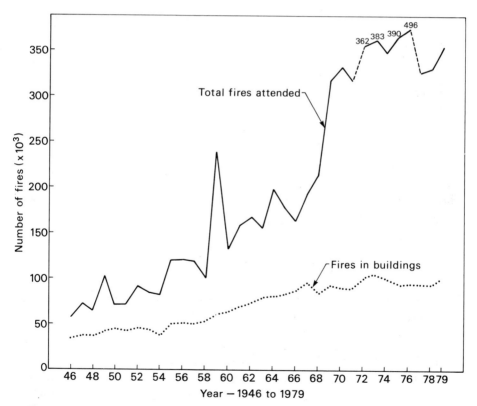

Figure 1.3 Fires in buildings (UK) compared with total number of fires.

Table 1.3   Fires ($\times 10^3$) in different types of building between 1958–1979

Type of building	1958	1960	1962	1964	1966	1968	1970	1972	1974	1976	1978	1979
Dwellings	24.3	27.6	32.5	35.0	35.9	43.1	45.3	52.9	55.1	51.1	53.3	58.6
Agriculture	2.6	2.9	3.3	3.6	3.3	3.7	3.7	4.0	3.3	3.2	2.8	2.8
Construction	1.5	2.7	3.7	5.2	4.5	2.0	2.2	2.1	2.0	1.5	1.3	1.3
Industrial[1]	5.9	7.1	7.8	9.1	9.8	10.6	12.3	11.3	11.4	10.0	9.3	9.9
Public buildings[2]	11.4	13.8	15.1	15.4	16.3	11.5	12.9	14.5	14.6	13.7	12.3	13.4
Others[3]	6.3	8.4	11.0	13.4	18.4	12.8	14.0	15.5	15.1	16.3	14.0	14.0
Total	52.0	62.5	73.4	81.7	88.2	83.7	90.4	100.1	101.5	95.8	93.0	100.0

[1] Excluding construction industry.
[2] Public buildings includes shops, offices, hotels, entertainment etc.
[3] Unknown and unclassified.

Table 1.4   Fire spread pattern for building fires in 1979

	All buildings	Dwellings	Construction industry	Other industrial	Hospitals	Schools	Shops	Hotels, hostels	Public assembly
Total fires	99 979	58 640	1 278	9 888	2 055	1 865	3 514	1 773	3 969
External fires	5 218	1 594	102	742	61	213	761	68	367
Internal fires	94 124	56 797	1 165	9 091	1 993	1 641	2 731	1 700	3 563
Contents only	55 787	36 026	242	6 233	1 669	740	1 237	1 144	1 927
Room structure affected	29 715	16 322	676	2 000	267	675	1 063	410	1 220
Spread to floor	2 959	1 710	49	253	13	112	112	44	135
Spread to other floors	3 928	2 391	32	437	25	82	205	81	220
Spread to other buildings	1 295	87	153	131	4	26	42	13	46

internally; of these 90% were confined to the room of origin (Table 1.4). Various statistical studies are available, including Thomas[20] and Baldwin and Fardell[21] the latter being based on differentiation between building types and the associated spread of fire. A related study[22] highlighted the consequences of preventing the spread of fires: a small reduction in the number of fires which become large was shown to substantially influence fire losses. Further studies on fire damage to buildings have been conducted by Baldwin and Allen[23] and North.[24]

1.3 Role of structural fire protection

The first concern when considering fire protection was to ensure the stability of the building. However, over the years fire protection has developed into a concept of which the five main components are:

(a) Preventing the initiation of fire
(b) Restricting the growth and spread of fire
(c) Containment of fire within specified boundaries—a compartment forming part of a building or the whole building
(d) Means of escape for the occupants of the building, and
(e) The control of fire by automatic devices and by active firefighting.

The fire protection objectives are realized by specifying requirements for passive as well as active measures. The former are part of the built system and are functional at all times, the latter come into operation on the occurrence of a fire. Passive measures include building layout, design and construction, while active measures comprise fire detection and fire control systems. For each of the objectives listed above the main fire protection measures are the following:

(a) Design and installation of energy sources and their proximity to combustible materials
(b) The nature and the quantity of combustible contents and the exposed surfaces in buildings
(c) Design and provision of compartmentation as well as separation between buildings and fire resistance of compartment boundaries
(d) Provision and design of escape routes, measures for smoke control and rescue facilities
(e) Fire detection and warning systems, sprinkler installations and the provision of firefighting facilities.

Items (a), (b) and (c) can be regarded as passive measures, part of item (d) is passive (escape route provision) and part active (some smoke control facilities) and item (e) is mainly an active measure. Measures may interact, i.e. the provision or the activation of one system can have beneficial effects on another.

Active measures	Passive measures
Detection	Contents and linings
Alarms	Escape provisions
Sprinklers	Compartmentation
Firefighting	Structural protection

It is thus seen that structural fire protection is intimately linked with other components of fire protection system, all of which interact and are influenced by the presence of other safety precautions. The main objectives of structural fire protection in a building can be considered to be:

(a) To maintain the integrity of safe areas in a building
(b) To restrict the size of fire and
(c) To prevent the building structure from becoming unstable.

The objectives are to some extent interdependent. Although the first is part of the measures to safeguard occupants, particularly in large and tall buildings, it also affects the others. The second is concerned with the division of buildings into smaller compartments to enable an easier control of fire but it also allows a more economic design of boundaries because of reduced fire resistance requirements. The third objective has occasionally been considered to be the sole aim of structural fire protection, probably due to the method of expressing requirements. Retention of stability is essential to achieve the other objectives, as it allows an easier control of fire and reduces the possibility of conflagrations. Chapter 3 discusses how requirements based on these objectives are applied to buildings.

References

1. Hamilton, S. B. *A short history of the structural fire protection of buildings particularly in England*. National Building Studies, Special Report No. 27, London, HMSO, 1958.
2. Reddaway, T. F. *The rebuilding of London after the Great Fire*. London, Jonathan Cape, 1940.
3. Davidge, W. R. The development of London and the London Building Acts. *J. R. Inst. Brit. Archit.*, 1914, 3rd series, 21 (11), London.
4. Stanhope. *Phil. Trans (A)*, 1778, 884.
5. Holland, H. *Resolutions of the Associated Architects in the Report of a Committee by them appointed to consider the causes of the frequent fires and the best means of preventing the like in future*—1793.
6. Burnell, H. H. *Description of the French method of constructing iron floors*. RIBA Paper 1853.
7. Holt, H. G. *Fire Protection in Buildings, a Practical Treatise for Engineers, Architects, Surveyors and Property Owners*. London, Crosby Lockwood, 1913.
8. Sachs, Edwin O. (ed). *The Testing Station of the British Fire Prevention Committee*. Red Book No. 13, London, 1899.
9. Sachs, Edwin O. *What is Fire Protection?* Red Book No. 1, London, 1898.
10. Sachs, Edwin O. (ed). *International Fire Prevention Congress—July 7–9, 1903. Record of the Organization, time table, papers and resolutions*. Red Book No. 75, London, 1903.
11. Royal Commission on Fire Brigades and Fire Prevention. *Report Cmd 1945*. London, HMSO, 1923.
12. BS 476: 1932. *British Standards Definitions for Fire Resistance, Incombustibility and Non-flammability of Building Materials and Structures*.
13. Ministry of Works. *Post-War Building Studies No. 20*. Fire Grading of Buildings—London, HMSO, 1946.
14. Babrauskas, V. and Williamson, R. B. The historical basis of fire resistance testing. *Fire Technology*, 1978 (Aug & Nov).
15. Sachs, Edwin O. (ed). *Some American Opinions on Fire Prevention*. Red Book No. 2, London, 1898.
16. *Engineering News*, Vol. 36 (August 6, 1896), pp. 92–94.
17. *Engineering News*, Vol. 56 (August 9, 1906), pp. 136–140.
18. Munro, John R. A history of fire prevention in buildings. *The Architect and Surveyor*. May/June 1970, pp. 17–20. July/August 1970, pp. 17–19.

19. *Fire Statistics— United Kingdom 1979*. London, Home Office, 1980.
20. Thomas, P. H. *Fires in old and new non-residential buildings*. Ministry of Technology and Fire Offices' Committee Joint Fire Research Organization. Fire Research Note No. 727/1968.
21. Baldwin, R. and Fardell, Lynda G. *Statistical analysis of fire spread in buildings*. Department of Trade and Industry and Fire Offices' Committee Joint Fire Research Organization. Fire Research Note No. 848/1970.
22. Melinek, Dr. S. J. *et al. The relationship between the chance of a fire becoming large and the chance of fire spreading beyond the room of origin*. Ministry of Technology and Fire Offices' Committee Joint Fire Research Organization. Fire Research Note No. 833.
23. Baldwin, R. and Allen, G. *Some statistics of damage to buildings in fires*. Ministry of Technology and Fire Offices' Committee Joint Fire Research Organization. Fire Research Note No. 805/1970.
24. North, M. A. *Fire damage to buildings, some statistics*. Department of the Environment and Fire Offices' Committee Joint Fire Research Organization. Fire Research Note No. 994/1973.

2 Meaning of fire resistance

2.1 Definition

It is not known when the expression 'fire resistance' was first used. There is evidence[1] that the term 'fireproof' was being used in the nineteenth century to describe constructions which would withstand the effect of fire. Although doubts were expressed about its validity, in the USA as late as 1907 ASTM issued a standard under the title 'Standard test for fire proof floor construction'. It seems that the expression 'fireproof' was used not only to denote some expected performance from a construction but also to indicate that the materials used were non-combustible. Insurance companies were in the habit of considering buildings as fireproof if non-combustible materials had been used. Fire Offices' Committee specifications spoke of steel doors as 'fire proof'.[2] The expression has also found its way into the electrical industry where until recently 'fireproof' motors were specified.

In 1914 a report of the ASTM Committee was described as 'Report of Committee on Fire-Resistive Construction', perhaps as a direct consequence of Edwin Sachs' initiative first expressed at the International Fire Congress in London in 1901. However at a later date an ASTM specification (E119) on fire resistance tests brought into vogue the expression 'fire endurance'. It had exactly the same meaning as fire resistance in the UK, but although it was considered by the technical committee of the British Standards Institution, it was not adopted.

A general dictionary definition of fire resistance is immunity to the effects of fire up to a required degree. The definition given by the British Fire Prevention Committee at the 1903 Congress[3] was more technically orientated but still lacked precision. A definition of fire resistance was introduced in 1932, when the first British Standard[4] (No. 476) was published, as 'that property by virtue of which an element of a structure as a whole, functions satisfactorily for a specified period whilst subjected to a prescribed heat influence and load'. It is implicit in this definition that the description 'fire resistance' cannot be applied to individual materials of which the element

10

is constructed but only to the complete element such as a beam, column, wall or floor. Reference is made to functions which these elements have to serve and conditions of heat and loading to which they may be subjected.

2.2 Testing for fire resistance

Tests for fire resistance conducted up to the beginning of this century were not standardized and each investigator devised his own technique. The first standardized approach was suggested by the British Fire Prevention Committee in 1903 at the International Fire Prevention Congress[3] as a testing plus classification system using a minimum temperature approach for periods varying between 45 and 240 minutes as shown in Table 2.1. The concept of duration of heating was used together with two levels of minimum temperature to be achieved giving six classifications. The descriptive classifications are not explained except that full classification meant resistance against the complete burnout of the contents of a building. A hose stream test was specified to simulate the additional damage caused by firefighting operations. No justification was provided for the temperatures specified.

A specification[5] issued in the USA in 1907 recommended a temperature of 926°C (1700°F) to be maintained for 4 hours, as specified in the New York building code, as approximating the heat of a burning building. Steven Constable, the superintendent of buildings in the city of New York, used this temperature in conducting a number of floor tests in 1896 and later, and it may be that the temperature represented the capability of the equipment used by him.

Meetings held in 1916 and 1917 in the USA by representatives of testing and research organizations, engineers and architects under the auspices of ASTM led to the issue of the first fire test standard[6] in February 1917 as C19, later renumbered as E119. The specification included a temperature time curve (Figure 1.2) extending to 8 hours. This demonstrated the first

Table 2.1 Fire test standard proposed by BFPC

Classification	Sub-class	Duration of test (min)	Minimum temperature °C (°F)	Hose stream application (min)
Temporary	A	45	816	
	B	60	(1500)	
Partial	A	90		2
	B	120		
			982	
Full	A	150	(1800)	
	B	240		

realization that a fire is a transient phenomenon and cannot be represented by a fixed temperature. The initial temperature rise was made more rapid than that obtained in tests conducted with wood fuel allowing for rapidly developing fires in certain occupancies. After 2 h the curve is a straight line with a slope of 41.7°C (75°F) per hour.

The first British standard on fire resistance testing was published in 1932 as BS 476 and described the method of test, criteria and a grading system. The constructions were expected to be 'full size', which means the size of an average room, roughly a 3 m cube. They were loaded to $1\frac{1}{2}$ times the maximum load they were designed to carry in practice, expected to support this load for 48 hours after heating as a reload test, and were subjected to the impact of a water jet if tested for 2 hours or more for a period in minutes corresponding to the hours of testing. The reason for the high test load was to allow for the fall of debris and the water used in fire fighting, also the reason for the application of the water jet. The reload test was supposed to take account of the loss in strength of materials during the cooling phase. There was no suitable test facility available in 1932, but the Fire Offices' Committee with the collaboration of the Building Research Station designed and installed three furnaces at Borehamwood to deal with columns, walls and floors, and these facilities came into operation in 1935.

The standard was revised in 1953[7] when changes were introduced to reduce the test load to the maximum permissible design load, as the overloading of elements in a fire could not be fully justified. A hose stream test and an impact test for non-loadbearing constructions were deleted owing to their non-representative nature—the phenomenon they were supposed to simulate did not occur in the manner employed in the test. A revision was made in 1972,[8] this time making use of the international standard, ISO 834,[9] issued in 1968 as a recommendation, under the guidance of the ISO technical committee TC92. The main changes were to introduce positive pressure in the furnace, as would usually be the case in a fire chamber, to specify an objective technique for measuring hot gas transfer through openings in walls or floors, and the deletion of a grading system for the tested construction. The main difference between the specifications was the retention of the reload test requirement in the British Standard. Table 2.2 shows the main changes made in BS 476 since its first introduction.

During 1981 the test specification will be considered for revision again and this time comparison is also being made with a draft directive (No. 1202) prepared by the Commission of the European Community through its directorate DG III responsible for eliminating trade barriers. The purpose of the Commission's activities is to harmonize the method of test for use in member countries over and above that possible or achieved by the international specification. The British Standards technical committee, FSB/1/6,

Table 2.2 Main changes in BS 476 test since its inception

Factor	1932	1953	1972
Standard curve	non-linear, similar to ASTM curve for 2 hours	no change	identical to ISO-834 curve
Specimen size:			
wall	3 m × 3 m	no change	2.5 m × 2.5 m
floor	3 m × 3 m		2.5 m × 4 m
column	3 m	3 m	3 m
beam	3 m		4 m
Load	1½ times design load	design load	no change
Reload test	after 48 hours	no change	after 24 hours or 80 % of heating period
Hose stream test	for tests > 2 hour	deleted	—
Impact test	for non-bearing partitions	deleted	—
Temperature measurement:			
furnace	no specification	bare thermocouples	no change
unexposed face	no specification	bare copper disc	asbestos covered copper disc
Criteria:			
insulation	ΔT 139°C at any point	mean ΔT 139°C	mean ΔT 140°C
integrity	no large cracks or fissures	crack or fissures ≯ 6 × 150 mm	cotton pad test
stability	no collapse	no collapse	for flexural member limit on deflection

has made a comparison amongst the three specifications and the main differences are shown in Table 2.3. One of the purposes of the current revision, which is expected to appear in 1982, is to provide greater technical detail in the specification to ensure that the procedure is not only repeatable but is capable of providing data for analytical estimation of fire resistance.

2.3 A rational approach

The earlier fire resistance test standards incorporated classification systems ranging from descriptive to alpha-numerical. The controlling authorities found it easy to make use of this system by specifying their requirements for fire protection directly in terms of the appropriate grades. Developments in the late sixties questioned the earlier assumptions about the relationship between fire load and fire severity and indicated the need for a more flexible system. This was partly made possible by indicating the precise performance

Table 2.3   Comparison of BS 476, ISO 834 and EEC 1202

Factor	BS 476: 1972	ISO 834: 1975	EEC 1202 (draft)
Furnace	No specification	No specification, recommendation in annexe on thermal inertia of lining	No specification, permissible fuels listed
Furnace pressure	Positive pressure in range of $15 \pm 5 \text{ N/mm}^2$ essential only when testing for integrity	Positive pressure 15 min after start of test $-10 \pm 2 \text{ N/mm}^2$	Positive pressure 5 min after start of test $-10 \pm 2 \text{ N/mm}^2$
Specimen	Conditioned to equilibrium	Conditioned to dynamic equilibrium	Conditioning to equilibrium for a minimum period, moisture content to be measured
Number	Single test acceptable	Single test acceptable	Average of two tests or single test with a positive tolerance
Loading	Maximum permissible loads used	Design load, preloading for at least 30 minutes	Design loads to be calculated and used, preloading as 834, details in loading and support conditions
Stability	No collapse, deformation limit for flexural members	No collapse	No collapse, rate of deformation for flexural members and columns
Performance expression	No grading system	No grading system	Semi-grading system

in test results without recourse to a grading system. Research was also started with the aim of analysing the behaviour of elements of construction in fire by studying their performance in the standard furnace tests and developing techniques for interpolation and extrapolation. As understanding increased there was a natural progression to the development of analytical design procedures for structural elements required to provide fire resistance for a specified period.

Most of the work so far has been based on tests conducted in furnaces on individual constructions or as a part of a research project. So the first objective has been to produce a mathematical model of the furnace test. These tests are not initially designed to provide an analytical basis for computing, and consequently difficulties have been experienced in completely correlating the calculated and the experimentally obtained performance. Witteveen and Petterson[10] have highlighted these differences in their studies and suggested the use of correction factors. The critical problem, which has not been fully resolved so far, is how to utilize the data from an individual test for computational purposes. Technical committees of national and international organizations are at present discussing improvements in the structural test method by establishing the precise properties of materials being subjected to the test and obtaining additional data on heat transfer and structural deformation during the test. With this type of additional data it should become possible to provide a mathematical model of each test, which will then facilitate interpolation and extrapolation of data, and also gain wide acceptability for the analytical approach.

References

1. Hamilton, S. B. *A short history of the structural fire protection of buildings.* National Building Studies Special Report No. 27, HMSO, 1952.
2. *Rules of the Fire Offices' Committee for the construction and installation of fireproof doors, lobbies and shutters.* Fire Offices' Committee, London, 1967.
3. *Standards of fire resistance of the British Fire Prevention Committee* (adopted at the international Fire Prevention Congress, London, 1903), British Fire Prevention Committee Publication No. 82.
4. British Standard Definitions No. 476: 1932 for fire resistance incombustibility. *Non-Inflammability of Building Materials and Structures,* British Standards Institution, London, 1932.
5. *Standard test for fire proof floor construction.* ASTM Proceeding, Vol. 7. American Society for Testing Materials, USA, 1907.
6. *Standard Methods of Fire Tests of Building Construction and Materials* (ASTM E119). American Society for Testing Materials, Philadelphia.
7. BS 476: 1953. *Fire tests on building materials and structures.* British Standards Institution, London, 1953.
8. BS 476: Part 8: 1972. *Fire tests on building material and structures Part 8: Test methods and criteria for the fire resistance of elements of building construction.* British Standards Institution, London, 1972.
9. ISO R834—1968—*Fire resistance tests. Elements of building construction.* International Organisation for Standardisation, Geneva.
10. Petterson, O. and Witteveen, J. On the fire resistance of structural steel elements derived from standard fire tests or by calculation. *Fire Safety Journal* 2 (1979/80), 73–87, Lausanne.

3 Fire resistance requirements

3.1 Regulatory control

All new buildings erected in the UK are subject to regulatory control for health and safety purposes. The safety requirements include provisions for fire protection but no single system applies to the whole of the country. In many countries, new buildings are subject to regulatory control, and provisions for fire protection are included. In Britain, four regulations apply[1-4] depending upon location, and there are additional specifications for schools[5] and hospitals.[6] Similar methods are employed by other countries, where either central regulations, or model codes which are adopted by local authorities, are applied.

Fire protection requirements include specifications for the fire resistance of buildings and the designer needs to be aware of the system so that he can satisfy the building authority. The architects' brief may include data on the fire resistance needs for various building components. It is nevertheless necessary for the designer to understand how the fire resistance requirements are arrived at, and to which elements they apply, as he may need to discuss with authorities his proposed solutions, particularly if these are unconventional. He has to satisfy the responsible authority as to the adequacy of his design, but if his proposed solution is not acceptable he can appeal to the higher authority responsible for their promulgation. The designer should also be aware of insurance considerations when dealing with commercial and industrial buildings. The insurance premiums are related not only to the nature of the risk but also the construction of the building and the provision of fire control systems, e.g. sprinkler installations.

The regulatory control for fire protection is concerned with safeguarding the occupants in the building where the fire may occur, minimizing risk to the adjacent buildings, and thereby avoiding conflagrations. To achieve these aims consideration is given to the planning, layout and construction of the building to control the growth of a fire, prevent its unrestricted spread, keep its size under control, safeguard escape provisions and prevent collapse of the building. To keep the fire under control it is necessary for the boundaries of the compartment in which it occurs to withstand fire attack without suffering collapse and without allowing it to spread to the adjacent compartment or building. The authorities are concerned with the size of a fire as large fires create serious problems for firefighting. Consequently where necessary provisions are made for the subdivision of a building into compartments. This is specially necessary for tall buildings and large industrial complexes. The risk to adjacent buildings can be minimized by spacing buildings a safe distance apart and by requiring the outer shell to resist fire penetration, although the latter cannot be achieved perfectly due to the presence of windows. Single storey buildings which are located a safe distance away from others and have good escape provisions for the occupants have a minimum of fire resistance requirements applied to them.

Although the control is concerned with the behaviour of the building as a whole, the requirements apply to individual elements of constructions. The assumption is made that if the individual elements are satisfactory, when together (as in a building) the whole should perform at least as well. In the England and Wales Regulations these are defined as 'elements of structure' and are identified as structural frame, beams or columns (excluding roof structures), floors and walls. Floors and walls are further sub-divided into normal floors and compartment floors; external walls, internal loadbearing walls, compartment walls, separating walls and enclosures for protected shafts.

In the regulations specific meaning is attached to the terms 'separating' and 'compartment'. Separating walls are those walls which separate houses in different ownership or occupancy, e.g. the wall between two semi-detached houses. Compartment walls and floors represent the boundaries of the compartment to which the fire resistance requirements apply. In some cases the division of a building into compartments in order to reduce the fire resistance requirements may be optional, in others it may be obligatory. Protected shafts contain the common services and access areas in multi-storey buildings, e.g. stairs and lift shafts. Figure 3.1[7] shows a building example identifying various construction elements to which fire resistance requirements apply. Terms used to describe some of the elements are not the same in all regulations but the concepts differ little.

The maintenance of structural stability is an important consideration of regulatory control. Consequently, not only all the main loadbearing members should retain their stability in a fire but also the others which provide structural support to them. If fire resistance requirements apply to a floor, the beam or column system or the walls which are providing structural support to that floor must all have fire resistance not less than that expected from the floor. The only exception is made for roof structures whose failure in a fire will not make the rest of the building unstable. This concept has led to some

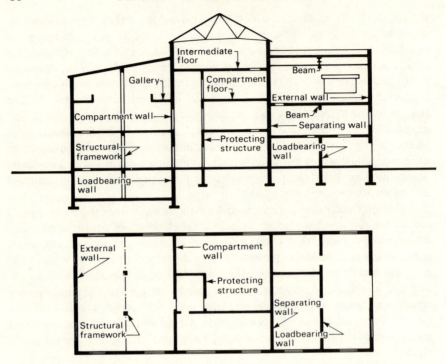

Figure 3.1   Various components of a building to which fire resistance requirements apply.

confusion with certain forms of roof constructions, e.g. portal frames for industrial buildings, and special instructions were issued to indicate the conditions under which the rafter section of a portal frame did not need to be considered for protection—see Chapter 12.

3.2 Methods of compliance

There are four ways by which it is possible to provide evidence of the ability of a construction to provide fire resistance, not all of these are acceptable to the authorities at present. These are:

(a) Standard tests to BS 476: Part 8
(b) Deemed to satisfy data
(c) Extrapolation and interpolation
(d) Analysis of structural performance.

The standard test has been the classic method of satisfying the fire resistance requirement. England and Wales regulations specify that if a specimen construction is subjected to the test specified in BS 476: Part 8: 1972 it should satisfy the relevant requirement of the test for not less than the specified period. This approach has tended to give the standard test a unique standing often not accorded to tests for other characteristics. Failure in the test by even one minute to satisfy the requirements for the period specified can lead to rejection of a construction. Authorities have to make assumptions about the performance of non-testable constructions, e.g. large systems.

The 'deemed to satisfy' data are provided in regulations and by-laws as an alternative to the standard test. These are supposedly test data expressed in generic terms but in their derivation much assessment has been done. The data are mostly tabulated and tend to be brief, consequently many necessary constructional details are missing. Tables of the same type are also included in various Codes of Practice. Not all of them have acceptability under the regulations. CP 110: Section 10[8] deals with the fire resistance of concrete structures; CP 121[9] includes data on masonry constructions; BS 5268: Part 4[10] describes the design of timber structures but no data on steel constructions are included in BS 449. None of these is directly acceptable under the regulations; the designer has to discuss with the authorities the adequacy of the construction. As data for various codes and schedules are proposed at different times they are not always fully compatible. A recent publication[11] from the Building Research Establishment includes not only tabulated data but essential information on constructional features.

There is no recognized technique at present for the extrapolation and interpolation of fire test data although in a few limited cases this has been done to produce tabulated data. The need exists and has been recognized by the standards organizations so that future test specifications can include guidance on suitable procedures.

The analysis of structural behaviour is not recognized at present by the authorities as a method of complying with requirements for fire resistance. In the GLC area it is possible for the designer to discuss such solutions with the building surveyor, in other parts of the country it could be done under the relaxation procedure. Until it becomes a recognized alternative to the other methods, designers will not have a strong incentive to use it except in special cases for large projects. In other countries, notably Sweden and France, the building authorities are more willing to consider analytical solutions. One of the purposes of this book is to promote this approach by making designers and local authority engineers aware of the possibilities of analytical techniques and therefore more amenable to their use.

References

1. The Building Regulations 1976. Statutory Instrument 1976 (No. 1676): Building and Buildings. HMSO, London, 1976.
2. The Building Standards (Scotland) Regulations 1971–1976. HMSO, London, 1976.
3. Building Regulations (Northern Ireland) 1977. Statutory Rules of Northern Ireland No. 149. HMSO, Belfast, 1977.
4. The London Building Acts 1930–1978 and the London Building (Constructional) Amending By-laws 1979. Greater London Council, London, 1979.
5. *Fire and the Design of Schools*—Building Bulletin 7. Department of Education and Science. HMSO, London, 1975.
6. *Fire Safety in Health Buildings*—Hospital Technical Memorandum 1. Department of Health and Social Security (to be published).
7. Mersey Regional Health Authority—private communication.
8. *British Standard Code of Practice for the Structural Use of Concrete.* CP 110, British Standards Institution, London, 1972.
9. British Standard Code of Practice CP 121: Part 1: 1973. *Brick and block masonry.* British Standards Institution, London, 1973.
10. *British Standard Code of Practice for the structural use of timber stud walls and jointed floor construction.* BS 5268: Part 4: Section 1.2. British Standards Institution, London (to be published).
11. Read, R. E. H. *et al. Guidelines for the construction of fire resisting structural elements.* Building Research Establishment report, HMSO, London, 1980.

4 Determination of fire resistance

4.1 Concept

The fire resistance of elements of construction in the United Kingdom is determined by conducting laboratory tests following the procedure laid down in BS 476: Part 8: 1972.[1] Most countries engaged in fire testing have standards for this purpose and over the last few years attempts have been made to harmonize these by the introduction of the international specification ISO-834. This chapter discusses features of the standard test in BS 476 with which a design engineer should be conversant so that he can use the test data with confidence.

The technique used for the determination of fire resistance is to expose a prototype construction to heating conditions of a standardized nature, simulating as far as practicable the use of the construction in a building. Measurements and observations are made to establish the duration for which the construction satisfied certain criteria related to its intended use in the building. The standard contains a specification for a standard temperature/time relationship representing the heating regime, data on the essential needs for the construction of specimens, methodology for the conduction of tests, instrumentation, criteria for assessing performance and the reporting of test results. The standard does not give any information on the use to which the test data can be put, the method of classifying constructions for their acceptability for regulatory purposes, or for the use of data for engineering design.

The fire resistance test is used primarily for three purposes: to be able to claim fire resistance for a given construction and hence have it accepted by the regulatory bodies, to assist with the development of new products and systems, and to establish essential parameters to predict behaviour by conducting tests as part of a research project. Much of the research in this field has been conducted by undertaking a planned series of standard tests with control on variables introduced. Often this requires measurements to be made in addition to those strictly necessary for the standard test. It is in this

21

area that some future developments are needed so that individual tests provide sufficient data for purposes of extrapolation and interpolation.

The results of fire resistance tests are expressed in units of time for which various performance criteria are satisfied. It needs to be understood that these times do not correspond to the duration of the real fire for which the particular construction may be specified. For example, it is misleading to suggest that a construction which has experimental fire resistance of 60 minutes will withstand exposure to an actual fire for the same period. As the duration of an actual fire cannot be precisely specified, the construction in a building may perform satisfactorily for a shorter or a longer period depending upon the characteristic of the fire.

4.2 Heating environment

The heating environment to which the sample construction is exposed is produced in specially designed furnaces with controlled fuel input to allow the

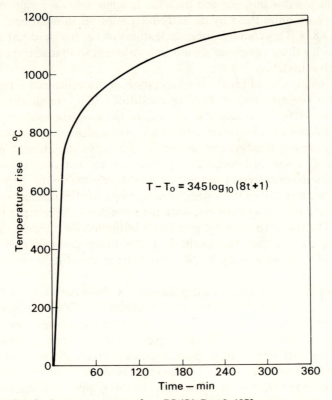

$$T - T_0 = 345 \log_{10}(8t + 1)$$

Figure 4.1   Standard temperature curve from BS 476: Part 8: 1972.

standard temperature/time relationship to be reproduced (Figure 4.1). The curve can be mathematically expressed as

$$T - T_0 = 345 \log_{10}(8t + 1), \text{ where}$$
$$t = \text{time from the start of the test in minutes}$$
$$T = \text{furnace temperature at time } t \text{ in } °C$$
$$T_0 = \text{initial furnace temperature in } °C.$$

Heating can continue for up to 360 minutes and the temperatures at a number of times are as follows:

Time, t (min)	15	30	60	90	120	180	240	360
Temperature rise, °C	718	821	925	986	1029	1090	1133	1193

A recent study by Castle[2] compares the heat transfer characteristics of three different furnaces by measuring total heat flux and the radiative flux for a 60-minute heating period. The results are shown in Figure 4.2 which clearly indicates that although in all three cases the standard temperature/time relationship was being followed by the furnace thermocouples, the heat received by the specimen constructions would be different.

The following heat flux values were found at 60 min for the three furnaces—

	Furnace A	Furnace B	Furnace C
Convective heat transfer, q_c	0.55	1.01	0.01
Radiative „ „ , q_r	2.2	3.15	·3.13
Total „ „ , q_T	2.85	4.16	3.14
Furnace thermocouple reading	917°C	927°C	965°C

This type of analysis shows that it is possible to obtain different heat transfer characteristics in fire test furnaces when the same standard temperature/time relationship is being followed because of differences in the type of fuel used, the location and distribution of burners, the arrangements for the evacuation of combustion gases and the thermal characteristics of the furnace walls.

A solution which has been examined and agreed by the ISO technical committee is to specify the exposed refractory material in terms of its thermal inertia (i.e. $k\rho c$ where k is the conductivity, ρ the density and c the specific heat for the material). An amendment[3] issued in 1980 suggests the following limit for this purpose:

$$\sqrt{k\rho c} \ngtr \frac{600 \text{Ws}^{1/2}}{\text{m}^2 \text{K}°}$$

The thickness of the lining with these characteristics does not need to be more than 50 mm. Walls of such low thermal inertia will increase in temperature

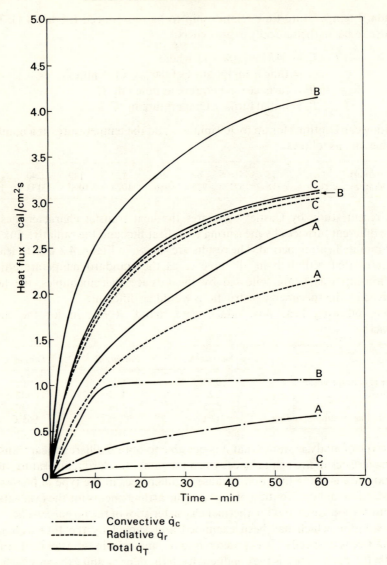

Figure 4.2   Heat transfer measurements in three furnaces.

quickly and therefore will radiate heat on to the specimen increasing the ratio of the radiant energy it receives in the early period of heating. In the example quoted in Figure 4.2, with such a lining all the three furnaces would have had similar radiative heat flux.

If the energy balance in a furnace is examined in a simple way (Figure 4.3) it

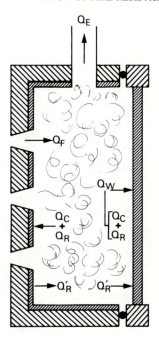

Figure 4.3 Energy balance in a furnace.

is seen that

$$Q_F = Q_W + Q_E$$

where Q_F is the total energy released by the fuel, Q_W is the energy received by the walls and the specimen and Q_E is the energy lost through exhaust gases and other leakages. Q_W is composed of radiative and convective components $(Q_C + Q_R)$. If the walls of the furnace have low thermal inertia they will not require much heat to raise their temperature to approximate to the gas temperatures and they will then be radiating heat (Q'_R) to the specimen. Consequently the specimen will acquire higher surface temperatures.

As Figure 4.2 shows, most of the heat transfer is by radiation and consequently differences in the heat transfer characteristics between furnaces will become smaller when low inertia linings are used.

Another desirable improvement would be to measure the value of the heat flux falling on the surface of the specimen. Whilst it is possible to fit a flux meter to the wall of the furnace, it may not indicate the precise flux received by the specimen. To be able to fix a flux meter to the specimen a special instrument is needed which is small, sensitive and capable of installation on the surface. Many of the present instruments require a recess to be cut which

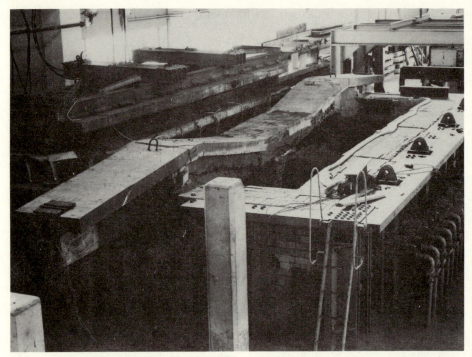

Plate 1 Development of plastic hinges in test on an R.C. beam.

Plate 2 Collapse of a concrete floor during fire test. (Plates 1 and 2 by courtesy of the Fire Research Station, Borehamwood, Herts.)

may not be possible in some cases and may damage the sample in others. Availability of suitable instruments could encourage the use of incident heat flux as a means of defining the heating environment in place of the present temperature/time curve.

4.3 Test specimens

The British Standard separates elements of construction into different categories and for each category requirements are laid down for size, method of support and the exposure conditions. The standard requires the boundary and support condition to be representative of those which exist in practice, but provides for simplified arrangements where these cannot be specified. The boundary conditions have an important influence on the behaviour of the construction and therefore need to be selected with care. In buildings, different elements are usually connected to each other so that interactions are possible and a redistribution of stresses and strains takes place. In tests only single elements are examined, hence the interaction with the adjacent members has to be simulated. Such simulations are not easy to realize because the precise interaction mechanism under fire conditions is difficult to predict, and problems also exist with mechanical reproduction of such conditions.

Another factor which has a bearing on the performance of elements concerns the level and the method of loading. The standard suggests that loads selected for test purposes should be those computed to generate maximum stresses in materials permitted by the relevant Codes of Practice. This has been interpreted as implying that for a given element the maximum permissible code loads are established. The standard does permit other, lower values to be employed where these represent more accurately the use condition. Loads are determined by using the characteristic or the mean values for material properties given in the codes or specified by the suppliers. These are not necessarily the actual material properties for the construction which may be superior in 95 % of the cases if the limit state concept is used.

The standard requires the load to be kept constant during the heating period. For loading systems using weights this creates no problems but with hydraulic loading there is a need to follow the deformation of the construction. When expansion of walls and columns takes place, controlled expansion is permitted to prevent any increase in load and when deformation or deflection occurs the jacking system must be able to follow the movement. This becomes particularly important when large deformations may occur before collapse. It is realized that in buildings the expansion of walls and columns is likely to be resisted by the adjacent components and increases in load are likely. As these cannot easily be quantified the standard has adopted the simple approach of keeping the loads constant.

Another feature which is virtually unique to the United Kingdom standard is termed the 'reload' test. The description is not precise, but the test construction is expected to retain sufficient strength to be able to withstand the continued application of the test load after it has cooled to ambient temperature. The first standard in 1932 suggested that this was to ensure that the building would not collapse after the fire had burnt itself out. However, the precise reasoning has not been made clear although references are made to firefighting and rescue services. The first standard in 1932 required the load to be reapplied after 48 hours, but the third issue (the current standard) has reduced the period to 24 hours and additionally a method of adjusted time is available as an alternative. If the construction fails during the heating period, its fire resistance can be construed to be 80% of this time on the assumption that had the test been terminated at this earlier point, the construction would have retained sufficient strength for it to support continued application of the test load. There seems little justification for this or the 'reload' test, but safety authorities find this additional safeguard a bonus. If the method has to be retained it needs to be termed the 'load maintenance' rather than 'reload' test, as laboratories do not want to remove weights and re-apply them. It would also be desirable to reduce the period to about 10 hours as by that time most constructions have cooled to ambient temperatures.

4.4 Performance criteria

Criteria for judging the performance of constructions are based on the premiss that the roles of different elements in a fire are well defined. This is linked to the basic fire protection concept of preventing collapse of the building and controlling the spread of fire by the maintenance of barriers forming fire zones or compartments. Fire barriers, i.e. walls and floors, can fulfil their function by preventing the transfer of flames or hot gases, and by restricting heat transfer through the construction in order to prevent ignition of combustible materials on the non-fire side. The formation of cracks and openings through which gas transfer can take place is restricted and limits are set on the transfer of heat by specifying temperature rise limits on the unheated face. These performance criteria have been named in the standard as *stability*, *integrity* and *insulation*, and can be expressed as below using limit state concepts:

Stability: the limit state is reached when the specimen collapses or unacceptable deformation occurs.

Integrity: the limit state is reached when cracks or other openings exist in a separating element through which flames or hot gases can pass which are capable of igniting a combustible material on the unexposed side.

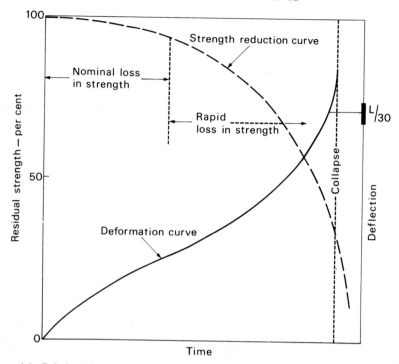

Figure 4.4 Relationship between deformation and strength reduction for simply supported flexural members.

Insulation: the limit state is reached when heat transfer through the construction raises the unexposed face temperature to a level considered unsafe for combustible materials in contact with the face.

The limiting conditions are defined as follows:

Stability: collapse, or the downward deformation of flexural members exceeding $L/30$ where L is the span.

Integrity: ignition of a cotton pad held close to an opening for 10 seconds.

Insulation: temperature of the unexposed face rising by more than 140°C as an average or by more than 180°C at any point.

The object of the limiting deflection specified for this purpose is to forestall actual collapse but to reach the point when collapse is imminent (Figure 4.4). Some countries[4] use the rate of deformation as an alternative or as an additional requirement. The usual relationship used for this purpose is

$$\frac{\Delta l}{\Delta t} \not> \frac{l^2}{9000d}$$

where $\Delta l/\Delta t$ is the rate of deformation per minute

l is the span, and

d is the depth of specimen

The limiting deflection is related directly to the span and the rate of deflection takes into account the depth of the element as well. However, both are more appropriate for simply supported rather than continuous or restrained constructions. The latter show greatly reduced deflections and rarely reach the limiting deflection values even when collapse is nearing.

The standard requires the results of fire resistance tests to be expressed in units of time for the duration for which various criteria have been met. This means that if all the criteria apply e.g. to a floor construction the results will be shown as minutes of compliance under each of the headings of stability, integrity and insulation.

4.5 International standards

Reference has already been made (in the previous chapter) to the international standard ISO-834-1975 which the British Standard closely resembles (Table 2.3). Other countries engaged on fire testing also have national standards, which were developed before the international standard came into existence, and consequently differences may exist between these and the ISO specification. Most countries are anxious to align their standards with international practice but in some the statutory provisions make it difficult to make the necessary changes. Countries differ for example in the number of tests and additional post-test requirements. Some countries require two tests for classification purposes, and take either the worst result or the mean value. Some specifications include a hose stream test of the type in BS 476: 1932, others also have an impact test for non-loadbearing partitions and doors.

The European Economic Community became concerned with differences between the member countries and asked the EEC Commission to prepare a common specification so that no trade barriers would exist on account of different standards. At the time of writing a draft directive reference 1202 had been prepared but not yet approved by the Commission. It is based on the ISO-834 specification but includes more detailed requirements. The ISO standard itself is subject to revision with a view to making it more detailed and improving its technical content.

One of the major changes that has been suggested is to provide a means for the extrapolation and interpolation of data. The current standards do not give any guidance on techniques to be followed for this purpose. Possibilities exist for dealing with some of the simpler situations where extrapolation is dependent upon computing heat transfer. Most heat transfer problems can be resolved, at least empirically, provided suitable additional measurements are made in tests. The extrapolation of factors which influence the integrity of the construction is not possible at present; systems need to be subjected to test to see if they have any design weaknesses.

References

1. Fire tests in building materials and structures—BS 476: Part 8: 1972. *Test methods and criteria for the fire resistance of elements of building construction.* British Standards Institution, London, 1972.
2. Castle, G. K. *The nature of various fire environments and the application of modern material approaches for fire protection of exterior structural steel. J. Fire and Flammability,* **8**, 1974 (American Institute of Chemical Engineers).
3. International Standard ISO-834—1975/4 Amendment 2. *Fire resistance tests—elements of building construction.* International Organization for Standardization, Geneva, 1980.
4. Van Keulen, J. *Comparison of heat transfer in several wall furnaces.* Report of the CIB Commission W14, No. 8, VI-74-17, February, 1974.

5 Fire resistance and fire severity

5.1 Fire severity

Unlike fire resistance, fire severity is not precisely defined in any standard or code. The expression is commonly employed to describe a fire in order to provide a basis on which it may be related to the fire resistance tests, i.e. tests using furnaces. Such a relationship is needed to assist designers as well as regulatory authorities to ensure that the correct safety needs are being met. Fire severity for this purpose may be defined as an aggregate measure of the heating conditions and their effect on a structure when exposed in a fire. It is not simply a measure of the temperature achieved in a fire nor of its duration. It takes into account both, as well as some other factors, such as the heat transfer characteristic of flames, temperature distribution etc.

It was the expectation of fire protection engineers when conducting early fire experiments that the data obtained were relevant to the general fire situation. The early experimenters saw no difference in the tests they performed on constructional elements and the exposure of such elements in a fire. Ingberg's work in the 1920s was perhaps the first acknowledgement that differences do exist and can be quantified. Since then other workers have developed improved correlations. More recently the need for clarification has been shown to exist when discussing fire effects. Most of the comparative work has been done by laboratories by conducting controlled experiments in purpose-built experimental rigs or old buildings. These are not necessarily a true replica of real fires but an attempt to simulate them. Therefore they could be regarded as an intermediate step, i.e. 'fire simulation' tests or experiments.

Most studies of real fire have to be made *post hoc*, i.e. the effects and consequences are studied by conducting post mortem exercises and tend to include subjective assessments. Fire simulation tests, on the other hand, are planned, fully instrumented and controlled to produce those conditions which are of interest. Data on correlation and the expression of fire severity are based mainly on such experimental investigations. Correlation with real fires is more difficult because of the random nature of such incidents and problems experienced in preparing an accurately detailed picture of such occurrences. Hence it is necessary to recognize that relationships for fire severity which have been developed and are used to predict the effects for fire occurrence are based mainly on fire simulation experiments, and whilst a stage nearer to the real fire situation they may not necessarily represent the complex system of a real fire. The knowledge so generated nevertheless represents an advancement on the mistaken notion of considering a standard furnace test as a replica of a fire.

5.2 Early experiments

The first experiments to relate the results of furnace tests to fire conditions were undertaken by Ingberg[1,2] using the facilities of the United States National Bureau of Standards. He simulated fire loads to be expected in offices, shops, warehouses etc. and made an attempt to correlate the fire severities in these experiments to those experienced by similar constructional elements in the furnace tests. He established a direct relationship between fire load density, i.e. the amount of combustible material available for combustion and fire severity. He also conducted a fire load survey for different type of occupancies and was therefore able to relate fire resistance needs for different types of buildings on the basis of the expected fire severity in them.

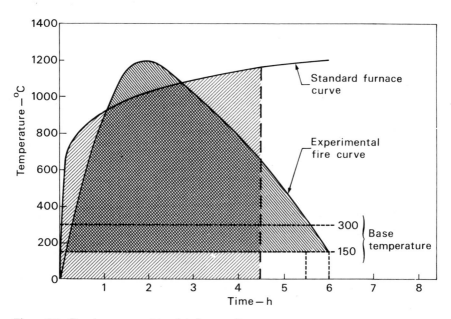

Figure 5.1   Equal area concept to relate fire severity.

These findings have been utilized by many building regulating authorities in arriving at the appropriate fire resistance requirement for buildings. The work has been analysed by Robertson and Gross[3] who defined the objective as obtaining information on the intensity and duration of fires in buildings so as to determine the appropriate conditions for testing materials and constructions and to provide guidance for applying results of such furnace tests to building design. Fire-loads used were in the range of 50 to 300 kg/m² of combustible materials per unit floor area. An equal area concept (Figure 5.1) was developed on the basis of this work by computing the area under the average temperature curve down to either the temperature of 150 or 300°C and equating it to the area under the standard temperature/time curve used in the furnace tests. As the figure shows, the difference between using either of the temperatures is less significant than variation between tests. Figure 5.2 shows the relationship between the fire load and the corresponding fire resistance times which has been used by many building authorities in drawing up their rules and regulations.

The buildings used in Ingberg's experiments were brick-built with rooms

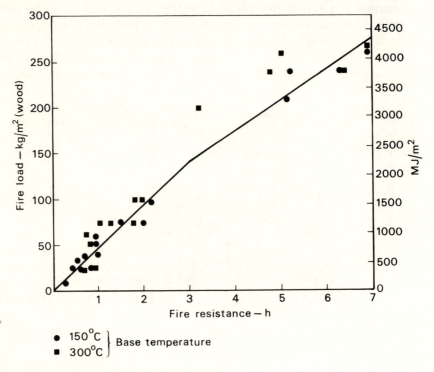

Figure 5.2   Relationship between fire load and fire resistance.

measuring $5 \times 10 \times 3$ m; later, rooms with four times the floor area were used. Whilst the distribution of the fire load and the ventilation conditions were important factors in the data obtained they were not identified as such. Ventilation was controlled by opening or closing window shutters to obtain the maximum fire severity at the height of burning. This was perhaps the first serious attempt at establishing correlation between the furnace tests and fires.

5.3 Recent work

It was not until the early fifties that fresh attention was paid to understanding the behaviour of fires in buildings. The work was initiated by Fujita[4] to show the possibility of modelling fire severity and was continued by Kawagoe[5] and Sekine[6] with the aim of developing basic procedures for numerical calculation of the heat balance. Kawagoe demonstrated the effect of ventilation, i.e. the area and the height of the openings through which air is made available to the fire for the combustion process to continue. The rate of burning of fuel was found to be related to the area of the opening (A) and the square root of its height ($\sqrt{H}$) and led to the expression $A\sqrt{H}$ which is consistently used in this connection.

In the early sixties experiments were conducted by Butcher et al.[7] in brick-built rooms ($3.7 \times 7.7 \times 3$ m) with controlled ventilation, and data were obtained (Figure 5.3) to show clearly the effect of ventilation on fire severity. The curves show average gas temperatures near the ceiling with fire loads of 7.5, 15, 30 and 60 kg/m^2 under two ventilation conditions 25% or 50% of the area of one vertical wall in which two windows 1.8 m high were located. This work demonstrated the need to explore in depth the effect of various factors on fully-grown fires. Under the auspices of a commission of the CIB (International Council for Building Research Studies and Documentation) eight research laboratories from different countries undertook collaborative research for studying fire severity, using models and burning wood cribs as fuel. This was the first serious international attempt to develop modelling techniques for fire and it has laid the foundation for most current concepts in this field. The experimental work and the findings have been detailed by Heselden[8] and Law[9]. Heselden showed that the rate of burning and temperature depend on the ventilation parameters, the size and shape of the compartment and the fuel density. He was able to relate the rate of burning of the fuel to the internal surface area of the compartment and the ventilation. Thomas et al.[10] had previously observed two types of fire regimes which were possible in compartments. With small ventilation openings the burning rate depended upon the availability of air, i.e. 'ventilation controlled fires' and with larger openings the burning rate was controlled by the fuel charac-teristics, i.e. 'fuel bed controlled fires'. A smooth changeover was found to

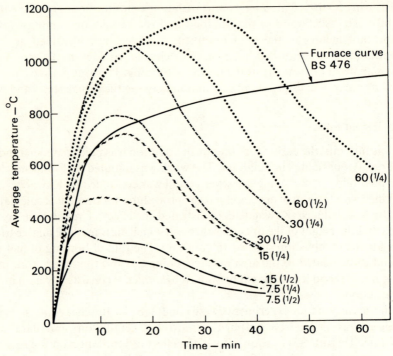

(60 (½) means fire load 60 kg/m² floor area and ventilation 50% of one wall)

Figure 5.3   Effect of fire load density and ventilation on fire temperatures.

exist between the two regimes (Figure 5.4). In the ventilation controlled fires R, the rate of burning,[8] was approximately $0.1A_vH_v$ kg s^{-1}. Law[9] used the data to develop an equivalent fire resistance concept by relating the temperature rise of steel sections in experimental fires and in furnace tests. The relationship suggested was of the form

$$t_e = \frac{N}{A_F} \times \frac{A_F}{A_v(A_t - A_v)} \qquad (5.1)$$

where t_e = equivalent fire resistance
        N = fire load A_F = floor area (m²)
        A_v = area of ventilation (m²)
        A_t = surface area of the compartment (m²).

The fire load has been expressed in terms of weight of wood or cellulosic based materials with a calorific value of 16–18 MJ/kg. However it is

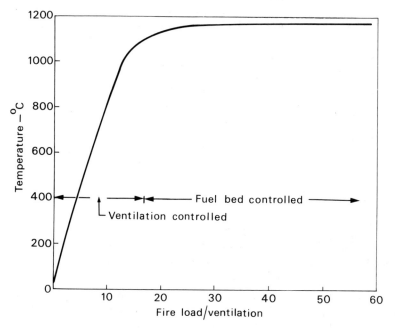

Figure 5.4 Fire temperature as a function of fire load/ventilation ($N/A_v\sqrt{H}$).

preferable to express it in appropriate heat units (MJ or MCal). Experimental and theoretical studies[11] undertaken in Sweden examined the heat balance in a compartment for a fully-developed fire and found that in addition to the factors already described, the thermal characteristics of the boundaries had an important role to play. A simple heat balance for an enclosure (Figure 5.5) shows that heat is produced by the combustion of the fuel and is lost to the walls and the outside through the exhaust gases

$$Q_F + Q_A = Q_G + Q_W + Q_E + Q_R$$

where Q_F is the heat produced by combustion
        Q_A is the heat content of the incoming air
        Q_G is heat used in raising ambient gas temperature
        Q_W is heat transfer to the walls, floor and ceiling
        Q_E is heat content of exhaust gases
        Q_R is heat loss by radiation from the window.

Ödeen[11] showed that the rate of burning was related to the 'opening factor'

$$\frac{A_v\sqrt{H_v}}{A_t}$$

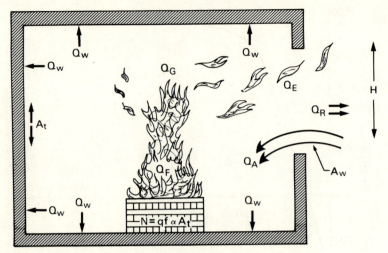

Figure 5.5 Heat balance for a compartment and its characteristics.

where A_v = window area, H_v = window height and A_t = total compartment surface area, and the thermal characteristics of the boundaries. Magnusson and Thelanderson[12] used the relationship to establish temperature/time curves for different opening factors and fire loads using a typical construction of concrete about 20 cm thick, having a thermal conductivity of 0.81 W/m°C and thermal capacity of 1.67 W/m³ °C. A typical example is shown in Figure 5.6. For compartment boundaries with different thermal properties, adjustments are made to the 'opening factor' and the 'fire load density'. The curves produced by this method are idealized, assume a constant temperature distribution within the compartment and a unique pattern of fire growth and decay. Pettersson[13] has used this approach and defined equivalent fire resistance by a simplified relationship which takes account of the thermal nature of the boundaries:

$$t_e = \frac{0.28N}{(A_t \cdot A_v\sqrt{H_v})^{1/2}} \text{ (min)} \tag{5.2}$$

The fire load can be expressed as a density $q_f = N/A_t$, then the relationship becomes

$$t_e = 0.067q_f \left(\frac{A_t}{A_v\sqrt{H_v}}\right)^{1/2} \text{ (min)} \tag{5.3}$$

$$t_e = \frac{0.057q_f \cdot A_t}{\sqrt{A_v(A_t - A_v)}} \text{ (min)} \tag{5.4}$$

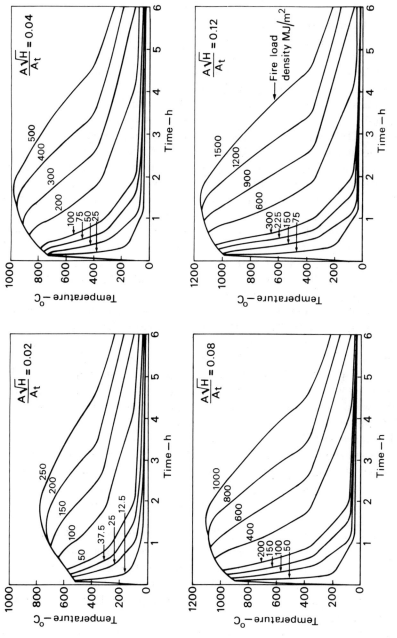

Figure 5.6 Theoretical temperature/time curves for different fire load densities and opening factors.

Experimental investigations which have been carried out so far have identified three main parameters which influence to varying degrees the severity of a fire to be expected in a given compartment. These are (1) fire load (quantity, type, distribution); (2) ventilation (area, height, location); (3) compartment (size—floor area, surface area; shape, thermal characteristics). The role of the *fire load* is critical and its rate of burning and the calorific potential determine the rate and the amount of heat that will be released in the compartment. Most of the experimental work has been on wood or wood-based products used as a fuel with more or less uniform distribution over the floor area. Only a limited number of experiments have been carried out with polymeric materials; these have different burning characteristics from wood and will in future be present in greater proportions in most buildings. In a large building used for storage or manufacturing purposes, the fire load may be distributed in a non-uniform manner with concentrations of the contents in certain areas. The role of *ventilation* has been studied extensively and data have been provided to show how account may be taken in computing its influence on the rate of burning. Most of the ventilation is provided by windows, hence it is a common practice to consider these as the primary source of ventilation. Openings in roofs can also be included in these calculations but sometimes it may be necessary to take account of other routes by which air may become available, e.g. doors. Doors, if assumed to be open from the beginning of the fire, can be treated as windows, but if closed and designed to have certain fire resistance they need to be included in calculations as a phased increase of openings. A normal assumption with reference to windows is that the glazing is destroyed soon after the start of the fire and full ventilation capabilities become available. With the increasing trend towards better energy conservation it is not known if this assumption is correct with double or triple glazed windows.

The *compartment size* is automatically taken into account when computing the fire load as fire loading is commonly expressed as a calorific content per unit floor area. The other important feature of the compartment is the surface area which is exposed to the heat released by the burning of the fuel. Some experimenters have taken the whole of the inside surface into account whilst others deduct the area occupied by windows. The thermal characteristics of the exposed boundaries have a role to play as boundaries of low thermal inertia ($\sqrt{k\rho c}$) will absorb heat at a lower rate, thus allowing the gas temperature to rise to higher values. Empirical methods have been developed which allow adjustments to be made to the other two characteristics, i.e. the fuel density and the ventilation, to compensate for the thermal properties of the compartment boundaries.

Most of the experimental work on fires has been carried out in small compartments representing typical dwelling/office rooms, of floor area

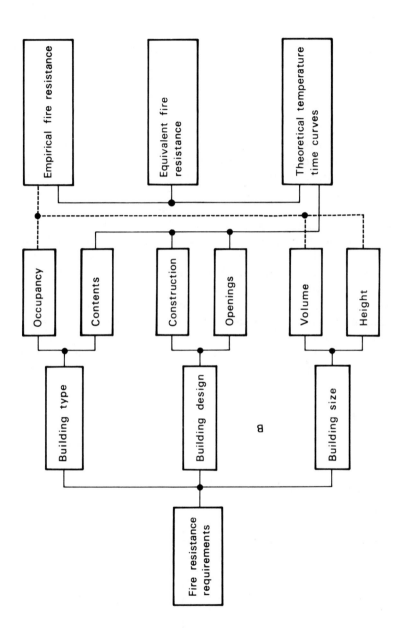

Figure 5.7 Methods of defining fire resistance need.

between 10 and 20 m². Industrial and commercial buildings have much greater floor areas and it is not known whether the burning pattern will remain the same. For example, in a large deep building, ventilation available for the fuel can be different near windows than it is in the depth of the building. It is known that in such buildings, as fire spreads progressively from one part to another, all contents do not become involved simultaneously.

5.4 Design approach

The main use that a designer can make of experimental data is to quantify the severity of fire which may be expected in a building and to match it to the design of the building so that it can be shown that the required level of protection is provided. He can make a number of choices, not all of which have an equal acceptability by the building authorities at present, but he should be in a position to consider these and put them forward as appropriate technical solutions, which can be of special value in certain unusual buildings.

Figure 5.7 shows three methods of expressing fire resistance needs and the factors which are taken into account. It indicates that a correlation is possible between them. The theoretical temperature/time relationship is an idealization based on estimation of the rate of burning of the fuel. It is not a true representation of a 'real' fire situation in which temperatures are likely to fluctuate in a random manner and vary from one part to another. The empirically based fire resistance requirements have been specified in the building codes for many years and have acquired a universal acceptability.

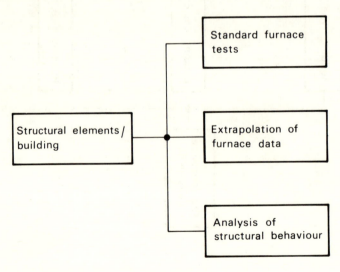

Figure 5.8   Methods of assessing structural performance.

Equivalent fire resistance allows the theoretical temperature/time relationships to be expressed in the empirical fire resistance units as shown in Example 5.1.

Figure 5.8 shows three approaches to ensuring that the structural performance of the building elements meets the requisite standards. The traditional method is to subject a prototype to the standard furnace test. Test data have been used to prepare 'deemed to satisfy' tables which for building regulation purposes have the same validity as test results. The analysis of structural behaviour from basic principles is being developed and solutions are possible for some of the simpler systems as explained in this book. As an intermediate step it is possible to develop empirical relationships derived from the furnace test data, their main function being to permit interpolation and extrapolation of data obtained from individual tests.

By matching the methods of specifying fire resistance requirements against compliance techniques (Figure 5.9) it is possible to see a number of possible routes which can be followed to satisfy safety requirements. They can be regarded as different levels of achievement or sophistication with Method 1 representing the traditional approach and Method 4 as a fully analytical process.

Method 1 is the current position in most countries where the empirical fire resistance requirements are satisfied either by the conduction of standard fire resistance tests or by the use of 'deemed to satisfy' data based on such tests. In Method 2 the specification of fire resistance follows the traditional pattern but two alternatives are possible for compliance purposes: (2a) represents the simpler approach of using interpolation/extrapolation techniques to extend the fire resistance data and (2b) introduces the concept of analysing structural behaviour of individual elements. In Method 3 the fire resistance specification is based on a knowledge of the combustible contents of the building and its other characteristics as shown in Example 5.1. Three possibilities are available for purposes of compliance, direct test data (3a) interpolation techniques (3b) or analysis of the structural behaviour (3c). Method 4 represents the highest sophistication possible and utilizes the theoretically determined temperature/time relationships as well as analysis of structural performance from first principles utilizing data on material properties and using behavioural models for materials and structures. Many of the current proposals have adopted a simplified approach for structural analysis by considering individual elements. As more sophisticated techniques are developed it should be possible to predict the behaviour of whole buildings.

At present in the United Kingdom, and most other countries, Method 1 is the normal approach although 2a is gaining a degree of acceptance. Method 2b is less common but some countries, e.g. Sweden and France, have officially recognized procedures and in others professional bodies are actively

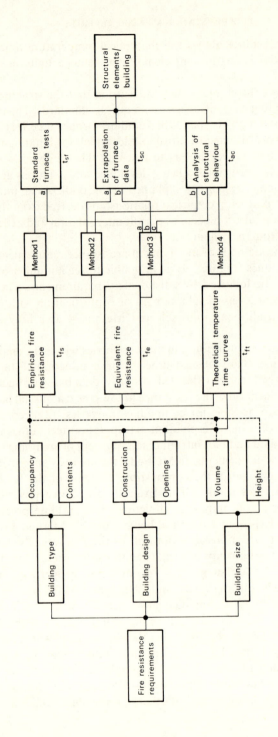

Figure 5.9 Different levels of sophistication in providing fire resistance.

encouraging the use of this approach. The publication[14] of the Institution of Structural Engineers has the aim of making designers familiar with this approach. Method 3a/3b has been used on rare occasions but as a matter of relaxation by the building authorities. This is the next logical step in the development of analytical procedures for structural fire protection. Once 3a becomes a practical possibility other developments will automatically lead to the acceptability of 3c. Method 4 is the objective of much research work which is presently in progress.

Example 5.1

Determine fire severity in a compartment of specified size and construction using the equivalent fire resistance method.

(a) Compartment size: $10 \times 5 \times 3$ m high
Windows in one wall: 4—2 m wide $\times$ 1.5 m high
Construction: dense concrete
Fire load: cellulosic based 50 kg/m² of floor area
Use relationships in Equations 5.3 and 5.4.
Window area $A_v = 4 \times 2 \times 1.5 = 12$ m²
Window height $H_v = 1.5$ m
Total internal surface area $A_t = (10 \times 5 \times 2) + (30 \times 3) = 190$ m²
Calorific value of cellulosic contents
$$= 4.3 \text{ MCal/kg} = 4.3 \times 4.18 = 17.974 \text{ MJ/kg}$$
Fire load density/unit surface area,

$$q_f = \frac{50 \times 50 \times 17.974}{190} = 236.5 \text{ MJ/m}^2$$

(i) Equivalent fire resistance t_e according to Equation 5.3

$$= 0.067 q_f \left(\frac{A}{A_v \sqrt{H_v}} \right)^{1/2} \text{ (min)}$$

$$= 0.067 \times 236.5 \times \left(\frac{190}{12 \sqrt{1.5}} \right)^{1/2}$$

$$= 56.9 \text{ min}$$

(ii) Equivalent fire resistance t_e according to Equation 5.4

$$= 0.057 q_f \frac{A_t}{\sqrt{A_v (A_t - A_v)}} \text{ (min)}$$

$$= \frac{0.057 \times 236.5 \times 190}{\sqrt{12(190 - 12)}}$$

$$= 55.4 \text{ min}$$

(b) If the compartment is constructed of lightweight concrete, Equation 5.3 allows an adjustment to be made. According to ref. 13, the opening factor $A_v\sqrt{H}/A_t$ and the fire load density q_f should be multiplied by a factor $K_f = 3.0$. Equation 5.3 then becomes

$$0.067 \times q_f \times \left(\frac{A_t}{A_v\sqrt{H_v}}\right)^{1/2} \times K_f^{1/2}$$

$$t_e = 56.9 \times \sqrt{3} = 98.5 \text{ min}$$

Equation 5.4 does not take this into account and the fire resistance remains at 55.4 min.

(c) The technique can be used to get an estimate of the fire severity to which a construction may have been exposed. In a multi-storey concrete building involved in fire in Brazil,
the floor area was $36.6 \times 18.9 \text{ m} = 584 \text{ m}^2$
the windows were 1.25 m in height, with a total area $A_v = 111 \text{ m}^2$

$$A_t = 584 \times 2.5 = 1460 \text{ m}^2$$

Assumed fire load for an office-type occupancy $= 30 \text{ kg/m}^2$
Total calorific value $30 \times 584 \times 17.974 = 314\,904 \text{ MJ}$

Fire load density $q_f = \dfrac{314\,904}{584} = 539.2 \text{ MJ/m}^2$

According to 5.3,

$$t_e = 0.067 \times 539.2 \left(\frac{1460}{111\sqrt{1.25}}\right)^{1/2}$$

$$= 124 \text{ min.}$$

According to 5.4,

$$t_e = \frac{0.057 \times 539.2 \times 1460}{\sqrt{111(1460-111)}} = 116 \text{ min.}$$

For the two cases studied when the construction is of dense concrete, the two equations give similar results.

References

1. Ingberg, S. H. *Fire Tests of Office Occupancies.* U.S. National Fire Protection Association Quarterly, **20** (1927).
2. Ingberg, S. H. *Tests of the Severity of Building Fires.* U.S. National Fire Protection Association Quarterly, **22** (1928) (1) 43–61.
3. Robertson, A. F. and Gross, D. *Fire load, fire security and fire endurance.* Fire Test Performance ASTM-STP 464. Philadelphia, 1970.
4. Fujita, K. *Research report concerning characteristics of fires inside non-combustible rooms and prevention of fire damage.* Building Research Institute Report 2N, Tokyo.
5. Kawagoe, K. *Fire behaviour in rooms.* Building Research Institute Project 7, Tokyo, 1958.
6. Kawagoe, K. and Sekine, T. *Estimation of fire temperature/time curve in rooms.* Building Research Institution Occasional Report 11—1963, Report 17—1961, Report 29—1967, Tokyo.
7. Butcher, E. G., Chitty, T. B. and Ashton, L. A. *The temperature attained by steel in building fires.* Fire Research Station Technical Paper No. 15, HMSO, 1966.
8. Heselden, A. J. M. Results of an international cooperative programme on fully-developed fires in single compartments. Symposium No. 5: *Fire Resistance Requirements for Buildings—a New Approach.* HMSO, London, 1971.
9. Law, M. Prediction of fire resistance. (Ibid.)
10. Thomas, P. H., Heselden, A. J. and Law, M. *Fully-developed compartment fires—two kinds of behaviour.* Fire Research Technical Paper No. 18. HMSO, London, 1967.
11. Ödeen, K. *Theoretical study of fire characteristics in enclosed spaces.* Bulletin No. 19, Division of Building Construction, Royal Institute of Technology, Stockholm, 1963.
12. Magnusson, S. E. and Thelanderssen, S. Temperature/time curves for the complete process of fire development. A theoretical study of wood fuel fires in enclosed spaces. Ci 65, *Acta Polytechnica Scandinavia,* Stockholm, 1970.
13. Pettersson, O. The connection between a real fire exposure and the heating conditions according to standard fire resistance test. *European Convention for Constructional Steelwork,* Chap. 11, CECM–111–74–2E.
14. Design 2. *Detailing of concrete structures for fire resistance.* Interim guidance by a joint committee of the Institution of Structural Engineers and the Concrete Society. Institute of Structural Engineers, 1978.

6 Properties of materials

6.1 Introduction

To understand the response of structures to the high temperatures experienced in fires it is important to have a knowledge of changes which occur in the properties of materials of which they are constructed. For simple systems it may be said that the rate of deterioration of material properties determines the fire resistance that the construction is capable of providing. As the structural systems become complex, the form of construction also becomes an important parameter. Normal design relies entirely on having data on material properties at ambient temperature, which is taken to be around 20°C for most buildings. Properties which will be considered in this chapter are those which influence the structural behaviour of the common constructional materials: concrete, steel, masonry and wood. Properties to be considered are not only those that affect structural performance but others which influence the temperature rise inside the construction. Protective materials will be examined in the appropriate chapter where their use is considered.

The material properties can be divided into four groups, as shown in Table 6.1 below, which includes properties which may not be temperature dependent, but may be useful in understanding fire behaviour. The division into different categories, e.g. physical or mechanical, is to some extent arbitrary, but it allows a convenient distinction to be made between

Table 6.1   List of material properties

Chemical	Physical	Mechanical	Thermal
Decomposition	Density	Strength	Conductivity
Charring	Expansion	Elasticity	Specific heat
	Softening	Strain	
	Melting	Creep	
	Spalling		

properties essential for loadbearing purposes and others which cause general physical degradation. Of the four materials listed only wood is subject to decomposition and charring, and only concretes of certain types and masonry constructions are liable to spall. Whilst some softening of steel will occur at temperatures in excess of 800°C, it is unlikely to melt at the maximum temperatures, around 1200°C, normally experienced in fires. A knowledge of mechanical properties is essential to understand the behaviour of loadbearing structures and to predict their performance by numerical methods. Thermal properties influence the rate of heat transfer into the construction, which under the transient heating conditions experienced in fires and in the standard furnace tests depends not only on thermal conductivity but also on the specific heat capacity of materials. This is often expressed as the thermal diffusivity of the material and is indicated as

$$\text{thermal diffusivity, } \psi = \frac{k}{\rho c} \, \text{m}^2/\text{h}$$

where k = thermal conductivity (W/m, °C)
        ρ = density (kg/m³)
        c = specific heat (J/kg, °C)

Another property which affects surface temperature during the early stages of exposure is expressed as thermal inertia, $k\rho c$, of the material. This is appropriate mainly for low density insulating layers and has been primarily considered in the design of the exposed surface linings of furnaces but may have some relevance for aerated concretes.

Engineers had been concerned with material properties for a long time but the effects of high temperatures had not attracted attention except in the design of furnaces, hearths and heating appliances. Structural materials were examined briefly by the British Fire Protection Committee and a publication[1] on concrete aggregates makes reference to properties of aggregates at high temperatures. During the mid-forties the Building Research Station issued a number of notes on the repair of damaged buildings and provided some data on the high temperature properties of concrete and steel. These were based on work carried out by Stradling[2] on concrete and steel. Most of the detailed experimental work on various materials has been undertaken by a number of institutes since the mid-fifties and a useful summary, particularly of the activity in North America, has been given by Abrams,[3] who deals with concrete, masonry and steel and makes reference to their use in fire-resisting construction. As the interest in the application of numerical methods for fire-resisting structures increased it was found that diverse data existed which needed to be co-ordinated. The international organization on testing and research on materials and structures (RILEM) set up a committee in 1979 under the chairmanship of the author to consolidate data on material

Table 6.2   Main materials and relevant properties

	Thermal deformation	Softening	Melting	Spalling	Decom-position	Charring
Concrete	✓	×	×	✓	×	×
Steel	✓	✓	✓	×	×	×
Masonry	✓	×	×	×	×	×
Wood	✓	×	×	×	✓	✓

	Conduc-tivity	Specific heat	Density	Strength	Elasticity	Creep	Stress/Strain
Concrete	✓	✓	✓	✓	✓	✓	✓
Steel	✓	✓	✓	✓	✓	✓	✓
Masonry	✓	✓	✓	✓	✓	✓	✓
Wood	✓	×	✓	✓	✓	×	✓

properties at high temperatures. With the assistance of international experts this committee will be publishing data in a few years' time on most constructional materials. One useful outcome of this work will be to identify differences in data obtained by various workers, caused primarily by the technique employed in the determination of properties. Gantvoort[4,5] has attempted a similar approach for concrete and steel data for use by a technical committee on the design of concrete structures in the Netherlands. The RILEM project is the most extensive one so far and it is intended to examine all the relevant properties for the four materials shown in Table 6.2.

One of the important results of recent work has been the recognition that in the application of such data a distinction needs to be made between studies conducted under steady state conditions and those under transient conditions. As a fire is a transient heating situation, properties under transient heating regimes are a truer representation of the behaviour pattern of materials in service. Some of the properties are different under the two conditions, particularly those dependent upon stress/strain relationships. RILEM[6] has recognized different methods of determining the mechanical properties of concrete (Figure 6.1). The most relevant can be described as follows:

1. *Stress/strain tests, stress rate controlled.* The specimen may or may not have a preload when heated at a constant rate (usually 1 to 10°C/min) to the test temperature, stabilized, and loaded at a constant rate to failure.

2. *Stress/strain tests, strain rate controlled.* As (1), but when loading after stabilization the strain rate is kept constant.

3. *Steady state, constant stress creep tests.* The specimen is heated to the required temperature, stabilized, and the load applied, temperature and load

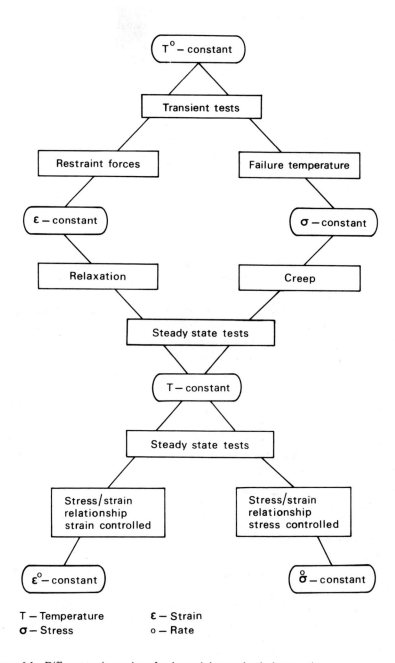

Figure 6.1 Different testing regimes for determining mechanical properties.

kept constant and strain measured over a long period. When the load is applied, instantaneous elastic deformation occurs followed by creep deformation.

4. *Steady state, relaxation tests*. As (3) up to the temperature of stabilization; when the load is applied the instantaneous strain is measured and kept constant by adjusting the load. The results show relaxation of the stress, i.e. final stress over a long period can be expressed as a percentage of the applied stress.

5. *Transient state, failure temperature tests*. The specimen is subjected to a constant load, and heated at a constant rate, and heating continued until failure occurs. The test duration is usually a few hours and the failure temperature is the critical temperature for the material.

6. *Transient state, restraint force tests*. When the specimen is initially loaded the strain is measured and maintained during the constant heating rate until the load approaches zero.

Stress/strain tests without a preload were customarily performed in the past but are not directly related to a practical situation, while tests following method (2) provide useful data on the residual strength after the maximum stress level is passed. The steady state creep tests are not relevant to real fires where heating may last only a few hours. The transient state tests have a direct application, with the constant stress approach (5), representing the majority of practical situations. In furnace tests, structural elements are required to be loaded to reproduce conditions considered normal for their use in a building, hence the relevant material properties should also be established under a similar condition for the data to be appropriate for predictive purposes. Consequently material tests for mechanical properties in which heating is applied without a preload on the specimen have less practical relevance. However, much information has been derived in the past under unloaded conditions and care is needed in its application to practical problems.

6.2 Concrete

Density. The density of concrete depends primarily upon the nature of the aggregate, and those made with dense aggregates have a density in the range 2 to 2.4 t/m^3. Lightweight aggregate concretes show a greater variation in density, as the aggregate covers a wider range, it can be as low as 1.0 t/m^3 and may approach 1.5 t/m^3 with certain materials. It is common to assume its density to be 1.2 t/m^3 for calculation purposes. One effect of heating concrete is to drive away free moisture as soon as the temperature in the section exceeds 100°C. Vapour migrates through capillaries to the outer surfaces, and on the heated side it would turn into steam, but on the cool side it can condense and appear as 'weeping'. The loss of moisture will reduce the density by a small amount, but for practical purposes this can be neglected.

Spalling. The likelihood of damage to concrete structures by spalling exists under the transient heating condition as steep temperature gradients exist across the section which can lead to damage in early stages of a fire. Three types of spalling are experienced in practice:

(a) Aggregate splitting, i.e. the bursting and splitting of silica containing aggregates due to physical changes in the crystalline structure at high temperatures. This is a surface phenomenon for dense concrete elements made with gravel or rock aggregates with high silica content. Its effect on structural performance is minimal and can be ignored.

(b) Explosive spalling—large or small pieces of concrete are violently pushed off the surface accompanied by loud noises. It usually occurs during the early part of exposure, e.g. during the first 30 minutes of a standard fire test. A number of detailed studies have been carried out but the precise nature of the complex phenomenon responsible for spalling is not fully understood. It is related to the nature of the aggregate, porosity of the concrete, its moisture content and the stress level to which the concrete is subjected. Siliceous aggregates, moisture content in excess of 2% by weight, section thicknesses below 70 mm and rapidly changing cross-sections induce spalling.

Dougill[7] has shown that explosive spalling is a complex reaction generated by the development of high vapour pressures in the pores of a concrete section causing cracks to be formed internally in a plane parallel to the surface. Under unfavourable stress conditions the exposed concrete layers are blown away with explosive force. Such occurrences can cause extensive damage and lower substantially the fire resistance of the structural elements.

The third type of spalling, known as 'sloughing off', occurs when the surface layers of concrete have become weak after prolonged exposure to high temperatures and are unable to retain themselves in position following the development of cracks. The arrises of beams and columns are the first to suffer such damage and continued heating causes outer layers to become detached. Most dense concretes are susceptible to this type of damage.

(c) The preventive measures against spalling are

    (i) Use of aggregates resistant to spalling (e.g. limestone and lightweight materials)

    (ii) Use of aerating agents

    (iii) Elimination of sharp corners and sudden changes in cross-section

    (iv) Insertion of anti-spalling reinforcement in the concrete cover

    (v) Use of plaster or other finishes to prevent a steep temperature gradient across the section.

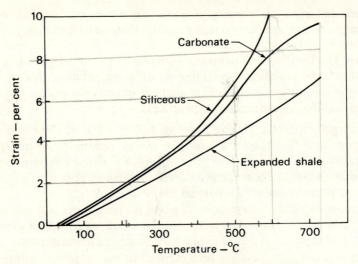

Figure 6.2   Thermal expansion of concretes made with different aggregates.

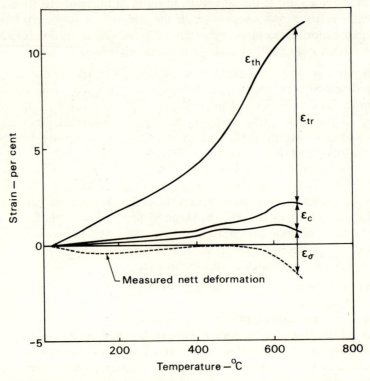

Figure 6.3   Different components of thermal strain.

Thermal deformation. The simplest form of thermal deformation is the expansion of concrete as its temperature is raised. Some of the early experiments by Cruz on the expansion of concrete using a dilatometer have been reported by Abrams[3] (Figure 6.2) and show that concretes can be divided into three groups on the basis of the aggregates used. At 500°C lightweight aggregate concretes expand by nearly half the amount shown by siliceous aggregate concretes. Data of this type have been obtained on specimens which are not subjected to any external forces during heating.

More recent work by Anderberg and Thellandersson[8] and Schneider[9] has shown that the total thermal strain exhibited by heated concrete consists of four components (Figure 6.3).

$$\varepsilon = \varepsilon_{th} + \varepsilon_\sigma + \varepsilon_c + \varepsilon_{tr}$$

where ε_{th} = thermal expansion undergone by concrete without external loads including drying shrinkage

ε_σ = elastic and plastic deformation caused by externally applied forces

ε_c = creep which is temperature/time/stress dependent

ε_{tr} = transient strain caused by heating underload due to chemical transformation in the cement paste

(Measurements on unloaded specimens of the type in Figure 6.2 show only ε_{th}.)

It has been shown that deformation of concrete is dependent upon a number of factors, such as type of aggregate, heating rate and the level of externally applied forces. Figure 6.4[8] shows the effect of external loads on siliceous aggregate concrete specimens when heated at 5°C/min under loads up to 67.5 % of their strength. The zero curve is the normal thermal expansion data on an unloaded specimen, and the effect of load can be seen to reduce this substantially at increasing values. At 35 % compressive load no net expansion occurred up to a temperature of 600°C, after which rapid contraction took place. For stressed specimens, deformation curves tend to become vertical as deformation rates approach infinity. Temperatures at which this occurs can be regarded as critical temperatures for that type of concrete under the specified loading conditions and the rate of heating. Data of this type are required as an input into the mathematical model to predict the deformation of concrete structures in tests.

Strength. As concrete is employed in structures primarily to resist compressive stresses, much interest has been shown in the effect of high temperatures on compressive strength. The results obtained from a number of such studies have been compared (Figure 6.5). Differences between the data on normal dense concrete are due primarily to differences in the experimental

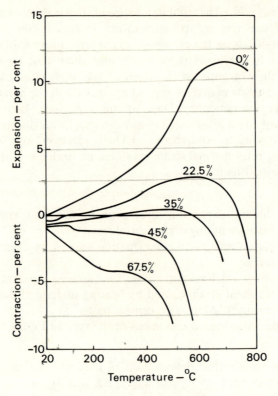

22.5% — per cent load, rate of heating
5°C/min, siliceous aggregate concrete

Figure 6.4   Thermal strain under different loading conditions.

techniques and to some extent to different locally available materials. These experiments were conducted by heating specimens to high temperatures without load, stabilizing the temperature and applying a load until failure occurred. It was appreciated that this does not represent a practical condition and tests were also undertaken by the author[10] by applying a preload of 20% during the heating period (Figure 6.6). This resulted in lower strength reduction at corresponding temperatures, possibly due to reduced deformation and crack formation. A similar pattern has been obtained by Abrams[3] on lightweight aggregate concrete although the rate of loss of strength is considerably less with the lighter density material. The strength of concrete is further reduced during the cooling phase and the residual strength can be as much as 50% lower than the hot strength.

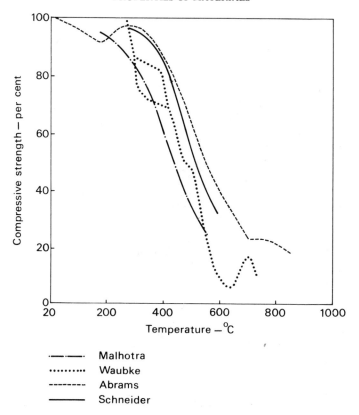

Figure 6.5 Compression strength of dense concrete at high temperature—no preload.

Elasticity. The modulus of elasticity of concrete is affected primarily by the same factors which influence its compressive strength. Only limited investigations have been made. Cruz[11] has examined the reduction in elasticity of three types of concrete (Figure 6.7) which shows a steady reduction for all three types. Schneider[9] obtained slightly more favourable results for lightweight aggregate concrete made with expanded clay. Anderberg's[8] results are also similar and extend to temperatures up to 800°C.

Creep. Creep data in the conventional sense have little practical application to the behaviour of concrete structures under fire conditions. They are obtained by heating specimens to a stabilized temperature, applying the load and maintaining it at a constant value for days to achieve consistency of strain. Structures are exposed to fires for a few hours only and temperatures are rarely stabilized. Short duration transient creep tests can however provide

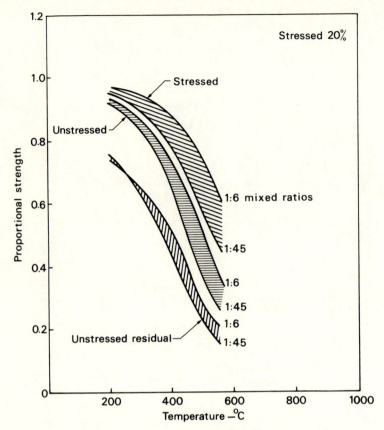

Figure 6.6   Effect of testing conditions on concrete strength (dense aggregate).

some useful information. Data on the basis of tests on gravel aggregate concrete are shown in Figure 6.8 for preloaded specimens. These show that up to a temperature of 400°C creep is not significant for short duration heating. It is affected by the level of the preload and becomes significant at higher temperatures.

Stress/strain relationships. A knowledge of the stress/strain characteristics of concrete is important in predicting its behaviour in a fire test. Anderberg and Schneider have both examined characteristics of a number of concretes under various test conditions. Figure 6.9 shows data for gravel aggregate concrete in which the specimens were not loaded during heating; consequently, up to the temperature of 400°C reduction in ultimate strength was small. With increasing temperatures higher strains and lower ultimate stresses were

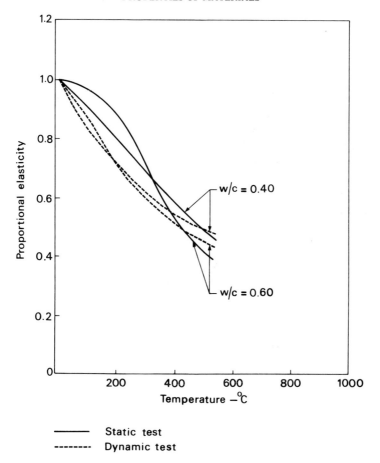

Figure 6.7 Modulus of elasticity of dense concrete at high temperatures.

observed. These data give information not only on compressive strength but also elasticity and ultimate strain. If however the strain rate is controlled during loading higher strains result (Figure 6.10) with a decrease of stress in the descending part of the curves.

Bond strength. Only a limited amount of work has been carried out on bond strength at high temperatures. There is no uniformity in test procedures and this has often led to differences in results. The surface of bars is a critical factor, deformed bars or plain bars with rusted rough surface showing higher bond strength at high temperatures than smooth plain bars. Type of concrete is another important factor; concretes with lower thermal strain charac-

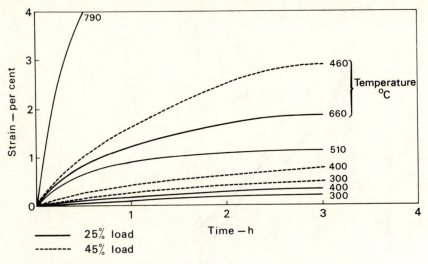

Figure 6.8   Short duration creep tests with preload (dense concrete).

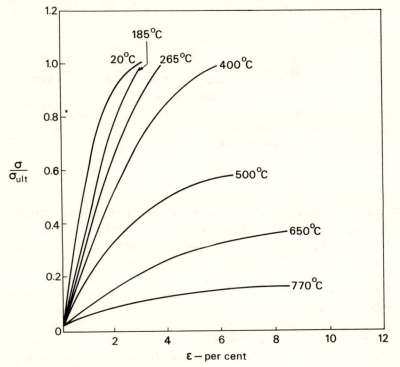

Figure 6.9   Stress/strain relationships for dense concrete (no preload—method 1).

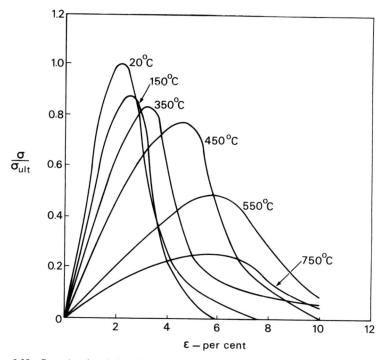

Figure 6.10 Stress/strain relationships for dense concrete (no preload—method 2).

teristics retain higher bond strength values. Figure 6.11 shows results obtained on a number of steels by Diederichs[12] at 400°C. Deformed bars retain twice as much bond strength as plain bars, and the decrease in bond strength follows the same pattern as the loss in compressive strength.

Conductivity. Thermal conductivity of concrete depends upon the nature of the aggregate, porosity of the concrete and, until dry, on the moisture content. In fires the moisture is driven out and therefore primary interest is in the conductivity of dry concrete. Harmathy[13] has examined various concretes and obtained performance bands (Figure 6.12). It can be seen that for dense concretes conductivity decreases with increasing temperature but for light-weight aggregate concretes the decrease is nominal. Other workers have found similar trends, although the actual values tend to differ between investigations due to variations in materials and experimental techniques.

Specific heat. In Figure 6.13 Harmathy's data on specific heat are compared with that obtained by Colette[14] and Ödeen.[15] It shows an increase in specific heat as temperature increases but also demonstrates the variability in results.

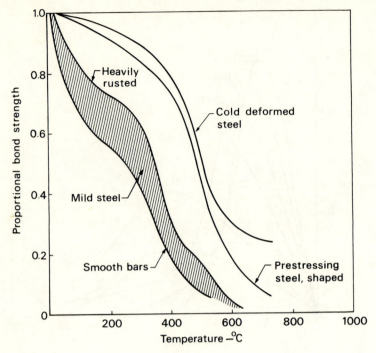

Figure 6.11   Reduction of bond strength for different steels.

Diffusivity. Thermal diffusivity data allow heat transfer to be computed for concrete structures. As thermal diffusivity values are derived from data on conductivity and specific heat, any difference in these will be reflected in the computed values. Figure 6.14 shows Harmathy's data plotted as two bands for dense and lightweight aggregate concretes. There is a decrease in diffusivity as temperature increases, i.e. rate of heat transfer is decreased, and after 600°C the differences between various concretes become less significant and only slight changes are indicated by the shape of the curves.

6.3 Steel

There are two distinct ways in which steel is used in building construction — either as a structural material or as reinforcement in concrete. In the first case the steel sections are of substantial size, rolled into various shapes and connected to steel or concrete elements. As reinforcement, the material is in the shape of bars, wires or tendons which may have a plain or deformed surface and in some cases these may have surface indentations or ribs to

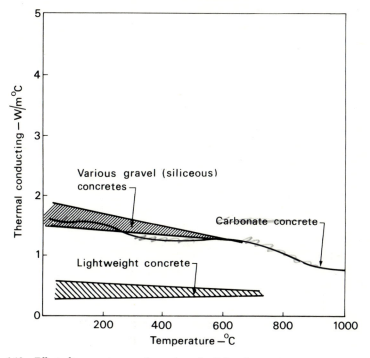

Figure 6.12 Effect of temperature on thermal conductivity of concrete.

improve bond. For purposes of considering their properties steel can be divided into three main categories.

(a) *Structural steel* (BS 4360), grades 43 and 50, having the following nominal properties:

Grade	Yield strength	Ultimate tensile strength	Design strength
43A	250 N/mm²	440 N/mm²	165 N/mm²
50B	350 N/mm²	580 N/mm²	230 N/mm²

(b) *Reinforcing bars* (BS 4449) may be of hot rolled mild steel or high yield steel; the latter are usually provided with ribs. Cold worked high yield steel (BS 4461) can also be used for such work, and is usually available as deformed bars. Mild steel is used less and less as main or primary reinforcement, as either high yield or cold worked steel provide more economic design.

Type	Yield strength	Ultimate tensile strength	Design strength
Mild steel	250 N/mm²	315 N/mm²	210 N/mm²
High yield steel	410 N/mm²	490 N/mm²	350 N/mm²
Cold worked steel	425–460* N/mm²	550 N/mm²	370–400* N/mm²

* depending upon the diameter of the bar.

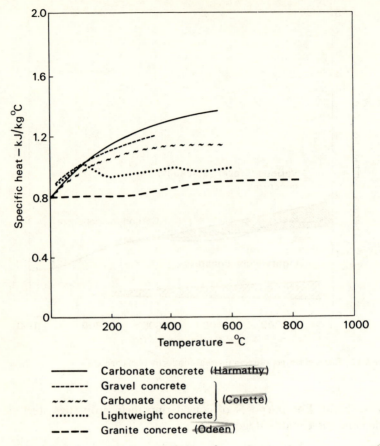

Figure 6.13   Effect of temperature on specific heat of concrete

(c) *Prestressing steel* (BS 2691, 3617) can be in the form of individual wires in diameters 3 to 7 mm or as strands, consisting of 7 or more wires, in diameters from 6.4 to 15.2 mm. In special cases alloy steel bars have also been used in post-tensioned systems.

Type	0.2% proof stress	Characteristic strength
Wire	1330 N/mm²	1570 N/mm²
Strand	38–193* KN	44–227* KN

* depending upon strand diameter.

The European system of steel specification is different—the steels are defined by their nature and the nominal strength characteristics; e.g. 230/340 hot rolled reinforcing bars have a nominal yield strength of 230 N/mm² and an ultimate strength of 340 N/mm². Prestressing steels are indicated by the

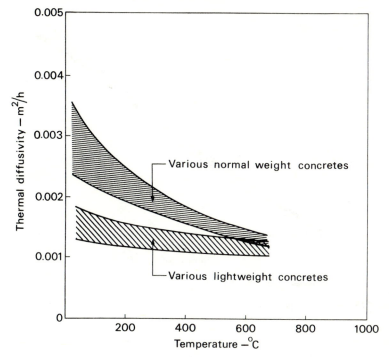

Figure 6.14 Effect of temperature on thermal diffusivity of concrete.

ultimate tensile strength only. Rolled sections have a letter abbreviation indicating the shape, followed by a figure denoting the design strength, e.g. IPE 140. The density of steel is unaffected by high temperature and is taken to be 7850 kg/m³.

Unlike concrete, steel has properties which are easily measured under either steady-state or transient heating conditions. Steady state tests have been more common in the past where the sample is heated, stabilized at a given temperature and loaded under constant stress or constant strain conditions to failure. Transient tests require a pre-application of the load and heating at a specified rate and establishing deformation characteristics, stress-strain relationships, or failure temperatures.

Thermal deformation. In measuring deformation of steel, the total strain consists of thermal strain, instantaneous stress-related strain and creep-strain which is time-dependent. Unlike concrete, it does not undergo transient strain. In this case,

$$\varepsilon = \varepsilon_{th} + \varepsilon_{\sigma} + \varepsilon_c$$

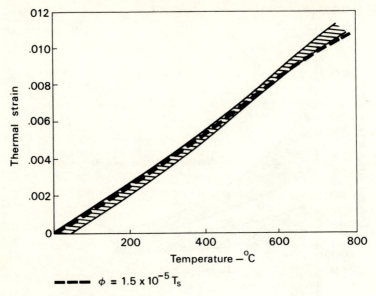

Figure 6.15   Thermal expansion of steel.

where ε_{th} is the thermal strain of the unstressed specimen
   ε_{σ} is the instantaneous strain, and
   ε_c is the time/stress dependent creep strain.

ε_{th} is also referred to as the *thermal expansion* of steel as commonly determined by heating steel specimens to various temperatures and measuring the increase in length. Figure 6.15 shows experimental data[16] which apply to most common steels.

$$\phi = \frac{\Delta l}{l} = (0.4 \times 10^{-8}T_s^2) + (1.2 \times 10^{-5}T_s) - (3 \times 10^{-4})\,\text{m/m}$$

where ϕ is the coefficient of thermal expansion
   Δl is the increase in length
   l is the original length, and
   T_s is the temperature rise of the steel.

An approximate simplification represented by a straight line is

$$\phi = 1.4 \times 10^{-5}T_s\,\text{m/m}$$

Strength. Strength properties of steel have been examined in great detail by many workers, but confusion often exists as to the precise implication of the measurements made. The classic stress/strain curves for mild steel are shown

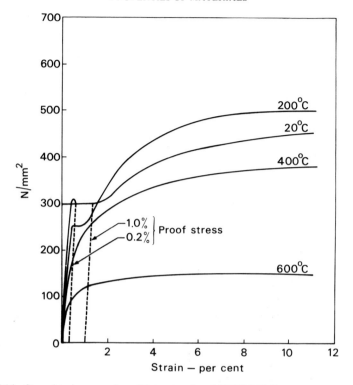

Figure 6.16 Stress/strain curves for mild structural steel (ASTM A36).

in Figure 6.16. Curves of this type allow three important parameters to be determined: the point at which first yielding of the section is observed (strain occurs without any increase in stress); 0.2 % proof stress (i.e. the stress under which strain of 0.2 % is recorded); and the ultimate strength (when rupture of the section takes place). The early part of the curve when the principle of proportionality applies allows the modulus of elasticity to be determined. Different steels have different stress/strain diagrams, and prestressing steels in particular (Figure 6.17) do not have a well-defined limit of proportionality or a yield point. In their case it is customary to consider the ultimate strength as the primary parameter and 0.2 % proof stress as a means for indicating permissible stresses.

On heating there is an increase in the ultimate strength of structural steel at temperatures up to 300°C, after which the strength is progressively reduced.[17,18] An important temperature effect is the gradual disappearance of a well-defined yield point and the limit of proportionality. This has also led to the development of the secant modulus of elasticity. Prestressing steels do not

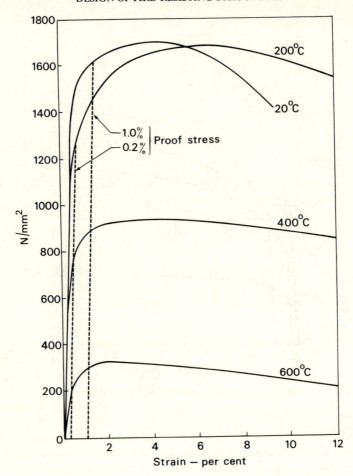

Figure 6.17 Stress/strain curves for cold drawn prestressing steel (ASTM A421).

show the increase in strength at low temperatures[19] and lose strength at somewhat faster rate. Abrams[3] has compared the strengths of three American steels (Figure 6.18) to show that cold drawn prestressing steel loses strength at a more rapid rate. Similarly data for different types of European reinforcing steels (reinforcing bars and prestressing tenders) have been given by Gantvoort[5] in a literature survey. More recently in the United Kingdom the British Steel Corporation Laboratories[20] have tested a number of Grade 43 and 50 samples, similar to that used in beams tested for fire resistance, this provided data (Figure 6.19) on their 0.2 % and 1.0 % proof stress. The data are comparable to those obtained by Skinner in Australia. The University of

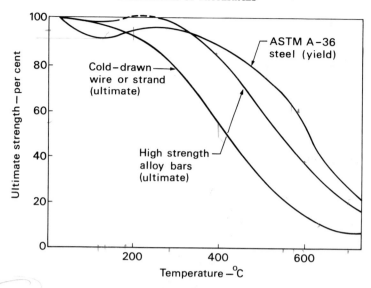

Figure 6.18 Ultimate strength of some steels at high temperature.

Aston in Birmingham[21] has examined the currently available reinforcing and prestressing steels in the United Kingdom and provided data on their ultimate strength as well as proof stress (Figures 6.20 and 6.21).

Modulus of elasticity. The modulus of elasticity has been examined by Copier[22] for structural steel and by Anderberg[17] for reinforcing steel (Figures 6.22 and 6.23). Both show a steady reduction and there are differences between the two groups as well as between individual steels in each group.

Creep. Although in fires transient creep strain is of interest, direct measurement of creep strain is possible only in steady state tests. It has been found that up to a temperature of 450°C strain due to primary and secondary creep is not very significant. Above this temperature stress and temperature history influence the amount of creep strain expected.

Figure 6.24 gives an example of data on structural steel and prestressing steel obtained by Harmathy.[20] Analytical models have also been developed initially by Down[23] and later improved by other workers. For each type of steel a creep model has to be developed.

Stress/strain relationships. Only a limited amount of work appears to have been done to establish stress/strain relationships for steel under transient heating conditions. In such tests load is applied before heating at a constant

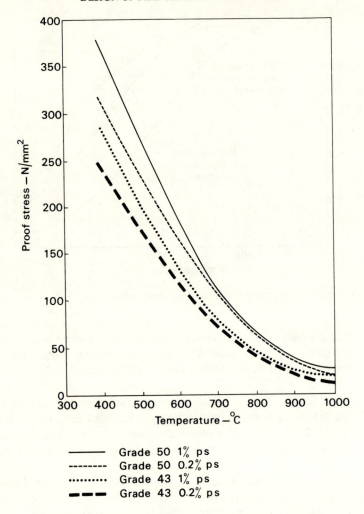

Figure 6.19   Effect of temperature on proof stress of typical British structural steels.

rate and the test continues until the failure point is reached. The strain monitored in the test is the total strain from which the sum of the creep and the instantaneous strain can be determined by subtracting free expansion ε_{th}. It is then possible to obtain relationships of the type shown in Figure 6.25. These illustrate the dependence of the creep strain on the heating rate as well as the stress level and the need to develop models which take such phenomena into account.

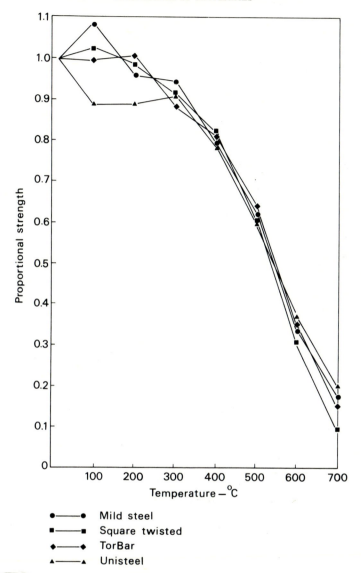

Figure 6.20 Strength reduction of typical British prestressing steel.

Relaxation. Creep strain (referred to in a previous section) can have a special significance for prestressed concrete flexural members. The resulting strain can lead to relaxation of prestress, or increase in deformation and lowering of the ultimate resistance. Figure 6.26 shows the type of relaxation that may

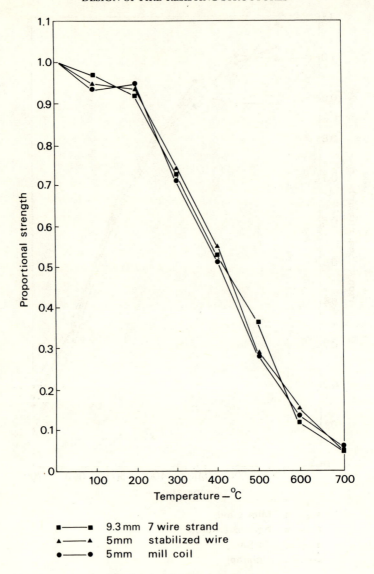

Figure 6.21   Strength reduction of typical British reinforcing bars.

result when wires are heated to 400°C. It is a time-dependent factor and indicates that at the end of a fire of one or two hours' duration further deformation may continue as long as the internal temperatures retain a high value.

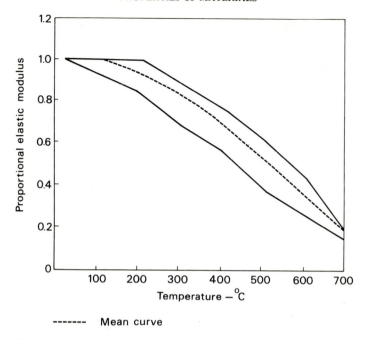

------- Mean curve

Figure 6.22 Modulus of elasticity of some reinforcing steels.

Residual strength. The re-use of structural elements in buildings which have not been irreparably damaged requires data on the residual strength after the materials have cooled down. Figure 6.27[21] shows the residual strength of hot rolled reinforcing bars which regain all their initial strength on cooling after being heated to 500°C. At higher temperatures there is a permanent loss in the yield as well as the ultimate strength. Figure 6.28 shows the data for prestressing steels which suffer a permanent loss at temperatures above 300°C with the residual strength reduced by nearly 50% at temperatures just above 600°C.

Conductivity. Thermal conductivity of steel is high in comparison with that of concrete; at room temperature it is about 50 W/m °C whereas for dense concrete it is below 2 W/m °C. It is commonly assumed that the conductivity of steel is high enough for normal size sections to have a uniform temperature throughout, but temperature differences exist in large sections as well as in sections which may be able to lose heat, e.g. the top flange of a beam in contact with a concrete slab.

Stirland[24,25] of the British Steel Corporation has collected data on steel properties (Figure 6.29) and shown that thermal conductivity decreases with

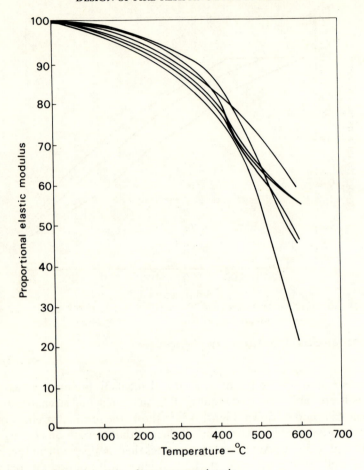

Figure 6.23   Modulus of elasticity of some structural steels.

increasing temperature and depends upon the composition of the material. The differences between the two grades of steel commonly used for structural purposes converge at 700°C after which the conductivity shows a slight increase. No explanation is available for this change.

Specific heat. Stirland[24] has also collated data on specific heat of steel from three different sources and found that negligible differences exist. This property can be considered to be independent of the nature of the steel. Specific heat increases progressively up to 700°C, where there is a sharp peak before it starts to decrease (Figure 6.30). Pettersson *et al.*[26] have observed

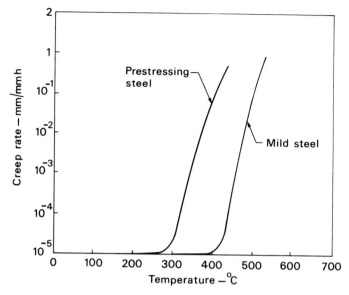

Figure 6.24 Creep rate for prestressing (ASTM A421) and mild steel (ASTM A36)—stressed.

similar properties, but without the sharp rise between 600 and 700°C. Stirland's curve can be expressed for temperatures up to 700°C as

$$\text{specific heat } c_s = (6.01 \times 10^{-7} T_s^2) + (9.46 \times 10^{-5} T_s) + 0.475 \text{ kJ/kg°C}$$

where T_s is the steel temperature.

Thermal diffusivity. Figure 6.31 shows thermal diffusivity of steel on the basis of data given in Figures 6.28 and 6.29. It has a value of 0.84 m²/h at 20°C and decreases, more or less linearly, to 0.28 at 700°C. It can be expressed with reasonable accuracy by the expression

$$\psi_S = 0.87 - (T_s \times 0.84 \times 10^3) \text{ m}^2/\text{h}$$

6.4 Masonry

Masonry construction comprises, in the main, walls made of clay or concrete bricks or concrete block walls. Only a little work has been done on thermal and structural properties at high temperatures, and although such constructions have been used for many years, computational techniques have not been developed to any great extent. Lie[27] has shown the thermal conductivity of clay bricks in the density range 700–2100 kg/m³; Figure 6.32 shows the conductivity increasing virtually linearly up to a temperature of 1000°C.

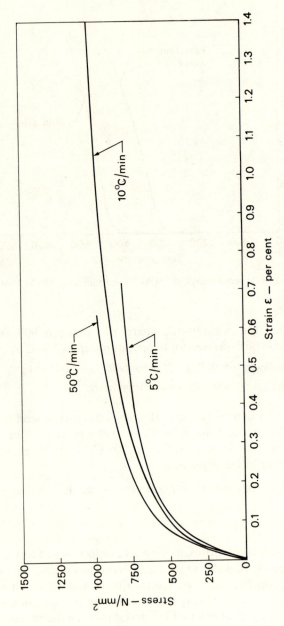

Figure 6.25   Stress/strain curves for steel at 600°C showing the effect of rate of heating.

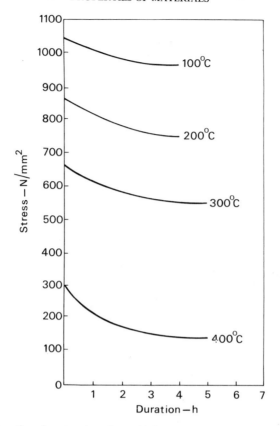

Figure 6.26 Relaxation of prestressing wires at high temperature.

Normal clay bricks have a density between 1600 and 2000 kg/m² whereas at the lower end the density is nearly that of aerated or cellular concrete.

Lie has also provided some data on the specific heat of clay bricks. This increases gradually in the temperature range from ambient to 1000°C, and only slight differences exist between clay bricks in the density range of 700 to 2100 kg/m³ (Figure 6.33). As masonry materials such as clay bricks are chemically stable, the changes in specific heat with increased temperature are likely to be slight.

6.5 Wood

Wood is a combustible material which consists essentially of cellulose, hemi-cellulose and lignin. It is a non-homogeneous and variable material, and even

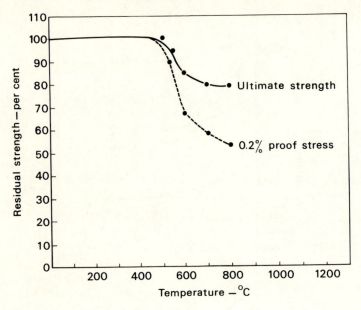

Figure 6.27 Residual strength of reinforcing bars.

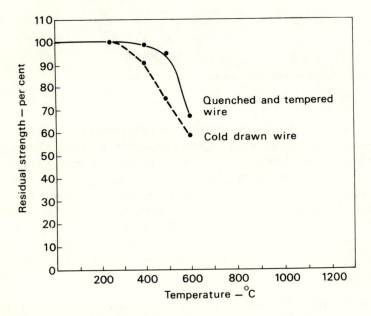

Figure 6.28 Residual strength of prestressing wire.

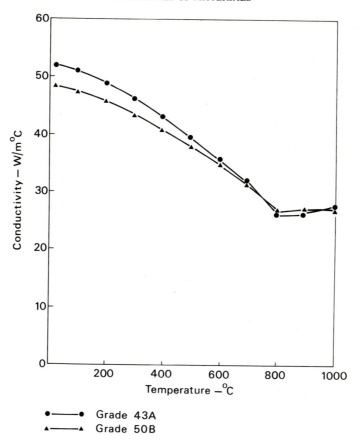

Figure 6.29 Thermal conductivity of steel.

for a given species the properties (particularly structural properties) are dependent upon the grain direction and the size and nature of discontinuities such as knots, shakes etc. Unlike other constructional materials it undergoes a dramatic change in its characteristics between the pre- and post-carbonization phases. On heating it expands up to a temperature of around 80°C, with an expansion coefficient of $3.50 \times 10^{-6}/°C$, and at this point shrinkage starts which continues until full decomposition has occurred. In inert atmospheres chemical degradation starts at 280°C and by 400°C carbonization is complete.

Ignition. On heating in air, ignition of wood occurs, depending upon the conditions of exposure. If an igniting source is present, e.g. a pilot flame, the

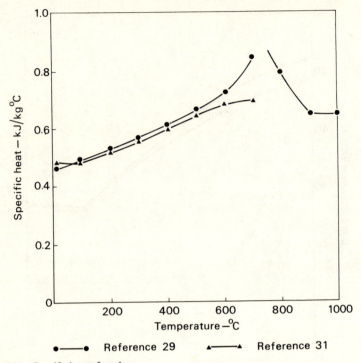

Figure 6.30   Specific heat of steel.

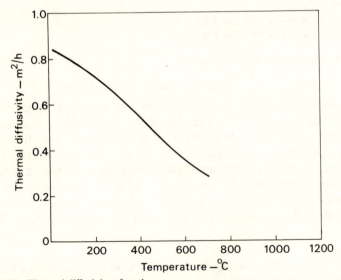

Figure 6.31   Thermal diffusivity of steel.

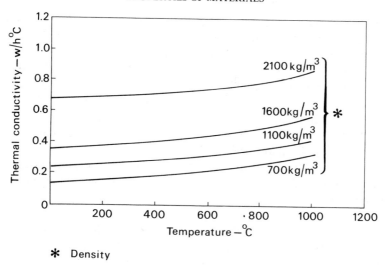

* Density

Figure 6.32 Thermal conductivity of clay bricks.

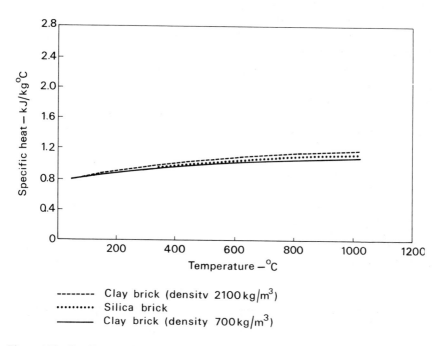

-------- Clay brick (density 2100 kg/m³)
.... Silica brick
———— Clay brick (density 700 kg/m³)

Figure 6.33 Specific heat of bricks.

flammable vapours emitted from the surface will ignite as soon as they are available in sufficient quantity. The surface temperature of wood may be in the range 150–350°C, although 250°C is generally assumed to be the average ignition temperature. If no pilot flame is present the gases will ignite at a higher temperature, in the range 350 to 550°C, by spontaneous ignition. Self-ignition, which is a form of spontaneous ignition, is also possible but has no relevance in a fire. Simms[28] has shown that ignition characteristics can be best expressed by defining the exposure conditions, and he established the critical intensity of radiant heat needed for the pilot and pilotless ignition to be 1.4×10^4 and 2.8×10^4 W/m^2 respectively. Ignition is dependent upon the species of wood and seems to be related to the density as well as porosity of the samples.

Charring. After ignition the surface layers of wood are fully decomposed and heat transfer takes place to the inside of the section. Owing to the low thermal conductivity of wood and the moisture content which requires a certain amount of heat energy to cause evaporation, heat transfer is at a low rate and the demarcation between fully decomposed, i.e. charred, and undamaged parts of section is well defined. Many workers have studied the rate of charring of wood sections in fire tests and produced relationships for different species and different conditions. Ashton[29] refers to early work which indicated that the average rate of charring for soft wood is 0.6 mm/min. Further work has shown that in fire tests it is also independent of the oxygen level in the range of 2–10% but is dependent upon the grain direction[30] (as in laminated constructions) and the intensity of exposure[31] (Figure 6.34). Shaffer[32] has related the rate of charring of Douglas fir as a function of its density (Figure 6.35), and the parallel nature of the curves indicates a direct influence of the moisture content on heat transfer within the section.

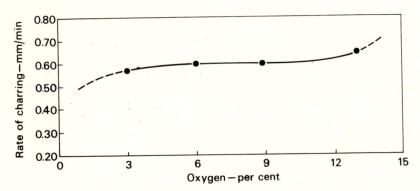

Figure 6.34   Effect of oxygen level on charring of wood in furnace tests.

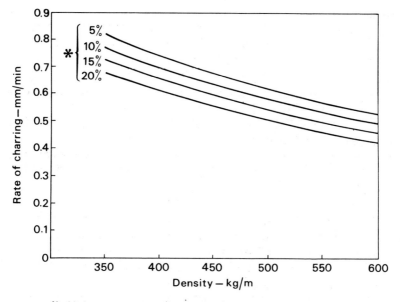

Figure 6.35   Rate of charring of Douglas fir as a function of its density and moisture content.

Strength. The strength properties of wood depend upon the orientation of the grain, but only a limited number of studies have attempted to establish these properties at low temperatures. Sano[33] found a linear relationship up to 60°C between compressive and tensile strength, with the strength decreasing gradually with temperature:

$$\sigma_t = -0.48T_w + 138$$

$$\sigma_c = -0.38T_w + 56 \text{ N/mm}^2$$

where σ_t and σ_c are the strengths in tension and compression, and T_w is the temperature of wood. The modulus of elasticity is also likely to decrease. However, the reductions are small in an uncharred section as the temperature drops rapidly to the ambient across the char boundary. In calculations a loss of 10% is considered to be adequate to cover such reductions, or alternatively, some increase in the charred area permits a safety factor to be introduced.

References

1. Holmes, A. *Geological and physical characteristics of concrete aggregates.* British Fire Prevention Committee, 'Red Book' No. 256, HMSO, London, 1921.
2. Stradling, R. E. and Brady, F. L. *Fire Resistant Construction.* Building Research Special Report No. 8, HMSO, London, 1927.
3. Abrams, M. S. *Behaviour of inorganic materials in fire* (Symposium on design of buildings for fire safety). ASTM Special Technical Publication, **685**, 1979. American Society for Testing and Materials, Philadelphia.
4. Gantvoort, G. J. *The mechanical properties of concrete during and after fire.* Report No. BI-78-60/72. 1.3210, Institute TNO for Building Materials and Building Structures, Delft, October, 1975.
5. Gantvoort, G. J. *The mechanical properties of reinforcing and prestressing steel during and after a fire.* Report No. BI-79-55/62. 1.3210, Institute TNO for Building Materials and Building Structures, Delft, September, 1979.
6. Schneider, U. *Effect of high temperature on concrete.* Paper of RILEM Committee 44—PHT (draft document).
7. Dougill, J. W. Modes of failure of concrete panels exposed to high temperatures. *Mag. Concrete Research* **24**, no. 79, pp. 71–6, June, 1972.
8. Anderberg, J. and Thelandersson, S. *Stress and deformation characteristics of concrete at high temperatures 2. Experimental investigation and material behaviour model.* Division of Structural Mechanics and Concrete Construction, Lund Institute of Technology, Bulletin 54, 1976.
9. Schneider, U. Behaviour of concrete under thermal steady state and non-steady state conditions. *Fire and Materials* **1** (3), 103–115, 1976.
10. Malhotra, H. L. The effect of temperature on the compressive strength of concrete. *Mag. Concrete Research* **8** (23), S. 84ff, 1956.
11. Cruz, C. R. Elastic properties of concrete at high temperatures. *J. PCA Research and Development Laboratories* **8**, No. 1, 1966.
12. Diederichs, U. and Schneider, U. *Untersuchung des Verbundverhaltens und der Verbundfestigkeit von Rippensträben und glatten Rundstaber bei hohen Temperaturen.* Institut für Baustoffkunde und Stahlbetonbau, Braunschweig, 1977.
13. Harmathy, T. Z. Thermal properties of concrete at elevated temperatures. *ASTM Journal of Material*, March, 1970, pp. 47–74.
14. Collette, Y. *et al. Etude de propriétés du beton soumis à des températures élevées.* Group de Travail, Comportement du Materiaux Béton en Fonction de la Température, Bruxelles, November, 1976.
15. Ödeen, K. and Nordström, A. Thermal properties of concrete at high temperatures. *Cement och Betong* **1**, Stockholm, 1972.
16. European recommendations for the calculation of the fire resistance of loadbearing steel elements and structural assemblies exposed to the standard fire, European Convention for Constructional Steel Work.
17. Anderberg, Y. *Mechanical properties of reinforcing steel at elevated temperatures* (in Swedish). Tekniska meddelande nr. 36, Halmsted Järnverk AB, Lund, 1978.
18. Skinner, D. H. *Measurement of high temperature properties of steel.* Melbourne Research Laboratories (MRL 6/10), May, 1972.
19. Harmathy, T. Z. and Stanzak, W. W. *Elevated temperature tensile and creep properties of some structural and prestressing steel.* Nat. Res. Council of Canada, Res. Paper 424, Div. of Eng. Res. NRC 11163, Ottawa, 1970.
20. Jerath, V. *et al. Elevated temperature tensile properties of structural steel manufactured by the British Steel Corporation.* Teesside Laboratories, Report No. T/RS/1189/11/80/C—July, 1980.
21. Crook, R. N. *The elevated temperature properties of reinforcement for concrete.* University of Aston in Birmingham, September, 1980.
22. Copier, W. J. *Creep of steel in fire.* Report No. BI-72-73/05.3.11.640. Institute TNO for Building Materials and Building Structures, Delft, 1970.

23. Down, J. E. Some fundamental experiments on high temperature creep. *Aust. J. Mech. Physics of Solids* **3**, 1954.
24. Stirland, C. *Steel properties at elevated temperatures for use in fire engineering calculations.* British Steel Corporation, Teesside Laboratory, Paper for ISO/TC92/WG15 Committee, October, 1980.
25. *Physical constants of some commercial steels at elevated temperatures.* The British Iron and Steel Research Association, Butterworth Scientific Publications, London, 1953.
26. Pettersson, O. *et al. Fire engineering design of steel structures.* Swedish Institute of Steel Construction, Publication 50, Stockholm, 1976.
27. Lie, T. T. *Fire and buildings.* Applied Science Publishers Ltd., London, 1972.
28. Simms, D. L. *Fire hazard of timber.* BWPA Convention Paper, pp. 72–90, Cambridge, 1951.
29. Ashton, L. A. *Fire and timber in modern building design.* Timber Research and Development Association, High Wycombe, Bucks, UK, 1970.
30. Rogowski, B. W. F. *Charring of timber in fire tests.* Paper No. 4, Fire Research Station Symposium No. 3, October, 1967. *Fire and structural use of timber in buildings.* HMSO, London, 1970.
31. Hadvig, S. *Wood in fires.* Brand Symposium, Borås, Sweden, May 9–17, 1978.
32. Schaffer, E. L. *Charring rate of selected woods, transverse to grain.* US Forest Service Research Paper FPL 69, US Department of Agriculture, Forest Products Laboratory, Madison, Wisconsin, 1967.
33. Sano, C. Effect of temperature on the mechanical properties of wood in compression parallel to grain. *J. Japanese Wood Res. Soc.* **7** (4), 147–150, 1961.

7 Computation of fire resistance

7.1 General structural behaviour

Computation of fire resistance means predicting the behaviour pattern of a
structural element were it to be exposed to the heating regime used in fire
resistance tests. It does not necessarily imply the capability to predict the
performance of that structural element when involved in a fire in a building.
The technique is primarily concerned with the computation of stability or the
loadbearing capacity of the construction and the prediction of excessive heat
transfer by conduction in the case of separating constructions. It is not
possible at present to apply computational techniques to predict the
formation of openings or orifices causing the loss of integrity. In certain
constructions, e.g. *in situ* slabs, masonry walls or metal decks, it can often be
assumed on the basis of experience that integrity will be maintained provided
the loadbearing capacity is not impaired.

The exposure of a structure to transient heating conditions in a furnace
results in the exposed surfaces receiving heat at increasing rates by radiation
supplemented by convective heat transfer. The increase in the surface
temperature of the structure causes heat to flow to the interior and leads to
physical and chemical changes with consequent effects on the structure.
Organic materials such as wood burn, materials with low softening temperatures melt and others may suffer some physical disruption, most will attempt
to expand and almost all undergo a reduction in strength.

The rate of heat transfer to the interior of the section will depend on the
thermal properties of the component materials, i.e. conductivity k, density ρ
and specific heat c; these are frequently combined as thermal diffusivity
$(\psi = k/\rho c)$.

In the case of conductive materials (such as steel) having high thermal
diffusivity, virtually uniform temperatures can exist across a cross-section,
whereas with low diffusivity materials a steep temperature gradient can be
expected (Figure 7.1). Thermal gradients will cause a material to tend to
expand by differing amounts through the section, inducing stresses ranging

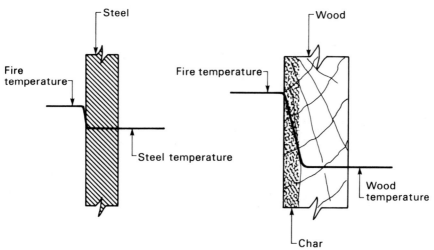

Figure 7.1 Heat transfer into steel and wood sections.

from compression at the hotter surfaces to tension within the section. The unequal expansion will cause deformation of the section, with a tendency to bulge towards the heat source, and this can induce internal cracking in brittle materials such as concrete. Restraint to deformation or movement can generate additional stresses (Figure 7.2) and add to those to which the structure is subjected by the external loads. In certain structural forms these additional stresses can acquire high values before plastic strains permit redistribution and if certain precautions are not taken, local failure can take place. Attention is drawn to this when dealing with continuous flexural members of reinforced concrete.

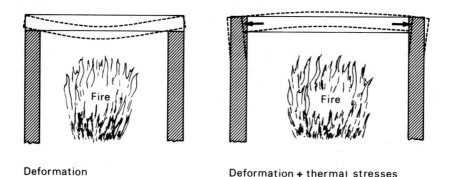

Deformation   Deformation + thermal stresses

Figure 7.2 Deformation and thermal stresses caused by fire.

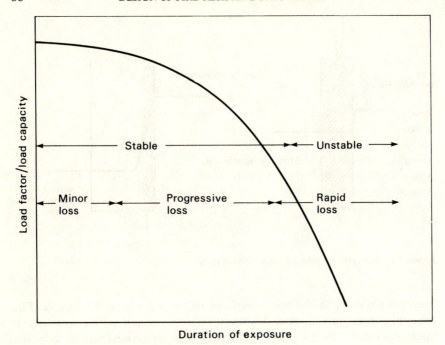

Figure 7.3   Reduction in loadbearing capacity caused by fire.

The global effect of all changes resulting from the high temperature exposure is progressively to lower the loadbearing capability of the structure. With some constructional forms, such as unprotected steel, this rate of decrease may be high, whereas with insulated constructions the reduction may proceed at a low rate. The reduction does not proceed at a constant rate—usually little change takes place in the early part of the exposure, then it may proceed at a constant rate followed by an accelerated decline. During this part a point is reached (Figure 7.3) when the reduced ultimate loadbearing capacity equals the imposed loads and failure occurs. In a building, whether this critical condition of a single element will lead to the collapse of the whole or a substantial part will depend upon the degree of redundancy in the structural design.

7.2 Limit state concept

Limit state concepts are becoming more widely accepted in structural design, and following the introduction of this approach in the concrete and the masonry codes, it has also been adopted for the proposed code on steel structures. The basic concept relates the performance of a structure to a specific limit state, and the design parameters are based on an acceptable probability against the structure or a part of it becoming 'unfit for use', within the context of appropriate criteria. Characteristic loads and strengths of materials are defined in statistical terms to take account of known variability. For each specified limit state, partial safety factors for loads and material properties are introduced to define design data relevant to that limit state. Two limit states are considered for normal design: the *ultimate* and the *serviceability* limit states. The concrete code,[1] CP 110, suggests that fire resistance should be regarded as a serviceability limit state. This does not fully agree with the report[2] of the Joint Committee of the Institution of Structural Engineers and the Concrete Society which considers the ultimate limit state approach as more appropriate to represent the consequences of a fire. It has been suggested that for structures exposed to attack by fire the two limit states used are the ultimate limit state of stability and the limit state of integrity; the last-named corresponds to the serviceability concept, as the structure remains fit to support imposed loads. Limit state of integrity is appropriate for those structures which separate spaces and therefore are required to act as barriers to the passage of fire, and this limit state is reached when the effectiveness of the barrier is breached because of the formation of undesirable openings or by the excessive transfer of heat to the unheated face (Figure 7.4).

The safety factors appropriate for normal design need some adjustment when designing for fire resistance.[2] Partial safety factors are normally specified for the dead and live loads (G_k and Q_k), and for material strength (f_c, f_y). It is desirable to have a higher partial safety factor for concrete strength in comparison with steel to ensure that in reinforced structures ductile failure of steel precedes failure of concrete in compression.

In addition, other partial safety factors may need to be introduced to deal with areas of uncertainty. A safety factor,[3] γ_c, to take account of the consequences and mode of failure, is needed to differentiate between different levels of risk, and a safety factor γ_d, to deal with the uncertainty of the design model. Furthermore, as some structures may need to be considered for re-use after a fire, a serviceability type of limit state is needed which controls deformation during the exposure.

It is proposed that the following values should be attached to various safety factors when calculating the high temperature strength of concrete and steel structures:

If G_k is the dead load and Q_k is the live load
 f_{cT} is concrete strength at $T°C$
 f_{yT} is steel yield strength at $T°C$

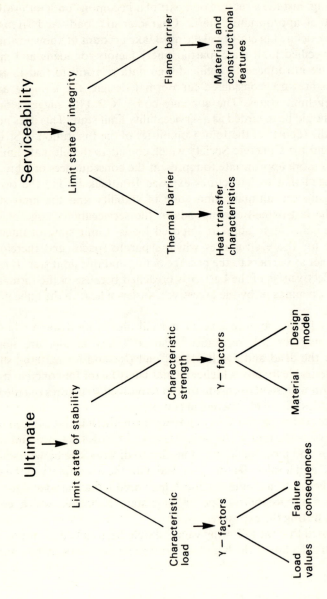

Figure 7.4 Limit state concepts for fire resistance.

γ_g and γ_f are partial safety factors for dead and live loads respectively
γ_{mc} and γ_{ms} are partial safety factors for concrete and steel respectively
γ_c and γ_d are partial safety factors to deal with consequences of failure and
the uncertainty of the design model; then

Load on the structure $= (G_k \times \gamma_g) + (Q_k \times \gamma_f)$
$$\gamma_g = 1.05 \text{ and } \gamma_f = 1.0$$

Material properties at ambient temperatures
$$\gamma_{mc} = 1.30 \text{ and } \gamma_{ms} = 1.00$$

Strength properties at critical temperatures
$$\text{Concrete} = f_{cT}/\gamma_{mc}$$
$$\text{Steel} \quad = f_{yT}/\gamma_{ms}$$

Consequences of failure
$\gamma_c = 1.0$ for normal risk, 1.2 for special risks and 0.95 for isolated
buildings or redundant design

Uncertainty of the design model
$\gamma_d = 1.0$ for simple design with non-communicating connections between
elements, or
1.05 for predictable degree of interaction, e.g. continuity.

7.3 Analytical procedure ᴛᴏ ᴀᴅᴅ

The main steps to be taken to establish if a given structure will satisfy the fire
resistance needs are shown in the flow diagram (Figure 7.5). With a
knowledge of the structural design and the exposure conditions (sub-routines
A and C), the reduced loadbearing capacity of the structure (sub-routines B
and D) is computed and if this is greater than the loading to which it is
subjected, no failure should occur. If failure is indicated then either the
structure should be redesigned or other protective measures taken to improve
its performance.

The detailed steps needed for each sub-routine will depend upon the nature
of the structure, design concepts employed, the material model for high
temperature properties and the structural model for residual loadbearing
capacity. Developments on the response of structures to fire have not
progressed uniformly for all forms of construction, as different national as
well as international committees have separately been considering design
codes for individual materials. More progress has been made with concrete
and steel constructions than with timber and masonry, but even with the first
two the approaches developed are somewhat different as the subsequent
chapters will show. However with a view to encouraging a common approach

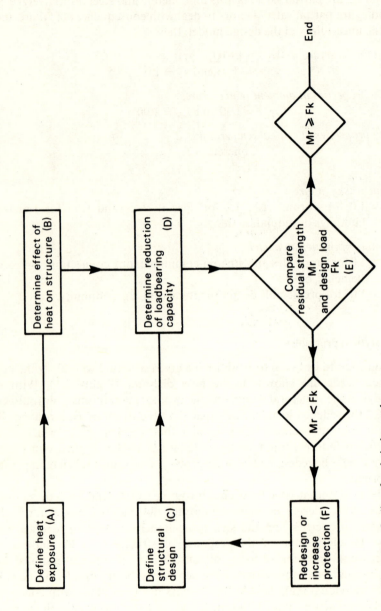

Figure 7.5 Outline of analytical procedures.

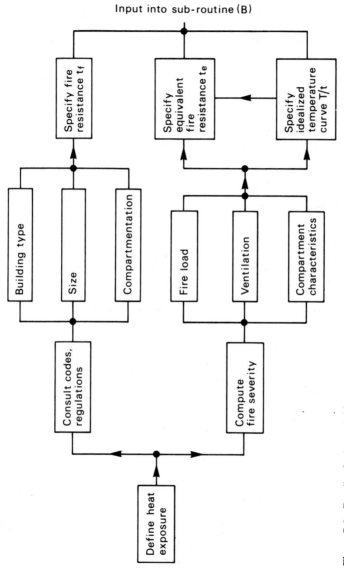

Figure 7.6 Details of sub-routine A.

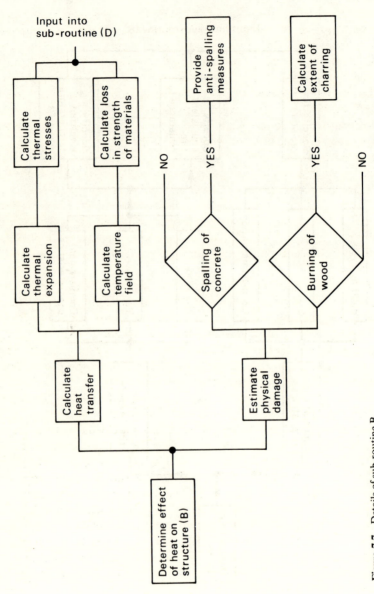

Figure 7.7 Details of sub-routine B.

in the long term, examples of detailed steps which may be necessary are shown in Figures 7.6–7.10.

Figure 7.6 shows sub-routine 'A' to establish the nature of the exposure conditions to which the structure under consideration is to be subjected for computational purposes. The concept of the sub-routine is virtually identical to that shown in Figure 5.7 for defining fire resistance. The most common approach is reference to the appropriate regulation or by-law; establishing the fire resistance requirement on the basis of building type, size and compartmentation provided. In certain cases the equivalent fire resistance approach is possible, by consultation with the regulating authority, in which account is taken of the fire load, ventilation conditions and the compartment characteristics, as illustrated in Example 5.1 in Chapter 5. The use of an idealized temperature curve other than that in BS 476: Part 8 will not be readily accepted by many authorities in the UK at present, though some consideration is being given to a temperature/time curve of greater severity than that in the British Standard for fires involving liquid fuels. The graded curves of the type shown in Figure 5.6 have little application at present but would find more use as the computation of fire severity becomes acceptable to authorities.

Sub-routine 'B' in Figure 7.7 considers two aspects of the effect of heat on the structure, firstly the calculable transfer of heat from the exposed surface to the interior of the construction and secondly the physical damage to which certain materials are prone. The former is dealt with later in the chapter, and is concerned with establishing the temperature distribution within the section under the transient heating conditions. It should also take into account thermal expansion and any consequent stresses and strains. The estimation of physical damage is related to the particular materials used in the construction, and the two examples given are that of concrete which may have a tendency to spall and the burning of wood. Both are dealt with in Chapter 6 as well as in later chapters dealing with concrete and wood structures.

The basis of structural design, sub-routine 'C' Figure 7.8, will be different for each type of structural form and the example shown is more appropriate for steel constructions although some features are common to other types. The engineer should have the appropriate information available to him if he is considering an existing structure, or he should consult the appropriate design codes when dealing with a new construction. If the design is based on simplified tables or graphs it would be necessary to undertake basic calculations to establish the yield strength or the ultimate load capacity of the element.

Sub-routine 'D' (Figure 7.9) brings together information from sub-routines 'B' and 'C' to establish the effects on the structure with a view to calculating its diminished loadbearing capabilities. Depending upon the use of elastic or

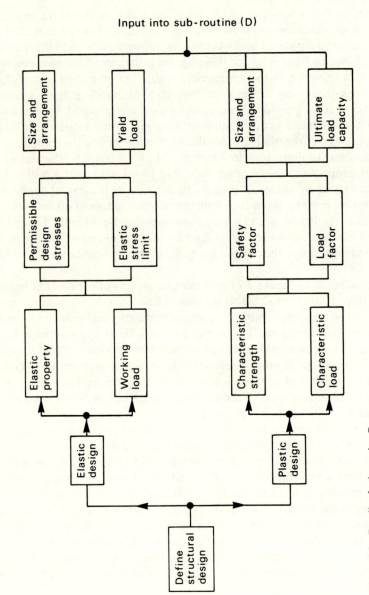

Figure 7.8   Details of sub-routine C.

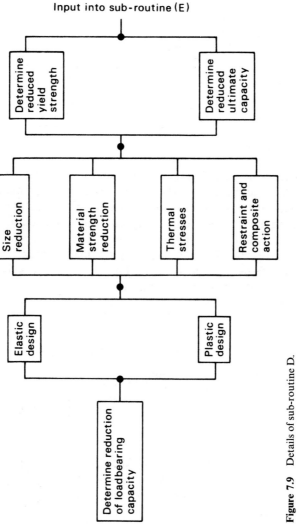

Figure 7.9   Details of sub-routine D.

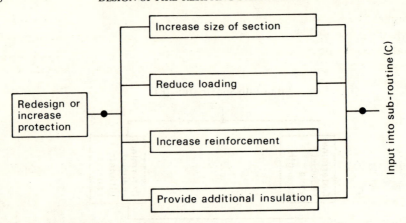

Figure 7.10   Details of sub-routine F.

plastic design principles, slightly different approaches are possible for steel and concrete flexural members. For timber and masonry constructions and for axially loaded members the elastic design methods are still most common. In establishing the reduced strength capacity, any reduction in the size of the section due to spalling or burning needs to be taken into account. Reduction in strength properties of materials and thermally induced stresses have already been referred to, and with composite systems the effect of restraint needs to be considered. For an engineer this is an important aspect of the problem, and is dealt with for each of the four constructional materials. The procedural details are not the same in each case, due partly to the nature of materials and the effect of high temperature on them. Nevertheless, the principle is identical—to compute the loadbearing capability of the heated element.

The next step is to compare residual loadbearing capacity with the design or the service load and if the residual strength is adequate the structure can be considered to be satisfactory. If not, some remedial measures have to be taken. Figure 7.10 shows four possibilities. If the load is reduced, no additional computation is necessary, but if any of the other three provisions are employed re-calculation would be needed to confirm the adequacy of the residual strength. In some cases it is possible to reverse the procedure and calculate the amount of protection or the dimensions of the section needed to retain a specified minimum residual strength.

In practice, when dealing with a structure the design engineer will find that some of the decisions have already been taken. The fire resistance needs for the building may have been defined by the architect; alternatively the engineer may have to consult the building authority to establish the fire resistance requirement. In a special case he may need to use the procedure in

Chapter 5 to establish the equivalent fire resistance, preferably in consultation with the building control authority. Once the level of fire resistance is established the design engineer has three options available to him to satisfy the authorities that his proposed construction will provide the necessary fire resistance:

(i) Use of fire resistance test results on an identical construction.
(ii) 'Deemed to satisfy' data included in regulations and by-laws — compliance with such data gains automatic approval from the building authorities.
(iii) Calculation of fire resistance in consultation with the building authorities.

Test data are generally appropriate when a proprietary system is being used as it is more than likely that the manufacturers have subjected their products to fire resistance tests. 'Deemed to satisfy' data consist basically of minimum sizes for the essential part of the construction such as thickness of concrete cover to reinforcement, amount of protection to a steel section, minimum sizes of timber joists or the thickness of a masonry construction. Reference is made to the availability of such data for each constructional material in the appropriate chapter. Calculation methods should in general provide a more economical and a more reliable solution, particularly when it is possible to take into account continuity and composite action.

7.4 Computation of heat transfer

The transfer of heat into a construction on exposure to the transient heating conditions which exist in a fire or its simulation as in a furnace test, depends not only on the temperature of gases and flames but also on the heat transfer characteristics of both the heating environment and the surface which is receiving heat. The subsequent heat flow by conduction from the surface is dependent on the thermal properties of the material, which may also be temperature-related. The basic relationship follows Fourier's laws of heat transfer, and in a three-dimensional mode can be expressed by the following partial differential equation:

$$\frac{\partial}{\partial x}\left(k_x \frac{\partial T}{\partial x}\right) + \frac{\partial}{\partial y}\left(k_y \frac{\partial T}{\partial y}\right) + \frac{\partial}{\partial z}\left(k_z \frac{\partial T}{\partial z}\right) + Q = \rho c \frac{\partial T}{\partial t} \qquad (7.1)$$

where k_x, k_y, k_z are thermal conductivity; ρ, density; c, specific heat; T, temperature; t, time and Q, any internal heat generation. For one-dimensional heat flow the equation can be simplified as:

$$\frac{k}{\rho c} \cdot \frac{\partial}{\partial x}\left(\frac{\partial T}{\partial x}\right) + Q = \frac{\partial T}{\partial t} \qquad (7.2)$$

The boundary conditions have to be defined for the above equations, either as a temperature history, or in terms of heat flow which depends on the heat transfer characteristics of the fire environment and the surface receiving the heat. The main modes of transfer are by convection and radiation, the latter being more predominant and temperature-dependent. This follows the Stefan–Boltzmann law and is proportional to the fourth power of the temperature difference. The convective transfer in tests is fairly consistent and is usually taken[4] as 25 W/m^2 °C.

The heat transfer coefficient for the exposed surface $\alpha = \alpha_c + \alpha_r$

where α_c is the convection transfer coefficient

and α_r is the radiative transfer coefficient

$$\alpha_r = \frac{5.77\varepsilon_r}{T_t - T_0}[(T_t + 273)^4 - (T_0 + 273)^4]\text{W/m}^2\,°\text{C} \tag{7.3}$$

ε_r is the resultant emissivity of the boundary surface and combustion gases and can be assumed to be 0.5 for furnace tests.

Heat transfer calculations for the simple cases where the thermal properties are not temperature-dependent and the boundary conditions are not complex can be made without much difficulty. However, as noted in Chapter 6, thermal properties of most materials *are* temperature-dependent and therefore solutions are complex. Numerical methods have been derived to solve these by using either finite difference or finite element techniques. In the first method, the structure is divided into squares of sides $\partial x, \partial y$ and temperature at the centre of each square determined at time intervals $\partial t = (c\rho/4k)\partial x^2$. A computer program based on this approach has been developed in France in connection with the design of concrete structures.[5] The boundary temperature is assumed to lag behind the standard curve such that its value is aT—the value of a for walls, slabs and beams is empirically established at 0.85.

In the finite element approximation, the structure is divided into elements of geometric shape connected at nodal points, and at each node the rate of entry of heat is equated to heat stored in the element and heat transferred to the adjacent element. The partial differential equation is transformed into a system of first-order differential equations, one for each node. Numerical methods have been devised to deal with one-, two- or three-dimensional heat flow systems; the best known are the FIRES-$T3$[6] and TASEF-2.[7]

In the case of unprotected steel sections the temperature rise is a function of the heat transfer characteristics as well as the 'shape factor'. The shape factor is the relationship between the exposed surface through which heat flow can take place and the mass of steel section which is being heated. It is commonly expressed as P_s/A_s where P_s is the perimeter over which heat flow is occurring and A_s the cross-sectional area of the steel section. Shape factors for some commonly-used sections are shown in Chapter 9 together with a simplified expression for measuring temperature rise in protected and unprotected sections.

7.5 Computation of stability

It has been pointed out earlier that the consequence of heating is to cause the structure progressively to reach the limit state of stability, and the purpose of computation is to establish when the ultimate condition occurs and the mode of instability. Alternatively computation can be used to show how the design may be improved to prevent the ultimate limit state being reached under the prescribed conditions of heating and composite action. Analysis of this type can at present be undertaken for individual elements of construction and for simple assemblies. Composite and complex systems representing a total building are more difficult to deal with. For practical purposes the individual element approach is an acceptable proposition as it conforms to the currently operative system of building control.

The loss in the strength of materials and some of the changes that may be involved due to thermal effects can lower the stress-resisting capacity of the element to the level of the load-induced stresses. Strain increases can cause deformations which lead to instability. The mode of failure for each type of element can follow a different route depending upon its design, boundary conditions and the rate of temperature increase. Elements can be divided into flexural and compression members, and some of the latter may in practice be subjected to a combination of compression and flexural loading, for example, the external columns of a building or portal frames.

The statically determinate flexural members (beams and slabs) reach the failure point when the tensile reinforcement is unable to resist the load-induced stresses, and a hinge is formed at mid-section (Figure 7.11). If the ultimate bending moment is M_u and the load-induced moment is M_a, failure occurs when $M_a = M_{uT}$ where M_{uT} is the new value of M_u when the tensile zone temperature is $T°$.

For statically indeterminate members, various modes of failure are possible. If hinges can be formed in the negative moment zones, followed by a third hinge in the middle, a condition of instability will be reached. On the other hand if the supports can provide sufficient rigidity and only a central hinge is formed, the flexural member will be transformed into two cantilevers and stability will be dictated by the high temperature behaviour of the compression zone, which is in a vulnerable position due to its location. In either case the ultimate point will be reached at a later stage in comparison with statically determinate members of essentially similar load capabilities. Com-

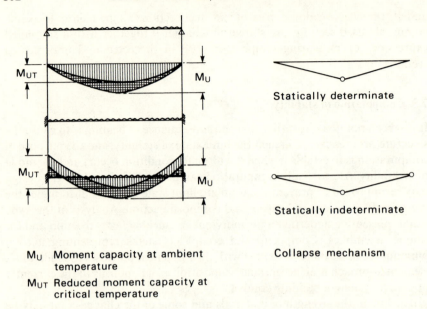

M_U Moment capacity at ambient
        temperature
M_{UT} Reduced moment capacity at
        critical temperature

Statically determinate

Statically indeterminate

Collapse mechanism

Figure 7.11 Bending moments and collapse mechanism for beams and slabs.

pression members may be designed to have hinged or fixed end conditions, and may be axially or eccentrically loaded. In practice pure hinges or complete concentricity may not be achieved; most members will have a degree of fixity and may often be subjected to some radial thrust by the expansion of beams or slabs. One of the consequences of heating of compression members is an increase in the slenderness ratio. In the case of columns fully exposed to heating, reduction of the effective section is uniform on all faces and the effect can be simulated by assuming removal of material from the faces. Walls exposed on one side suffer an uneven reduction, and furthermore the expansion of the heated face leads to an eccentric loading condition. Figure 7.12 shows three possibilities for the failure mode of columns. However, in practice most walls and columns, unless very thick, will fail in buckling rather than compression.

The classic Euler formula gives the failure load of slender pin-jointed columns as

$$F_e = \frac{\pi^2 E}{\lambda^2} = \frac{\pi^2 EI}{l_e^2}$$

where λ is the slenderness ratio and l_e the effective length. The Euler formula gives high buckling load values at low slenderness ratios as it ignores the effect of direct compression. Rankine's relationship for structures allows both

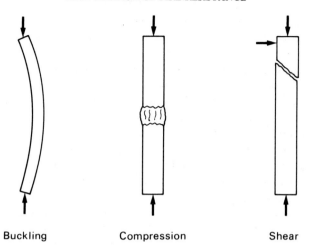

| Buckling | Compression | Shear |

Figure 7.12 Modes of failure of columns.

buckling and compression loads to be taken into account by using the relationship

$$\frac{1}{F} = \frac{1}{F_c} + \frac{1}{F_e}$$

where F is the failure load

  F_c is the failure load under direct compression, and

  F_e is the Euler buckling load.

This can be expressed as

$$F = \frac{A \cdot fc}{1 + a\lambda^2}$$

where a is the Rankine constant, $fc/\pi^2 E$.

The Rankine formula shows lower failure loads for columns with lower slenderness ratios and approaches the Euler loads at higher slenderness values. When using this relationship, the theoretical effective length for the column needs to be used to take account of different end conditions. Both formulae were originally derived for steel sections with a homogeneous cross-section. For use with concrete columns the E and I values are derived for both concrete and steel and added together, or by the transformation of the steel section into an equivalent concrete area a single calculation could be made.

A number of problems need to be resolved before data can be applied to complete structural systems other than simple frames, such as column beam assemblies, portal frames etc. The expansion of the horizontal or near-horizontal section subjects the vertical components to side thrusts and, depending upon the rigidity of the connection, can induce rotational moments. The deformation characteristics depend upon the relative rigidity of the elements. A rigid horizontal member will push the top of columns and generate shear forces capable of causing local failure. Rigid uprights will lead to the upward deformation of the horizontal members. In a continuous system, deformation of members away from the seat of fire can lead to the occurrence of local hinges causing cracking and failure.

An unknown in analysing a real building structure is the rate of progress of fire from part to part, and the horizontal and vertical routes that may be dictated by the internal subdivision of a building. Consequently more confident predictions are possible for single-storey buildings or where assumptions can be made of the 'instantaneous' involvement of all parts within a compartment. Much work needs to be done to relate the predicted behaviour of individual elements to that of the whole system.

References

1. CP 110: *The structural use of concrete*. British Standards Institution, London, 1972.
2. *Fire resistance of concrete structures*. Report of a joint committee of the Institution of Structural Engineers and the Concrete Society, Institute of Structural Engineers, London, August, 1975.
3. *A treatment of structural safety of buildings taking account of the consequences of failure*. Building Design Partnership CP 63–74, Building Research Establishment, Garston, June, 1974.
4. *The basis of design for the fire protection of steel structures*. Draft recommendation by M. Law and O. Pettersson to the Code Advisory Panel of the CIB Commission W14. (To be published.)
5. *Méthode de prévision par la calcul du comportement au feu des structures en béton*. Document Technique Unifié (DTU), Centre Scientifique et Technique du Bâtiment, Paris, October, 1974.
6. Iding, R. M. *et al.* FIRES-RC-II. *A computer program for the fire response of structures—reinforced concrete frames*. Report No. UCB/FRG77–88, Department of Civil Engineering, University of California, Berkeley, 1977.
7. Wickström, V. TASEF-2. *A computer program for temperature analysis of structures exposed to fire*. Report No. 79-2, Lund Institute of Technology, Lund, Sweden.

8 Design of concrete elements

8.1 Introduction

The normal design of concrete elements will generally follow the procedure laid down in CP 110,[1] or in some cases some of the older codes, such as CP 114, 115 etc., may also be utilized. The current issue of CP 110 deals with fire resistance of concrete structures in a 'deemed to satisfy' manner, i.e. it lists various constructions with minimum requirements for thickness, width and cover, as appropriate for beams, columns and floors which can be assumed to have a specified fire resistance. Additional information is provided on factors to be taken into account when designing various elements particularly provision of supplementary reinforcement to minimize damage by spalling. The data are more extensive than those in the regulations but still not comprehensive enough to prevent weaknesses. The data are similar to that contained in an international recommendation prepared by a Commission of the International Federation of Prestressed Concrete (FIP).[2] These data have been updated and issued (1980) as a BRE technical report.[3]

In practice a design engineer may find that for a large number of projects computation of fire resistance is not needed owing to the nature of the project and the need to save time. Experience shows that for many constructions requiring a fire resistance of not more than two hours the sections normally used to satisfy the loading requirements may possess sufficient fire resistance. This can be checked quickly by reference to the 'deemed to satisfy' tables. However, with precast elements, particularly ribbed or troughed floors, computation may be needed to confirm that adequate fire resistance is possible.

Concrete structural elements can be divided into two main types, flexural members (beams and floors) and compression members (columns and walls). The former have been studied in greater detail in comparison with the latter, and a number of procedures have been developed. The most detailed treatment has been given in the interim guidance issued by the Joint Committee of the Concrete Society and the Institution of Structural

Engineers *Design and detailing of concrete structures for fire resistance.*[4] The procedure given in this chapter is essentially that described in this publication. The conventional elastic design approach has been described in a recent publication of the American Concrete Institute: *Guidance for determining the fire endurance of concrete elements.*[5] A similar approach has also been adopted in France and is described in *Méthodes de prévision par la calcul du comportement au feu des structures en béton.*[6]

8.2 Heat transfer

After the exposure conditions for the structural element have been decided, the next step is to estimate temperatures within the section or at some predetermined critical point, e.g. the tensile reinforcement. Reference has been made in Chapter 7 to available computer programs which may be used for this purpose. Empirical relationships are also available which permit a quick check to be made of the temperature for simple configurations. Figures 8.1 and 8.2 show the temperature gradient in concrete slabs up to a distance of 100 mm from the exposed surface when exposed to the heating conditions in the furnace tests up to 4 hours. The temperature rise within lightweight aggregate concrete is at a lower rate owing to the lower thermal diffusivity of the material.

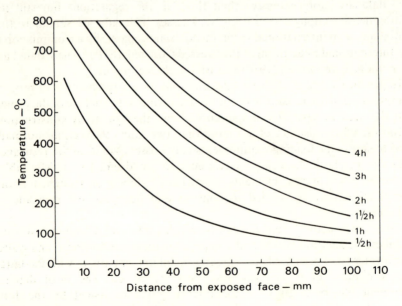

Figure 8.1 Heat transfer in a dense concrete slab.

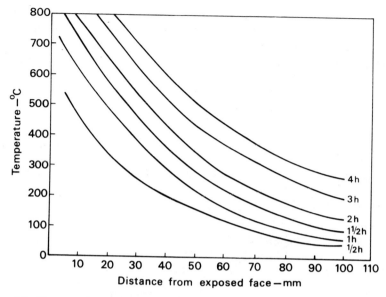

Figure 8.2 Heat transfer in a lightweight concrete slab.

In the case of beams with heat transfer from three faces, the temperature rises at a more rapid rate as compared to a slab, and the isotherms have a U-shape (Figure 8.3). If the shape of the beam is altered resulting in a smaller mass of concrete, still higher temperatures will occur. In Figure 8.3, an I-

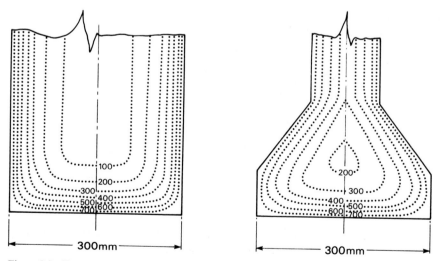

Figure 8.3 Temperature distribution in dense concrete beams.

section beam of the same width is compared with a rectangular beam. Whilst temperatures close to the exposed surface are similar, higher temperatures exist in the central part of the I-section beam. Consequently the reinforcement will also reach higher temperatures in the latter case. Figures 8.4 and 8.5 show

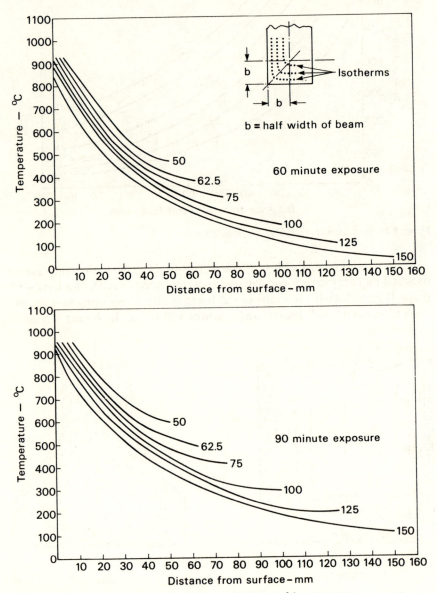

Figures 8.4 and 8.5   Temperature rise in rectangular beams of dense concrete.

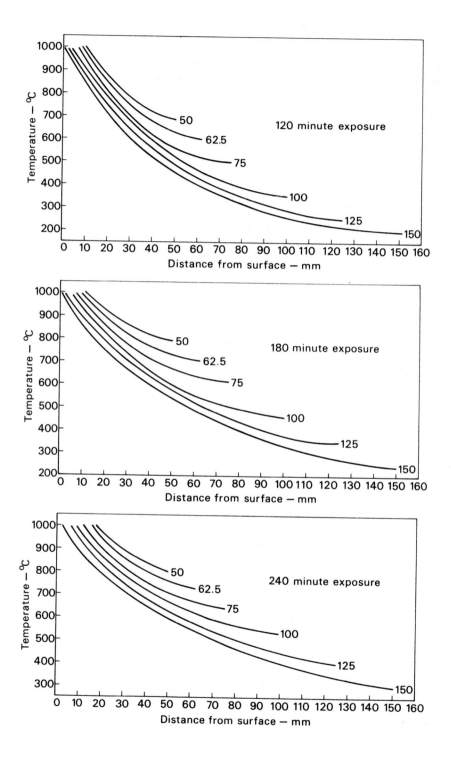

temperature distribution in dense concrete rectangular beams in the range of 100 to 300 mm width. For beams of larger cross-section, isotherms can be drawn for 150 mm wide vertical edge strips from the diagram for 300 mm wide beams and the isotherms joined by horizontal lines.

Temperature rise inside columns is likely to be more rapid than for a beam of the same width; four typical examples are shown in Figure 8.6 of isotherms

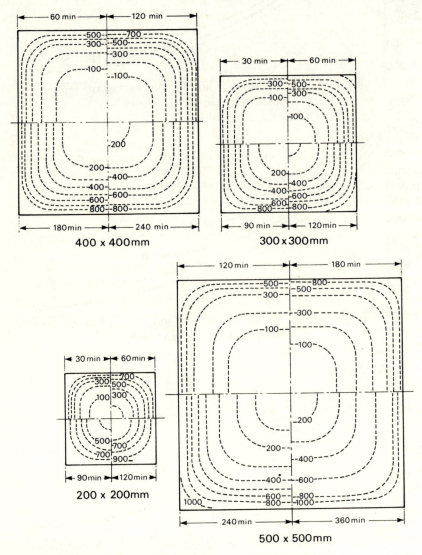

Figure 8.6 Isotherms in dense concrete columns.

in columns of varying widths from 200 to 500 mm square when exposed to heating in a standard furnace.

In the case of flexural members, the temperature rise data are needed to estimate the temperature of the reinforcing bars or prestressing wires. For slabs with plane soffit and single layer of reinforcement the temperature can be determined from Figure 8.1 or 8.2 by using the appropriate exposure curve and by noting temperatures at the depth equal to concrete cover. If the reinforcement is present in multi-layers the average cover to the reinforcement is computed as below:

$$C_{av} = \frac{A_{s_1} \cdot c_1 + A_{s_2} \cdot c_2 \ldots + A_{s_n} c_n}{A_{s_1} + A_{s_2} \ldots + A_{s_n}} = \frac{\Sigma A_s \cdot c}{\Sigma A_s}$$

where A_s is the area of the reinforcement or tendon and
c its distance from the exposed face.

All reinforcement with concrete cover less than $0.5\,C_{av}$ is likely to be too hot to make any significant contribution to the loadbearing capability of the element and should therefore be ignored. This is likely to be particularly important with corner bars or wires in beams.

For rectangular beams cover is to be measured to the nearest face. For I-section beams the average cover is reduced to 60% of the value obtained above to compensate for the additional heat transfer through the upper face of the bottom flange.

Floor slabs also need to be checked for expected temperature rise on the unheated face. Figure 8.7 shows the minimum thickness necessary for solid slabs of dense and lightweight aggregate concretes to satisfy the insulation requirements of the standard on fire resistance tests. For hollow slabs the actual thickness is reduced to an effective thickness to allow for the presence of voids in the cross-section.

$$d_{\text{effective}} = D\sqrt{S}$$

where D is the actual thickness, and
S is the ratio of solid material to voids per unit width.

Flexural members

A simplified procedure for the design of flexural members can consist of the following essential steps:

(1) Calculate the maximum design load or the service load for the element (F_d)
(2) Calculate maximum applied moment (M_a)
(3) Calculate the ultimate moment capacity (M_u)

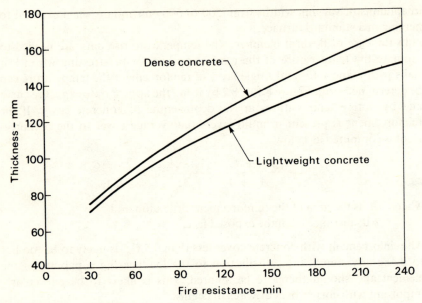

Figure 8.7 Thickness of slabs for various fire resistance periods.

(4) Determine the average temperature of steel reinforcement (T_s°)

(5) Calculate the reduced tensile force capacity (F_{sT})

(6) Determine the average temperature of concrete in the compression zone (T_c°)

(7) Calculate the reduced compressive free capacity (F_{cT})

(8) Equate tensile and compressive forces (F_{sT} and F_{cT})

(9) Calculate the reduced moment resistance (M_{uT})

(10) Compare 9 with 2. If $M_{uT} > M_a$ the design is satisfactory, if not, redesign.

For elements restrained at the boundaries or of a continuous nature, the basic procedure is the same but sub-routines are introduced to take account of the redistribution of stresses and the modified behaviour pattern on the development of hinges. A flexural member fixed at ends when a central hinge develops can behave like two cantilevers. It is then necessary to consider if the modified section retains sufficient moment capacity. Practical examples follow, showing how these steps are applied.

8.3 High temperature properties of materials

For steps 5 and 7 above it is necessary to have data on the reduction of strength of steel and concrete at high temperature. The relationship shown in

Chapter 6 for the appropriate type of concrete or steel may be used for this purpose. For the majority of usages it is possible to idealize these relationships and rectilinear curves of the type shown in Figures 8.8 and 8.9 can be

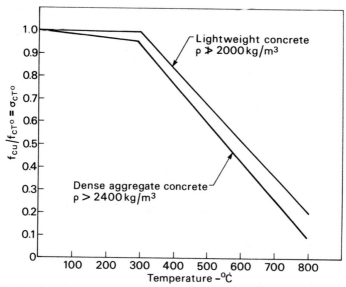

Figure 8.8   Idealized compressive strength reduction curves for concrete.

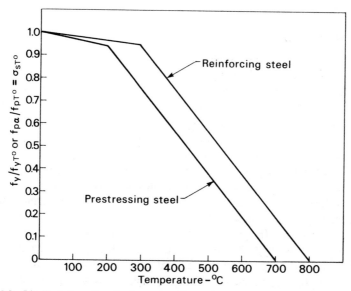

Figure 8.9   Idealized strength reduction curves for steel.

Table 8.1 Strength reduction factor (σ_T)

Material	Temperature range	σ_T
Dense concrete	20–300	$1 - \dfrac{T^\circ}{6000}$
	300–800	$0.95 - \dfrac{T^\circ - 300}{588}$
Lightweight concrete	20–300	1.0
	300–800	$1.0 - \dfrac{T^\circ - 300}{625}$
Steel reinforcement	20–300	$1 - \dfrac{T^\circ}{6000}$
	300–800	$0.95 - \dfrac{T^\circ - 300}{421}$
Prestressing steel	20–200	$1 - \dfrac{T^\circ}{4000}$
	200–700	$0.95 - \dfrac{T^\circ - 200}{526}$

used for concrete and steel. Table 8.1 shows the value of the strength reduction factor σ.

8.4 Worked examples

The first example is that of a reinforced concrete beam which was part of a research project on concrete beams.[7] It was tested as a simply supported beam with 4-point loading. Figure 8.10 shows the average reinforcement temperature and the central deflection. The second example shows the application of the general principles to the design of a simply supported slab which is required to provide fire resistance for two hours. The design follows the procedure specified in CP 110 and it is shown that the reduced moment capacity is not adequate to deal with moments due to the applied load. One solution is to increase the concrete cover. The alternative solution is to anchor the slab at the ends to the edge beams so that a redistribution of moments can take place. With nominal negative reinforcement of just over 0.15% of the cross-sectional area sufficient moment capacity is developed to resist the total applied moment of 7.227 KNm. It should be noted that in calculating the applied moment during the fire, the partial safety factors for loading are given new values; γ_g for dead load is 1.05, i.e. the characteristic load may be 5% in excess, but it is highly unlikely that the live load will increase, in fact it may be

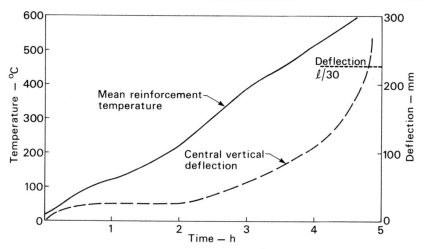

Figure 8.10   Temperature and deflection curves for R.C. beam.

considerably reduced if the occupants have escaped and the contents are burning. Hence the γ_f is given a value of 1.0.

The third example is a simplified version of that given in the ISE document[4] and considers the possibility of improving fire resistance by the provision of edge restraint to precast double-tee units of prestressed concrete made with lightweight aggregate concrete. The shape and the size of the tee stems makes this type of construction suffer a greater reduction in its loadbearing capacity at high temperatures. However as the units are provided with a structural topping of dense concrete and they are intended to be structurally tied to the edge beams, so the units will act as a restrained construction.

After exposure to the standard heating conditions for two hours the mid-span moment resistance is inadequate to support the applied moment under service load. However, with some contribution from the moment capacity of the negative moment zone, the construction can provide fire resistance for two hours with an ample margin.

It should be noted that with restrained constructions, with the redistribution of moments the points of contraflexure move towards the centre of the span. In Example 8.2 the point of contraflexure is 1.17 m from the support, hence it is important to ensure that the negative reinforcement is anchored at least 12 diameters beyond this point. If this is not done, cracking will develop close to the end of the reinforcement, leading to failure. The FIP recommendation[2] suggests that at least 20% of the negative reinforcement should be continued over the whole span. The ISE document[4] draws attention to the need to ensure that the flexural members will not be weak in shear in the limit

Calculation*

Example 8·1   <u>Check the fire resistance of a reinforced
concrete beam, previously subjected to a fire test.</u>
Design data :

Cross section as shown
Tensile reinforcement 6Y28
   fy = 410 N/mm²

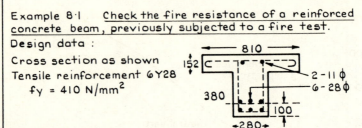

Compression reinforcement 2Y11
fy = 240 N/mm²

Simply supported span
4 point loading ⅛, ⅜, ⅝, ⅞ span.

$A_s = 6 \times 380 = 2280 \text{mm}^2$
$f_{cu} = 34.48 \text{ N/mm}^2 (\text{actual})$
age factor = 1·2
$1·2.f_{cu} = 41.37 \text{N/mm}^2$

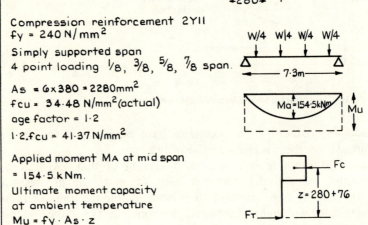

Applied moment M_A at mid span
= 154·5 kNm.
Ultimate moment capacity
at ambient temperature
$M_u = f_y \cdot A_s \cdot z$
   $z = 280 + 76$, assuming the top flange to be under compression.
∴ $M_u = 410 \times 2280 \times 356 = 333$ kNm.

Allowable strength reduction co-efficient
for tensile reinforcement $= \dfrac{154}{333} = 0·46$

Fig.8·8   Strength reduction of 0·46 occurs at 600°C
Fig.8·9   In the test, steel temperature of 600°C reached
at 4hr. 35mins.

*Sketches not to scale

Calculations

Example 8·2   Design an R.C. slab for a fire resistance
of 2 hours.
Design data :
Span = 2700mm
Thickness = 125mm.

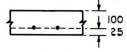

Load :
$\quad$ Self-weight = $\dfrac{125 \times 23\cdot6}{1000}$ $\quad$ = 2·95 kN/m

$\qquad$ Partitions etc $\qquad$ = 1·27 kN/m
$\qquad$ Gk $\qquad\qquad$ = 4·22 kN/m
$\qquad$ Live load, Qk $\qquad$ = 3·5 kN/m
$\qquad$ γ_g = 1·4, γ_f = 1·6

$\therefore$ Design load = 1·4 Gk + 1·6 Qk = (1·4 × 4·22) + (1·6 × 3·5)
$\qquad\qquad\qquad$ = 11·51 kN/m

Max. applied moment Ma = $\dfrac{wL^2}{8}$ = $\dfrac{11\cdot51 \times 2\cdot7^2}{8}$

$\qquad\qquad\qquad\qquad$ = 10·79 kNm

C.P110
vol. 2

Reinforcement $\dfrac{100 As}{bd}$ = 0·3

As = 300 mm², use 10 Y 250 = 314 mm²

fy = 460 N/mm²
fcu = 25 N/mm², age factor – 1·2
1·2 × fcu = 30 N/mm²
Service load = Gk + Qk = 4·22 + 3·5
$\qquad\qquad$ = 7·72 kN/m

Actual steel stress under service load
$\qquad$ = 460 × $\dfrac{7\cdot72}{11\cdot51}$ × $\dfrac{300}{314}$ = 295 N/mm²

CP110
Table 10

Steel percentage = $\dfrac{314 \times 100}{1000 \times 100}$ = 0·31%

Modification factor = 1·36
Allowable span/depth ratio l/d < 20 × 1·36 = 27·2
Actual span/depth ratio = $\dfrac{2700}{100}$ = 27

$\therefore$ l/d ratio O.K.

Calculations

Effect of exposure to heating for 2 hours :
Partial safety factors to be used :

γ_{gT} – 1·05   (dead load)

γ_{fT} – 1·00   (live load)

γ_{mc} – 1·30   (concrete strength)

γ_{ms} – 1·00   (steel)

Load during fire : $Gk \cdot \gamma_{gT} + Qk \cdot \gamma_{fT}$
$$= (4 \cdot 22 \times 1 \cdot 05) + (3 \cdot 5 \times 1 \cdot 0)$$
$$= 7 \cdot 931 \text{ kN/m}$$

Max. bending moment $M_A = 7 \cdot 227$ kN/m 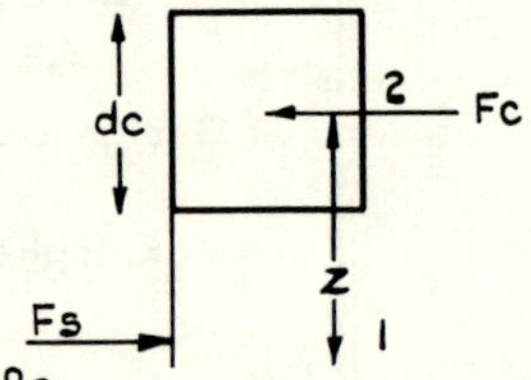
Temperature and strength
reduction factors after
2 hours exposure.

Fig 8·1
8·8
8·9

Position	Temp T °	σ_{cT}	σ_{sT}
1	670°C	0·44	0·32
2	<300°C	1·00	1·00

σ_{cT} - reduction factor for concrete at T°C
σ_{sT} - reduction factor for steel at T°C

$F_{sT} = f_y \cdot \sigma_{sT} \cdot A_s / \gamma_{ms} = \dfrac{460 \times 0 \cdot 32 \times 312}{1 \cdot 0}$ $= 46 \cdot 22$kN

$F_{cT} = 0 \cdot 67 \cdot f_{cu} \cdot \sigma_{cT} \cdot d_c \cdot b / \gamma_{mc}$

$= \dfrac{0 \cdot 67 \times 30 \times 1 \cdot 0 \times 1000 \times d_c}{1 \cdot 3}$ $= 15 \cdot 46 \times d_c$ kN

$\therefore d_c = 2 \cdot 99$ mm

$z \not> 0 \cdot 95 d$ (95mm) or $d - \dfrac{d_c}{2} = (100 - 1 \cdot 5 = 98 \cdot 5)$

$\therefore z = 95$ mm.

Reduced ultimate moment resistance $M_{ut} = F_{sT} \times z$

$= \dfrac{46 \cdot 22 \times 95}{1000} = 4 \cdot 39$ kNm

$M_{ut} < M_A$ $\therefore$ slab likely to fail before 2 hrs.
hence design not O.K.

Calculations

Fig8·9 | Minimum value of M_{UT} needed = M_A = 7·227 kNm
This requires F_{ST} = 76 kN,
possible if $\sigma_{ST} \not< 0·53$, corresponding to an average
steel temperature of 560°C.

Fig.8·1 | After 2 hours exposure, temperature rise is $\not> 560°C$
when the concrete cover is 36mm.
An alternative solution is to anchor the slab at the
ends to provide restraint and develop additional
moment resistance.

 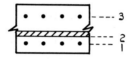 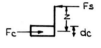

Assume slab to be anchored at the ends to rigid beams
capable of resisting torsion with adequate anchorage
and sufficient negative reinforcement.

To determine the moment capacity at the supports,
cover to the bottom reinforcement is ignored as it
would be seriously reduced in strength.
The contribution of the bottom reinforcement
is also ignored.

Fig.8·1 | Temperature and strength reduction factors
8·8 | for steel and concrete are as follows :
8·9 |

Position	TempT°	σ_{cT}	σ_{sT}
1	670	0·44	−
2	640	0·49	−
3	< 300	1·00	1·00

Calculations

$$F's = \frac{fy \times A's \times \sigma_{ST}}{\gamma_{ms}} = \frac{0.67 fcu \times 1000 \times dc \times \sigma_{CT}}{\gamma_{mc}}$$

A's, negative reinforcement is $\geqslant$ 0.15% of cross-section.

$$A's \geqslant \frac{0.15 \times 1000 \times 100}{100} \geqslant 150 mm^2$$

Use 8Y300 bars $\therefore$ A's = 168mm²

$$\therefore F's = \frac{460 \times 168 \times 1.0}{1.0} = 77.28 kN$$

$$dc = \frac{77.28 \times 1.3}{0.67 \times 30 \times 0.49 \times 1000} = 10.2 mm.$$

z $\not\geqslant$ 0.95d (d = 75) or d - $\frac{dc}{2}$

$\not\geqslant$ 71.25 or 75 - 5.1 ie. 69.9mm

Moment capacity at supports at high temperature
= F's . z = 77.28 × 69.9 × 10⁻³ = 5.4 kNm

Total moment capacity (M'$_{UT}$)
= 4.39 + 5.4 = 9.79 kNm

$\therefore$ M'$_{UT}$ > MA ; design O.K.

The point of contraflexure is shifted towards
mid-span, that is x = 1.17m, $\therefore$ the negative moment
reinforcement must extend $\simeq$ 1.3m from the supports
to prevent cracking and collapse.

Example 8·3 <u>Check fire resistance of the double-tee beam with structural topping</u>

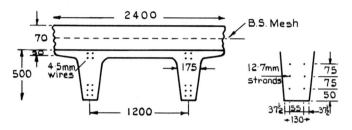

Span : 12 m, ends built into an edge beam to resist torsion.

Concrete : lightweight aggregate for the tee-beam $f_{cu} = 50 \text{ N/mm}^2$, f_{ci} (transfer) 36 N/mm^2

Topping, dense concrete $f_{cu} = 30 \text{ N/mm}^2$

Steel : Prestressing strands 12·7mm diameter. Characteristic breaking strength = 165 kN

Reinforcement, high yield $f_y = 460 \text{ N/mm}^2$

Loads : Dead load $G_k = 5·75 \text{kN/m}^2 \times 2·4 = 13·8 \text{ kN/m}$

      Live load $Q_k = 4·00 \text{ kN/m}^2 \times 2·4 = 9·6 \text{ kN/m}$

      Service load $= 1·05 G_k + 1·0 Q_k$

                  $= 14·5 + 9·6 = 24·1 \text{kN/m}$

   Ultimate load $= 1·4 G_k + 1·6 Q_k = 34·68 \text{ kN/m}$

 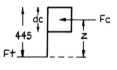

$f_{cu} = 30 \times 1·2$ (age factor) $= 36 \text{ N/mm}^2$

Design concrete strength in compression block

$= 0·4 f_{cu} = 0·4 \times 36 = 14·4 \text{ N/mm}^2$

Rupture strength of steel $= \dfrac{165 \times 12}{\gamma_m} = \dfrac{1980}{1·15} = 1722 \text{ kN}$

Calculation

Area of compression zone = $\dfrac{1722 \times 10^3}{14 \cdot 4}$ = 119 583 mm^2

Depth of compression block = d_c = $\dfrac{119\,583}{2400}$ = 49·82mm

$\therefore$ z = 445 - $\dfrac{49 \cdot 82}{2}$ = 420 mm.

Ultimate moment of resistance = $1722 \times 420 \times 10^{-3}$ = 723·24 kNm

Maximum applied moment = $\dfrac{34 \cdot 68 \times 12^2}{8}$ = 624·24 kNm

Maximum moment under service load = $\dfrac{24 \cdot 1 \times 12^2}{8}$ = 433·8 kNm

Assume exposure to standard heating condition for 2 hours.

Width of rib at c.g. of steel

= $\left(\dfrac{175-130}{450} \times 125\right)$ +130 = 142·5 mm

Fig.8·3 | Temperature after 2 hours

150 mm. rib - 570°C $\left.\begin{array}{c}\\\\\end{array}\right\}$ dense concrete
125 mm rib - 630°C

By extrapolation for 142·5 mm rib temperature rise

= 570 + $\left(\dfrac{60}{25} \times 7 \cdot 5\right)$ = 588°C

Fig.8·9 | For lightweight concrete 588 × 0·8 = 470°C

Strength retention factor for steel σ_{ST} = 0·42

$\therefore$ steel rupture strength = $122 \times 12 \times 0 \cdot 42$ = 816·5 kN

Concrete stress in the compression zone = $\dfrac{0 \cdot 67 \times 36}{1 \cdot 3}$ = 18·55 N/m^2

Concrete area needed = $\dfrac{816 \cdot 55 \times 10^3}{18 \cdot 55}$ = 44016 mm^2

Depth of compression zone, d_c = $\dfrac{44016}{2400}$ = 18·34 mm.

Lever arm z = 570 - 125 - $\dfrac{18 \cdot 34}{2}$ = 436 mm

Reduced mid-span moment of resistance
= $816 \cdot 5 \times \left(436 \times 10^{-3}\right)$ = 356 kNm

This is less than the service load moment of 433·8 kNm

$\therefore$ fire resistance less than 2 hrs.

The tee-beam as a simply supported construction is
not satisfactory. Assume the ends to be built in
and therefore restrained, leading to a redistribution
of moments:

Moment capacity needed at support = 433·8 - 356 = 77·8 kNm

Steel in the negative moment zone - 10Y150 = 523·3 mm²/m

$$A's = 2·4 \times 523·3 = 1256 \text{ mm}^2$$

If the temperature rise of this steel is $< 300°C$, $\sigma_{ST} = 1·00$

Tensile force $F_t = 1256 \times 460 \times 10^{-3} = 578 \text{ kN}$

To determine the area
of concrete in compression,
ignore 20mm concrete
surface layer as too weak.

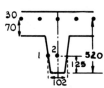

Fig 8·3   Temp at 1. 20mm from surface = 850°C

Temp. at 2. 70mm from surface = 580°C

Average temperature = 715°C

Average for lightweight concrete = 715 × 0·8 = 572°C

Fig.8·8   Residual concrete strength factor, $\sigma_{CT} = 0·85$

$$f_{CUT} = \frac{0·85 \times 50 \times 1·2}{1·3} = 39·2 \text{ N/mm}^2$$

Size of compression zone = $F_t / f_{CUT} = \dfrac{578 \times 10^3}{39·2} = 14745 \text{ mm}^2$

Width of ribs in compression = 102 × 2 = 204 mm.

Height of compression block dc = $\dfrac{14745}{204}$ = 72·3 mm.

Depth d = 570 - 20 - 30 = 520 mm.

Lever arm z = 520 - $\dfrac{72·3}{2}$ = 484 mm

Moment capacity at support = $F_t \times z = 578 \times 484 \times 10^{-3} = 279.7 \text{ kNm}$

Moment capacity needed at supports = 77·8 kNm

Hence the double-tee beam can provide 2 hours fire
residence with adequate margin in hand.

state condition. Shear failure of flexural members in fire is a rare occurrence nevertheless a simple check can be made by determining the ratio of the bending moment to the shear force at a given section $l_v = M/V$ (commonly known as the shear span). Factor $K_v = M/v \cdot d$ (where d is the effective depth of the section) can be used to determine whether shear resistance needs to be investigated. If the factor has a value of 6 or more no shear problem is expected. When its value is less than 2, shear will be a problem and provision will need to be made to prevent shear failure. In between the failure may be due to a combined effect of shear and flexure. The ISE document provides guidance on the provision of additional shear reinforcement. In practice the main areas where special provision has to be made are end blocks and brackets with concentrated loads and small shear spans.

8.5 Compression members

The behaviour of compression members has been studied in furnace tests and reports are available on series of experiments performed. These indicate that the behaviour pattern of reinforced concrete columns falls into two distinct categories, as with ambient temperature tests: one where the failure is predominantly in compression and the other where buckling leads to collapse. The main difference between ambient and high temperature behaviour lies in the demarcation between the two. For normal design purposes distinction between short and long columns is made on the basis of slenderness ratio. If it is more than 12, a column is considered to be slender. However, during the course of exposure to fire conditions the outer layers of concrete attain higher temperatures than the inner section, consequently the strength of outer layers reduces at a faster rate. It may be assumed that with most columns after exposure to standard heating for one hour or more the layer of concrete outside the reinforcement cage makes little structural contribution. This in consequence leads to an increase in slenderness ratio and columns assumed to be short under normal design considerations can fail in buckling. The exposed height of columns in furnace tests is generally 3 m and a square column with sides 200 mm wide, assuming it to be properly retained in direction at both ends, will have a slenderness ratio of $(0.7 \times 3000)/200 = 10.5$ and will be designed as a short column. If the concrete cover is 20 mm and links are 10 mm in diameter, the core will measure $200 - 60 = 140$ mm. The effective slenderness ratio will increase to $(0.7 \times 3000)/140 = 15$, making the column behave as a slender section.

A simple approach was used in the early fifties[8] on the basis of fire resistance tests on R.C. columns ranging in size from 200×200 mm to 480×480 mm. The columns were designed as axially loaded compression members, with the permissible loads on the concrete and the steel sections added together using the allowable stresses. Reduced strength was similarly computed by using reduction factors for concrete and steel derived empirically from the test data.

The strength of a column after the furnace test was expressed as

$$F'_c = 0.65 f_{cu} \cdot A_c \cdot \sigma_{cT} + f_y \cdot A_s \cdot \sigma_{sT}$$

where σ_{cT} and σ_{sT} were the high temperature proportional strength factors for concrete and steel respectively. It was found that the temperature of steel reinforcement in the corners was virtually independent of the size of the column with the cover in the range 25 to 37 mm but the temperature gradient within the concrete section was a function of time and the section size. Figure 8.6 shows idealized temperature curves within different sections to assist in computations. Research paper No. 18,[8] however, assumed an average concrete temperature related to the size of the section and the duration of exposure and related the factor σ_{cT} to this temperature.

Lie,[9] in a more recent study, utilizes the basic Euler concept for the strength of columns and integrates the residual properties of concrete and steel over the cross-section using temperature-dependent relationships. The section rigidity $EI = E_s I_s + a_c E_c I_c$ is the sum of the rigidities of concrete and steel components; a_c is a factor related to the ratio between the failure load and the axial strength of the cross-section and has a value between 0.2 and 0.7. The American Concrete Institute (ACI Code 318-71) design concept is used for material strengths, modulus of elasticity and the eccentricity of loading which is assumed to be at least 25 mm (or $0.1b$, where b is the width of the column).

The temperature rise within a fully exposed section is established by using a finite element method by a process of iteration and the residual strength of these elements is aggregated for the whole cross-section. Resistance to axial force as well as bending moment is established and the estimates have been compared with test data on columns of 150×150, 200×200 and 300×300 mm. The correlation is good with the calculated results being about 10% lower than the test data.

Computations have shown that thermal properties of concrete, concrete cover to the reinforcement, the amount of reinforcement and the ratio between the applied load and the ultimate load are the main critical factors. Assuming notional concrete covers and steel reinforcement, the fire resistance for various columns of dense and lightweight aggregate concrete has been computed under service loads developing permitted maximum material stresses. These show that in general terms the fire resistance of columns is proportional to their size. This has led to the tabulation of data for columns related to the minimum width and in Figure 8.11 the specifications given in CP 110, FIP recommendations,[2] the Canadian data[9] and the more recent recommendations in France by DTU[6] are reproduced. There are minor

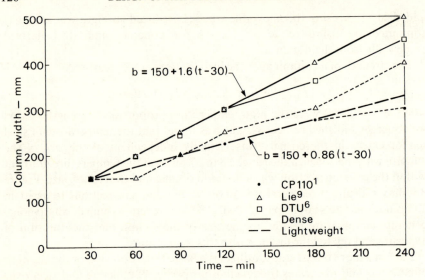

Figure 8.11   Column width versus fire resistance.

differences for fire resistance periods of three and four hours, for dense concrete and a fairly significant difference for the four-hour period for lightweight aggregate concrete. The data can be idealized as two straight lines such that

$$b = 150 + 1.6 \ (t - 30) \ \text{mm for dense concrete, and} \qquad (8.1)$$

$$b = 150 + 0.86(t - 30) \ \text{mm for lightweight aggregate concrete,}$$
$$\text{where } b \text{ is the column width and } t \text{ fire resistance.} \qquad (8.2)$$

Until computational techniques are developed to establish the fire resistance of R.C. columns, it is suggested that the empirical relations in Equations 8.1 and 8.2 be used to check if a given design of R.C. column has the required fire resistance.

8.6 Detailing

Proper detailing of reinforcement, layout and sizes of members and of joints is essential to ensure that the required performance can be obtained, composite action between elements can develop and the pattern of failure will follow a predictable course. Detailing is particularly essential to minimize damage by spalling, where fire resistance of two hours or more is being provided and the boundaries are required to provide adequate restraint. The Institution of Structural Engineers document gives illustrations on detailing of joints between a variety of elements. Some of the important points to note are as follows:

1. As mentioned on page 115, one effect of exposure to high temperatures is to shift the point of contraflexure towards the centre; consequently continuity reinforcement should be extended to prevent the occurrence of flexural shear cracks. It is a good principle to have at least 20% of the top reinforcement covering the whole span.

2. Where the edge beams provide restraint against rotation, slab reinforcement should be tied in and ends looped or given sufficient anchorage length.

3. Junctions of slabs and intermediate beams should be provided with sufficient reinforcement to provide composite action but not too much, to prevent ductile failure. Mild steel is ideal for top reinforcement. Use of stirrups near supports will prevent bond failure and slippage particularly with pretensioned prestressed units.

4. Attention should be paid to the design of bearings for simply supported members; a minimum bearing of 75 mm for 60 minute fire resistance and 100 mm for greater periods is desirable. The bearing stress should not exceed $0.4f_{cT}$, and if it does additional precautions are necessary.

5. Columns should be well bonded to beams with reinforced joints with precast as well as *in situ* construction. Links or dowels may need to be provided when *in situ* and precast units are used in composite construction.

8.7 Additional protection

If on the basis of analytical design or by reference to the tabulated data it is found that the construction is unable to provide the necessary fire resistance then either the elements may be redesigned as shown in the examples, or particularly when dealing with precast units, additional protection will be necessary. The presence of such protection provides a barrier to the passage of heat and delays the temperature rise within the concrete section and the temperature gradients are less steep. Additional protection can be considered in two ways, either as a substitution for an equivalent thickness of concrete or as providing additional fire resistance. The first approach is usual when computations are made and the thickness of the protective material is estimated by comparing its thermal properties with that of concrete. The following approximations have been suggested in various codes including the FIP recommendations:

$$d_p = \text{thickness of protection}, \ d_c = \text{thickness of concrete}$$

Dense cement rendering: $\qquad d_p = d_c$

Gypsum plaster: $\qquad d_p = 1.5d_c$

Lightweight gypsum plaster: $d_p = 2.0d_c$
Sprayed mineral fibre: $d_p = 2.0d_c$

The protection may be applied directly to the surface of concrete, or to a metal membrane to provide a horizontal ceiling below flexural members. In the latter case, due to the air gap the value of protection is increased to the equivalent of 1.5 times the values shown above. When applied directly it is necessary to have data to show that under high temperatures the adhesion can be maintained and the protection will stay in place. Its integrity can be improved by the introduction of a light reinforcing membrane in the thickness. This is necessary if the thickness of dense protection exceeds 15 mm.

8.8 Spalling

The spalling of concrete from the exposed surfaces has been described in Chapter 6. It can seriously affect the loadbearing capacity of structural elements particularly if it occurs during the early stages of exposure. Generally concretes made with siliceous aggregate are susceptible, and where the thickness of concrete cover on an exposed face is excessive, its dislodgement can be prevented or the damage limited by the use of supplementary reinforcement. The reinforcement is inserted in the mould before casting so that it occupies a mid-position in the cover, but not more than 20 mm from the face. It may consist of expanded metal lath or a wire fabric not lighter than 0.5 kg/m² (2 mm diameter wires at not more than 100 mm centres) or a continuous arrangement of links at not more than 200 mm centres and not more than 20 mm from the face. Such reinforcement is not needed with lightweight aggregate concrete or where suitable additional protection is used. It is needed when cover to the reinforcement exceeds 40 mm for dense concrete and 50 mm for lightweight aggregate concrete. It is not required where additional protection is provided (as listed in the previous section).

References

1. CP 110. *The structural use of concrete, Part 1: Design, materials and workmanship, Section 10: Fire resistance.* British Standards Institution, London, 1972.
2. *FIP/CEB Report on methods of assessment of the fire resistance of concrete structural members.* Cement and Concrete Association, Wexham Springs, Slough, UK, 1978.
3. Read, R. H. *et al. Guidelines for the construction of fire resisting structural elements.* BRE Report, HMSO, London, 1980.

4. *Design and detailing of concrete structures for fire resistance.* Interim guidance by a joint committee of the Institution of Structural Engineers and the Concrete Society. The Institution of Structural Engineers, London, 1978.

5. Guidance for determining fire endurance of concrete elements. (Report by ACI Committee 261.) *Concrete International*, February, 1981.

6. Méthode de prévision par la calcul du comportement au feu des structures en béton. DTU (Document Technique Unifié) No. 208, April, 1980. Centre Scientifique et Technique du Bâtiment, Paris, 1980.

7. Malhotra, H. L. *Fire resistance of structural concrete beams.* Fire Research Note No. 741, Fire Research Station, Borehamwood, Herts, UK.

8. Thomas, F. G. and Webster, C. T. *The fire resistance of reinforced concrete columns.* National Building Studies Research Paper No. 18, HMSO, London, 1953.

9. Lie, T. T. and Allen, D. E. *Calculation of the fire resistance of reinforced concrete columns.* Technical Paper No. 378, National Research Council of Canada, Ottawa, 1972.

9 Design of steel elements

9.1 General

The general design approach outlined in Chapter 7 can be applied to steel elements. There are differences in their response to fire conditions in comparison with concrete structures, and hence the detailed treatment for their design is different. The fabrication of different shapes during manufacture or on site permits maximum use to be made of the material, but elimination of the excess material reduces the benefit of thermal capacity to delay temperature rise during the transient heating conditions experienced in fires. Additionally, the high thermal conductivity of steel means that heat flow within the section is rapid and temperature gradients across the section are less steep than with other materials.

Steel elements do not need to be combined with other materials for structural reasons, and consequently their behaviour in the unprotected form is of interest to design engineers and will be examined first. The use of special protections imposes an economic disadvantage on steel structures, and therefore the conditions under which they may be used without protection, inside or outside a building, need to be established. In addition to the conventional techniques of providing an external encasement, other methods of providing fire resistance, for example by water cooling, will also be considered in this chapter.

Two publications give detailed data on the fire resistance of steel structures. One, published by the Swedish Institute of Steel Construction,[1] covers the complete subject of determining fire severity, expressing it as a number of temperature/time relationships and establishing the behaviour of steel constructions in most building situations. The other document prepared by a Committee of the European Convention for Constructional Steelwork[2] provides a simple approach on the basis of the standard furnace test exposure conditions and represents a common approach by a number of European countries. In this chapter relevant data from both publications is considered

130

but the design approach is based on that described in the latter and outlined in a paper by the author.[3]

Properties of steel at high temperature were discussed in Chapter 6 but for purposes of a simplified design approach the following values may be used:

Coefficient of thermal expansion a $= 1.4 \times 10^{-5}$ m/m °C
Specific heat c_s $= 0.52$ kJ/kg °C
Density ρ_s $= 7850$ kg/m³
Thermal conductivity k_s $= 50$ W/m °C

Grade 43A structural steel (BS 4360)
Elastic limit   at 20°C $f_{y_{20}} = 250$ N/mm²
Ultimate strength   „ $F_{t_{20}} = 450$ N/mm²
Modulus of elasticity   „ $E_{20} = 206$ kN/mm²

The effect of temperature on the yield strength and the modulus of elasticity of structural steel is shown in Figures 6.23 and 6.31 in Chapter 6. For a simpler approach the curves can be considered to be rectilinear, having the shapes shown in Table 9.1 and Figure 9.1.

'Deemed to satisfy' data for steel structures are less extensive than those for concrete. Most are contained in generic form in the schedules to the Building Regulations for England[4] and in a publication from Constrado[5] giving details of some proprietary systems. The data contained had a limited application as little account was taken of the shape and size of the steel sections, and consequently the presentation of such data has been altered in the more recent BRE publication.[6] Manufacturers of protective materials produce technical leaflets containing the appropriate data on their particular products.

The main outline for the determination of the fire resistance given in Chapter 7 can be applied to steel structures with small modifications to suit the particular characteristics of steel construction. Often it will be found that the reduced loadbearing capacity is related to a particular temperature, referred to as a critical temperature. It is therefore possible to rearrange the

Table 9.1   Effect of temperature on elastic properties of steel

Elastic properties	Temperature range		
	20–300°C	300–700°C	700–900°C
$\dfrac{f_{yT}}{f_{y_{20}}}$	$1 - \dfrac{T°}{3000}$	$0.9 - \dfrac{T° - 300}{500}$	$0.1 - \dfrac{T° - 700}{200}$
$\dfrac{E_T}{E_{20}}$	$1 - \dfrac{T°}{3000}$	$0.9 - \dfrac{T° - 300}{611}$ (300–900°C)	

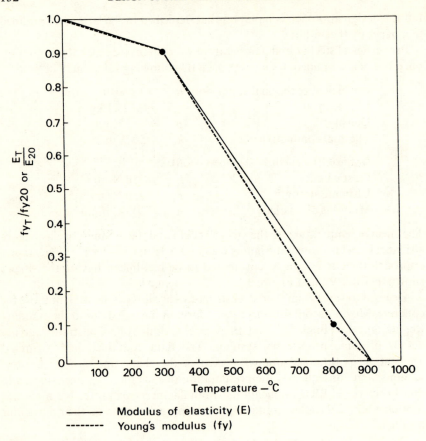

Figure 9.1   Simplified relationship between steel strength and temperature.

basic routine in such a way that the critical temperature for the steel section can be established under the relevant design concepts, then the time at which unprotected steel sections will reach the critical temperature is estimated and if this is less than the fire resistance required protection becomes necessary. A simplified approach is shown in Figure 9.2 for solving simple problems (see later examples) on the basis of fire resistance requirements in regulations or by-laws. The structural elements which can be dealt with in this way are beams and columns.

9.2 Heat transfer

The quantity of heat transferred to a section of steel exposed to the hot gases and flames has been referred to in Chapter 7, and Figure 7.1 illustrates

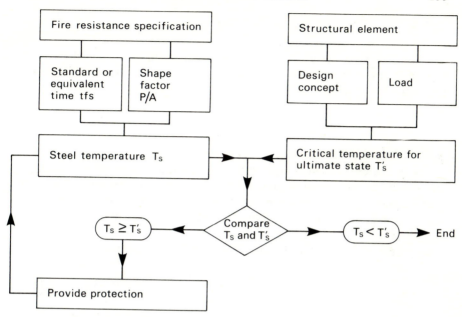

Figure 9.2   A modified approach for steel structures.

unidirectional flow showing a small drop from the gas temperature close to the surface of the section and a uniform temperature within the section, assuming high conductivity and instantaneous flow of heat. The quantity of heat transferred per unit length over a short interval of time Δt is

$$q = \alpha \cdot S \cdot (T_f - T_s) \cdot \Delta t \tag{9.1}$$

where α = total heat transfer coefficient (W/m² °C)
    S = surface area exposed to fire (m²/m)
    T_f = temperature of hot gases (°C)
    T_s = temperature of steel section (°C)

The temperature of the unit length steel section is increased by ΔT_s when q units of heat are absorbed, such that

$$q = c_s \cdot \Delta T_s \cdot m_s \tag{9.2}$$

where c_s = specific heat of steel (J/kg °C)
    m_s = mass of steel (kg/m)

As the quantity of heat is the same in two expressions, the temperature rise is

$$\Delta T_s = \frac{\alpha}{c_s} \cdot \frac{S}{m_s} \cdot (T_f - T_s) \cdot \Delta t \qquad (9.3)$$

The surface area S per unit length corresponds to the perimeter of the steel section P_s (m), and as the mass of steel is directly proportional to its cross-sectional area A_s (m^2), expression 9.3 can be rewritten as

$$\Delta T_s = \frac{\alpha}{c_s} \cdot \frac{S}{m_s} \cdot (T_f - T_s) \cdot \Delta t \qquad (9.4)$$

P_s/A_s is known as the shape factor of the steel section.

The coefficient of heat transfer α has two components, α_c and α_r, i.e. heat transfer due to convection from the fire gases to the exposed surface (α_c) and heat transfer by radiation from the flames and hot gases (α_r). It has been experimentally shown that in gas-fired furnaces of the type used in the United Kingdom, $\alpha_c = 25$ W/m^2 °C. α_r on the other hand is related to the flame temperature and follows the Stefan–Boltzman law for radiation, i.e.

$$\alpha_r = \frac{5.77\omega_r}{T_f - T_s}\left[\left(\frac{T_f + 273}{100}\right)^4 - \left(\frac{T_s + 273}{100}\right)^4\right] \text{W/m}^2\,°\text{C} \qquad (9.5)$$

ω_r is the emissivity of flames, hot gases and the exposed steel surfaces. The emissivity of luminous flames is between 0.8 and 0.9 and of the steel surfaces slightly lower, so that the net emissivity is of the order of 0.7. In many furnaces the flames are non-luminous during the early part of heating, and screening of parts of sections is possible by the flanges (a function of width/height ratio). For practical purposes the value $\omega_r = 0.5$ has been found to give reliable results for beams carrying concrete floor slabs.

9.3 Shape factor

The shape factor P_s/A_s is a measure of the ease of rise of temperature of a steel section. The perimeter P_s indicates the surface through which heat is flowing to the steel, and A_s the mass of steel which has to be raised in temperature. Increase in P_s for a given A_s means more rapid increase in temperature and conversely increase in A_s for a given P_s means slower increase in temperature. For a given mass of steel the most favourable section is a round bar, but structurally a tube or a shaped section will be preferable. The lower the value of the shape factor, the lower the rate at which its temperature will increase.

Most of the experimental data are available for shape factors in the range 10 to 300. If the shape factor is greater than 300, the steel temperature can be assumed to be the same as the furnace gases, and when less than 10, temperature distribution across the section is unlikely to be uniform.

Figures 9.3 and 9.4 show how the shape factor P_s/A_s is determined for some

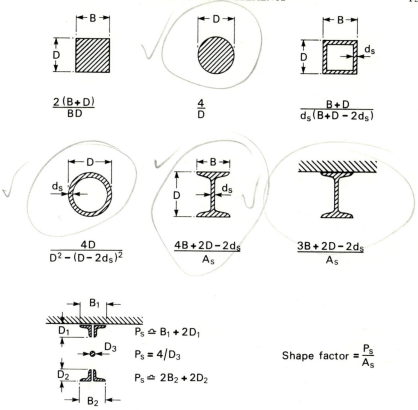

$$\frac{2(B+D)}{BD}$$

$$\frac{4}{D}$$

$$\frac{B+D}{d_s(B+D-2d_s)}$$

$$\frac{4D}{D^2-(D-2d_s)^2}$$

$$\frac{4B+2D-2d_s}{A_s}$$

$$\frac{3B+2D-2d_s}{A_s}$$

$P_s \simeq B_1 + 2D_1$

$P_s = 4/D_3$

Shape factor $= \dfrac{P_s}{A_s}$

$P_s \simeq 2B_2 + 2D_2$

Figure 9.3   Shape factor for unprotected steel sections.

common steel shapes exposed to heating in relation to their use in a building. With unprotected steel P_s is the whole of the exposed perimeter, whereas with protected sections, it is the perimeter of the inner face of the protection.

9.4 Steel temperature

(a) *Uninsulated section*

The temperature rise of an uninsulated steel section is determined by using Equation 9.4.

$$\Delta T_s = \frac{\alpha \cdot P_s}{c_s \cdot \rho_s \cdot A_s} \cdot (T_f - T_s) \cdot \Delta t$$

As $\alpha = \alpha_c + \alpha_r$ and α_r is dependent upon the furnace and the steel temperature its value increases as heating proceeds, for this reason the time interval Δt

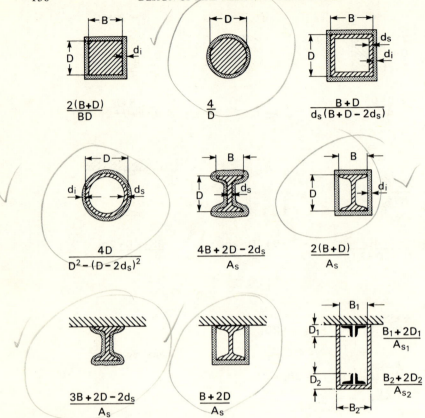

Figure 9.4 Shape factor for protected steel sections.

should not have a large value. The ECCS document suggests that

$$\Delta t \not> \frac{25\,000}{P_s/A_s} \tag{9.6}$$

Temperature rise of the steel section is found step by step as demonstrated in Example 9.1, until the end of the heating period or until it exceeds a specified temperature.

The temperature rise of a range of steel sections having shape factors (P_s/A_s) in the range 10 to 300 is shown in Figure 9.5 when exposed to heating in a furnace having a resulting emissivity (ω_f) of 0.5. The curves demonstrate the influence of the shape factor on temperature rise, as its value increases the steel temperature gets closer to that of the furnace gases. The curves can be replotted to show the relationship between the shape factor and the duration of heating necessary for a critical temperature of 550°C. It demonstrates

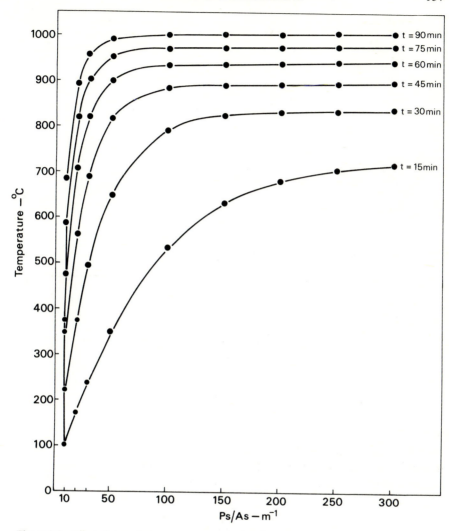

Figure 9.5   Effect of shape factor on temperature rise of unprotected steel.

clearly the advantage of a low shape factor for unprotected steel; to remain below this temperature for at least 30 minutes the shape factor needs to be less than 35 (Figure 9.6).

(b) *Insulated section*

The temperature rise of the insulated steel section depends upon the steel characteristics listed in the previous section as well as the resistance provided

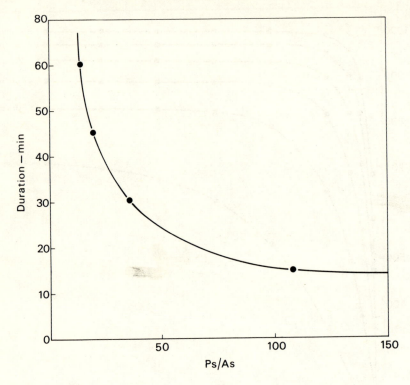

Figure 9.6   Relationship between P_s/A_s and t_f for unprotected steel when $T_s = 550°C$.

by the insulation to the flow of heat. If it is assumed that the rate of heat flow through the insulation results from a linear temperature gradient, the quantity of heat received by the insulated section in time Δt is

$$q = \frac{1}{1/\alpha + \dfrac{d_i}{k_i}} \cdot P_i(T_f - T_s)\, \Delta t \; \text{J/m} \qquad (9.7)$$

where α = coefficient of heat transfer $(\text{W/m}^2\,°\text{C})$
        d_i = thickness of insulation (m)
        k_i = thermal conductivity of insulation $(\text{W/m}\,°\text{C})$
        P_i = surface of the insulation facing the steel section (m^2/m)
        T_f = fire temperature at time t $(°\text{C})$
        T_s = steel temperature at time t $(°\text{C})$
        Δt = time interval.

CALCULATIONS

Example 9·1

Find the temperature rise of a fully exposed steel column.
Size : 203mm. x 203mm. I - section, wt 60 kg/m.
Use the following equation to determine the temperature

Eq.9·4
$$\Delta Ts = \frac{\alpha}{Cs \cdot Ps} \cdot \frac{Ps}{As} (Tf - Ts) \; \Delta t$$

Ps = 1·24 m
As = 7·6433 × 10^{-3} m^2

Eq. 9·3
$$Ps/As = \frac{1·24}{7·6433 \times 10^{-3}} = 162·23 \; m^{-1}$$

Eq.9·6
$$\Delta t = \frac{25000}{162·23} = 154·3 \; sec$$

use Δt = 150 sec. in eq. 9·4

$$\therefore \Delta Ts = \frac{\alpha \times 150 \times 162·23}{520 \times 7850} \times (Tf - Ts)$$

$$= \frac{\alpha}{168} (Tf - Ts)$$

Eq.9·5 Assuming ambient temperature of 20°C, emissivity wr = 0·5,
αc = 25, then equation 9·5 can be used to obtain
the values of α. Tf is the furnace gas temperature.
Tf = 745 $\log_{10}$ (8t +1) (t is in minutes)
The first value of Tf is obtained at 75 sec. (1·25min.)
and subsequent values at 150 sec. (2·5 min.) intervals.
Tf at 1·25mins = 399°C   Ts at 0 = 20°C
$\therefore \alpha r$ from equation 9·5 = 15
$\therefore \alpha$ = 15 + 25 = 40 W/m^2 °C

Subsituting values of Ps/As, c_s and ρs in equation 9·4

$$\Delta Ts = \frac{\alpha}{c_s \rho s} \; \frac{Ps}{As} \cdot (Tf - Ts) \cdot \Delta T \;°C$$

$$= \frac{\alpha \times 162·23}{520 \times 7850} (Tf - Ts) \cdot 150 = \frac{\alpha}{168} (Tf - Ts) \;°C$$

at 1·25 min, when Tf = 399°C, Tf - Ts = 399 - 20 = 379°C

$$\therefore \Delta Ts = \frac{40 \times 379}{168} = 90°C$$

$\therefore$ the average steel temperature at 2·5mins = 110°C

CALCULATIONS

This step by step procedure is continued until 15 minutes
and results obtained are shown in the table below :

Time mins.	Tf °C	α W/m³ °C	Tf - Ts °C	Δ Ts °C	Ts °C
0	399	40	375	90	20
2·5	534	52	424	132	110
5·0	609	67	367	146	242
7·5	658	85	270	136	388
10·0	696	105	172	107	524
12·5	714	125	81	60	631
15·0					691

If the steel column was subjected to full design loads,
its collapse would be imminent between 550°C and 600°C.
According to temperature rise values shown above it
could fail between 10 and 12·5 minutes.

Heat quantity q raises the temperature of the steel section by T_s assuming the heat flow to be unidimensional, uniform and instantaneous, such that

$$q = c_s \cdot \rho_s \cdot A_s \cdot T_s \qquad (9.8)$$

where c_s = specific heat capacity of steel (J/kg °C)
  ρ_s = density of steel (kg/m³)
  A_s = area of steel section (m²)

By equating 9.7 and 9.8

$$\Delta T_s = \frac{P_i}{(1/\alpha + d_i/k_i) c_s \cdot \rho_s \cdot A_s} (T_f - T_s) \cdot \Delta t \qquad (9.9)$$

Under fire temperatures the value of $1/\alpha$ is small in comparison with the thermal resistance of the insulation (d_i/k_i) and may be ignored, which simplifies Equation 9.9 to

$$\Delta T_s = \frac{k_i}{d_i} \cdot \frac{P_i}{A_s} \cdot \frac{1}{c_s \rho_s} (T_f - T_s) \cdot \Delta t \qquad (9.10)$$

$\dfrac{k_i}{d_i}$ is a measure of the thermal conductance of the insulation

$\dfrac{P_i}{A_s}$ is the shape factor for a protected steel section as shown in Figure 9.4

$c_s \rho_s$ is the thermal capacitance of the steel section, and

$(T_f - T_s)$ is the temperature gradient between the fire gases and the steel.

This relationship is based on the assumption that the insulation has no thermal capacity, i.e. it does not absorb any heat, and is completely dry. The effect of both would be to delay the rise in temperature of steel. As a simple rule the insulation should be considered as a low thermal capacity material, when

$$c_s \cdot \rho_s \cdot A_s > 2c_i \cdot \rho_i \cdot d_i \cdot P_i \qquad (9.11)$$

where $c_s \cdot \rho_s$ and $c_i \cdot \rho_i$ are the thermal capacities of the steel and the insulation respectively.

If the insulation has greater thermal capacity than indicated by Equation 9.11, heat needed to raise its temperature has to be taken into account. If it is assumed that over a given time interval Δt, the fire temperature rises by ΔT_f and the steel temperature by ΔT_s and the insulation temperature increases by $(\Delta T_f + \Delta T_s)/2$, the quantity of heat needed is the sum of the heat needed to raise the steel temperature by ΔT_s and that needed to raise the insulation temperature is $(\Delta T_f + \Delta T_s)/2$.

Equation 9.10 is amended to

$$\Delta T_s = \frac{k_i}{d_i} \cdot \frac{P_i}{A_s} \cdot \frac{1}{c_s \rho_s} \left[\frac{1}{1 + \dfrac{c_i d_i \cdot \rho_i \cdot P_i}{2 c_s \rho_s \cdot A_s}} \right] \cdot (T_f - T_s)\,\Delta t - \frac{\Delta T_f}{1 + \dfrac{2 c_s \rho_s \cdot A_s}{c_i d_i \rho_i \cdot P_i}} \qquad (9.12)$$

Equation 9.12 can be further simplified by assuming that the effect of the heat capacity of the insulation can be simulated by increasing heat capacity of the steel section by $\frac{1}{2}(c_i \rho_i d_i P_i)$. This amends Equation 9.10 to

$$\Delta T_s = \frac{k_i}{d_i} \cdot P_i \cdot \frac{1}{\left(A_s c_s \rho_s + \dfrac{c_i d_i \rho_i \cdot P_i}{2} \right)} (T_f - T_s)\,\Delta t \qquad (9.13)$$

$$= \frac{k_i}{d_i} \cdot \frac{P_i}{A_s} \cdot \frac{1}{c_s \rho_s} \left[\frac{c_s \rho_s}{c_s \rho_s + \dfrac{c_i d_i \rho_i \cdot P_i}{2 A_s}} \right] (T_f - T_s)\,\Delta t \qquad (9.14)$$

The factor

$$\frac{c_s \rho_s}{c_s \rho_s + \dfrac{c_i d_i \rho_i P_i}{2 A_s}}$$

Table 9.2   Typical thermal properties of insulating materials

Material	Density kg/m^3	Specific heat J/kg °C	Thermal conductivity W/m °C	Moisture content % by weight
Sprayed mineral fibre	250–350	1050	0.10	1.0
Vermiculite slabs	300	1200	0.15	7.0
Vermiculite/gypsum slabs	800	1200	0.15	15.0
Gypsum plaster	800	1700	0.20	20.0
Mineral fibre sheets	500	1500	0.25	2.0
Aerated concrete	600	1200	0.30	2.5
Lightweight concrete	1600	1200	0.80	2.5
Dense concrete	2200	1200	1.50	1.5

has a value of less than 1 and as a consequence delays the temperature rise of the steel section. Depending upon whether the steel section is protected or not, and whether the insulation has a negligible or high heat capacity, Equation 9.4, 9.10 or 9.14 is used to calculate the steel temperature.

The thermal conductivity (k_i), specific heat (c_i) and the density (ρ_i) of the insulating materials are temperature-dependent properties, and of these the specific heat and the density do not alter significantly. Thermal conductivity, however, does vary and in some materials can increase by a factor of four when the temperature is increased from 100 to 1000°C. Ideally the calculation method should allow for this, but this requires the use of a computer for calculation purposes. For simple calculation it is possible to use an average value of the conductivity based either on the mean temperature of insulation when the steel section has reached a maximum safe temperature, or, to introduce a greater factor of safety, its value at the maximum acceptable steel temperature (say around 600°C).

Typical properties for a range of materials which may be used to protect steel are given in Table 9.2. If more precision is needed the thermal properties for a given material should be established by means of separate tests.

The calculation of steel temperature for protected sections is illustrated in Examples 9.2 and 9.3. Example 9.3 deals with a steel beam supporting a roof slab of concrete and protected with a light density mineral fibre insulation. The other example examines the temperature rise of a steel column protected with slabs of vermiculite bonded with a silicate-based adhesive. The first step is to determine if the insulation has a significant heat capacity. The encasement in the second example is shown to have a sufficiently high thermal capacity to influence the rate of temperature rise of the steel section.

Example 9.3 shows that steel temperature after 100 minutes exposure rises to 554°C. The insulated column on the other hand shows a less rapid temperature rise despite exposure on four sides but a lower value of the shape factor P_s/A_s. Calculations of this type can be made using a desk top calculator and the flow diagram in Figure 9.7 shows the basis for developing a suitable program. Figures 9.8 to 9.12 illustrate the use of such programs to obtain data for graphical representation of the effect of insulating materials with different d_i/k_i values and shape factor P_s/A_s. Such data can be used for a rapid check on

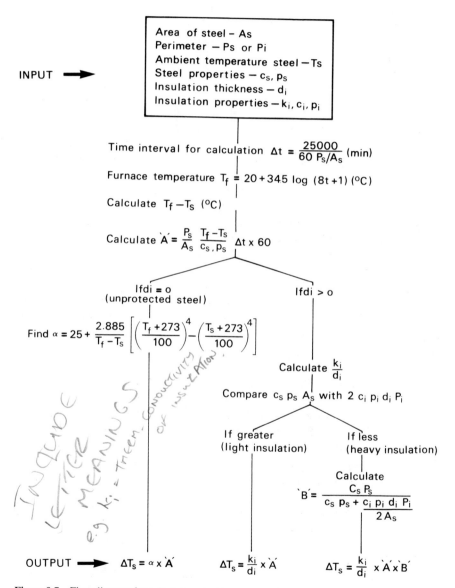

Figure 9.7 Flow diagram for calculating steel temperatures.

Example 9·2

<u>Determine the temperature rise of a protected steel column</u>.

Duration of heating - 60 mins.
Steel dimensions = 203 x 203 x 60 kg.
Insulation : vermiculite slabs 25mm. thick.

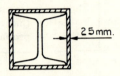

25mm.

Fig 9·7 | Area of steel, As = 75·8 x 10^{-4} m^2
Inside insulation perimeter, Pi = 0·8296 m

$$\frac{Pi}{As} = 109 \ m^{-1}$$

Ambient temperature = 20°C
Steel properties C_s = 250 J/kg°C
$$\rho s = 7850 \ kg/m^3$$

Table 9·2 | Insulation : Thickness, di = 0·025 m.
Conductivity, ki = 0·15 W/m°C
Heat Capacity, ci = 1200 J/kg°C
Density, ρi = 300 kg/m^3

$$\frac{di}{ki} = 0·16$$

Time interval for calculation steps,

Eq. 9·6 | $\Delta t = \dfrac{25000}{60 \times Pi/As} = \dfrac{25000}{60 \times 109} = 3·8$, say 4 mins

Is thermal capacity of insulation significant?
Compare $c_s \, \rho s \, As$ with $2 \, ci \, \rho i \, di \, Pi$
250 x 7850 x ·00758 $\longleftrightarrow$ 2 x 1200 x 300 x 0·025 x 0·8296
14875 $\longleftrightarrow$ 14932

The insulation can be assumed to have significant heat capacity.

Fig 9·7

Calculate 'A' $\dfrac{Pi}{As} \cdot \dfrac{Tf - Ts}{Cs \cdot \rho s} \cdot \Delta t \times 60$

$$= \dfrac{109 \times 4 \times 60}{520 \times 7850} \ (Tf - Ts) = 0.0064(Tf - Ts)$$

Calculate 'B' $= \dfrac{Cs \ \rho s}{cs \ \rho s + \dfrac{ci \ \rho i \ di \ Pi}{2 As}} = 0.799$

Calculate $\dfrac{ki}{di} = \dfrac{0.15}{0.025} = 6$

$\Delta Ts = 'A' \times 'B' \times \dfrac{ki}{di} = 0.0064 \times 0.799 \times 6 \ (Tf - Ts)$

$$= 0.031 \ (Tf - Ts)$$

The furnace temperature Tf at 1min. for initial calculation.

$$Tf = 20 + 345 \log (8t + 1) = 349°C$$
$$Tf - Ts = 349 - 20 = 329°C$$

$\therefore \Delta Ts = 0.031 \times 329 = 10°C \quad Ts = 20 + 10 = 30$

The calculations are then repeated at 4 min intervals as shown below.

Time mins	Tf °C	Tf-Ts °C	ΔTs °C	Ts °C
0				20
2	349	329	10	30
6	576	546	17	47
10	645	598	19	66
14	705	639	20	86
18	748	662	21	107
22	781	674	21	128
26	808	680	21	149
30	831	682	21	170
34	851	681	21	191
38	869	678	21	212
42	884	672	21	233
46	899	666	21	254
50	905	651	20	274
54	924	650	20	294
58	935	641	20	314
62	945	631	20	334

Fig.9·10 | At 60mins. steel temperature is 334°C
9·11 | Using the data in Figures 9·9 and 9·10 for
Pi/As = 109

$$\frac{di}{ki} = 0·1 \quad Ts = 460°C \text{ at } 60min.$$

$$\frac{di}{ki} = 0·2 \quad Ts = 310°C \text{ at } 60mins.$$

when $\frac{di}{ki} = 0·16 \quad Ts = 400°C$

If the thermal capacity of the insulation is ignored

$$\Delta Ts = \text{'A'} \times \frac{ki}{di} \quad \therefore \quad Ts \text{ at } 60mins = 368°C$$

Example 9·3

Determine the time for the temperature of a
protected steel beam to rise to 550°C.

Steel section: 460 x 152 x 60 kg.
Insulation : 25mm. sprayed fibres.
Area of steel $A_s = 75·8 \times 10^{-4}$ m²
Fig.9·7   Perimeter $P_i = 1·2538$m. $\dfrac{P_i}{A_s} = 165$ m⁻¹

Insulation thickness $d_i = 0·025$m.
          conductivity $k_i = 0·1$ W/m°C
                   $c_i = 1050$ J/kg°C
                   $\rho_i = 300$ kg/m³

Ambient temperature, c_s, ρ_s as in example 9·2
Time interval for calculations

$$\Delta t = \frac{25000}{60 \times 165} = 2·5 \text{ mins.}$$

compare $c_s \, \rho_s \, A_s \longleftrightarrow 2 \, c_i \, \rho_i \, d_i \, P_i$
              14875 $>$ 13590

∴ the insulation has low heat capacity
∴ $\Delta T_s = A \times \dfrac{k_i}{d_i}$

Fig.9·7

$$A = \frac{165 \times 2·5 \times 60}{520 \times 7850} \quad (T_f - T_s) = 0·006 \,(T_f - T_s)$$

$$\frac{k_i}{d_i} = \frac{0·1}{0·025} = 4$$

$$\Delta T_s = 0·024 \,(T_f - T_s) \quad °C$$

The first calculation of the furnace temperature T_f is at
1·25 min., then at 3·75 mins. and continues at 2·5 min. intervals
until the steel temperature exceeds 550°C

Time min.	Tf °C	Tf-Ts °C	Δ Ts °C	Ts °C
0				20
1·75	469	449	11	
2·5				31
5·0	534	503	12	43
7·5	609	566	14	57
10	569	602	14	71
30				188
60				349
90	1008	501	12	507
92·5	1012	493	12	519
95	1016	485	12	531
97·5	1020	477	11	543
100				554

The steel temperature reached 550°C at

$$97.5 + \frac{2.5 \times 7}{11} = 99 \text{ minutes}$$

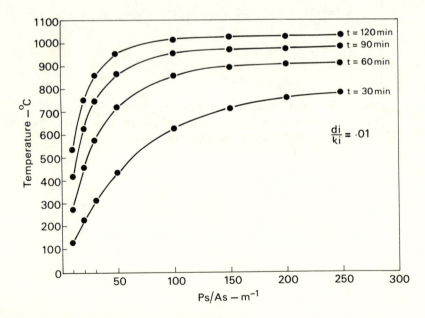

Figures 9.8–9.12   Steel temperature of insulated sections.

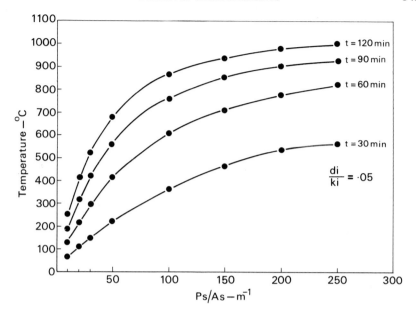

Figure 9.9

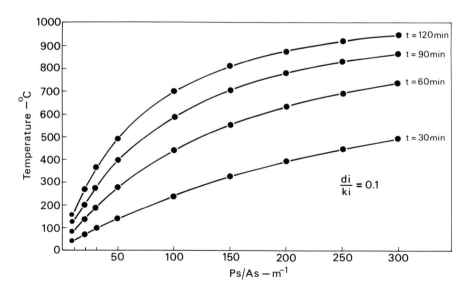

Figure 9.10

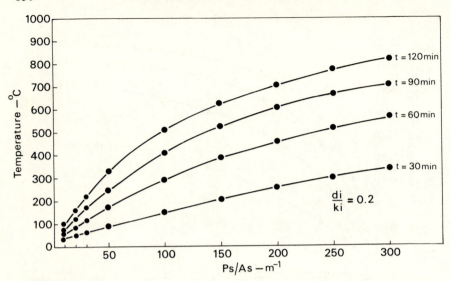

Figure 9.11

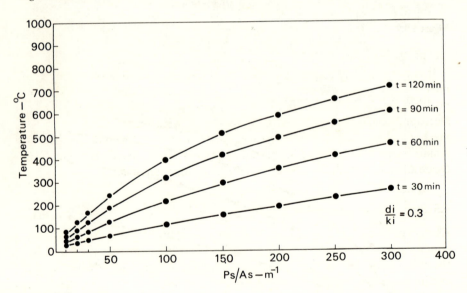

Figure 9.12

the suitability of a given protective material provided reliable data on its thermal properties are available.

Figure 9.13 shows graphically the relationship between P_i/A_s and d_i/k_i for a range of shape factors up to a maximum heating period of 120 minutes.

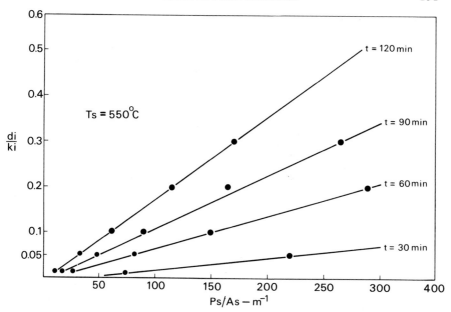

Figure 9.13   Relationship between P_s/A_s and d_i/k_i.

It is important to appreciate that actual fire test data will be required in most cases to demonstrate the ability of the protective materials to stay in position. Sprayed low density materials rely on the retention of the bond with steel and boxed encasements on the fixing system which may consist of mechanical means as well as adhesives. Ideally a system should be tested for a maximum period for which it may need to be employed and the test data also used to check the validity of assumed thermal characteristics.

9.5 Structural behaviour—beams

As steel beams are heated, their stress resisting capacity decreases, and failure condition is reached when the reduced capacity equals stresses produced by the imposed load. This limit state of failure causes a condition at which strain can increase at a rapid rate without any increase in stress. Another limit state which may be imposed is that of deformation (i.e. the downward deflection) and can be expressed as either a critical rate of deformation or a limiting value of deformation.

The limit state of structural failure is a function of the stress level, sectional properties, the interaction of the beam with the adjacent members and the temperature profile. With steel structural members the failure condition can

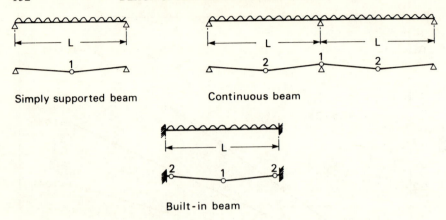

Simply supported beam   Continuous beam

Built-in beam

Figure 9.14   Formation of hinges in beams.

be related to the attainment of a particular temperature at a critical part of the system, hence the concept of a 'critical steel temperature' has developed. However, it needs to be borne in mind, as already pointed out, that there is no unique temperature to describe all failure conditions and for each structural system a suitable value has to be established. The final collapse of an element when 'free' strain, i.e. without increase of stress, is occurring is also dependent upon the rate at which the temperature is increasing.

The failure of steel members follows an elasto-plastic behaviour—after passing through the elastic limit, collapse does not take place until a mechanism is formed with plastic hinges. In the case of a statically determinate system, the formation of a single hinge at the point of greatest stress can cause failure to occur as the section is unable to offer any resistance to rotation. With statically indeterminate systems more than one hinge is needed for the mechanism to fail. Figure 9.14 shows the formation of hinges in a simply supported and a continuous beam to illustrate the difference. Hinge 1 is formed first, in the centre of a simply supported uniform section or over the support for the symmetrically loaded continuous beam, allowing each side to rotate. However, failure of the continuous beam does not occur until a second hinge has been formed at mid-span. Consequently statically indeterminate systems give an improved performance in case of a fire and the determination of their behaviour pattern is more accurately done on the basis of plastic analysis.

If we consider a prismatic beam, simply supported with a load of W per unit length and a span of L, the maximum bending moment is

$$M_a = \frac{WL^2}{8}$$

and the elastic moment capacity $M_e = f_y \cdot Z_e$ where f_y is the yield strength and Z_e, the elastic section modulus.

At failure the stress in extreme fibre is f_p and the plastic moment $M_p = f_p \cdot Z_p$ where Z_p is the plastic section modulus. For a rectangular section

$$M_e = f_y \cdot \frac{bd^2}{6} \text{ and } M_p = f_p \cdot \frac{bd^2}{4} \text{ as } Z_e = \frac{bd^2}{6} \text{ and } Z_p = \frac{bd^2}{4},$$

therefore the ratio of plastic to elastic modulus

$$= \frac{bd^2}{4} \times \frac{6}{bd^2} = 1.5.$$

For I-sections the ratio is about 1.15, i.e. the load on the section can be increased by 15% before full plasticity occurs. The calculation of the structural stability of a simply supported beam and of a continuous beam is illustrated in Examples 9.4 and 9.5.

The basis of design under normal conditions will influence the reserve of plastic capacity available before failure becomes imminent. If we take the example of a uniformly loaded beam which is restrained at its ends, where the service load is W_s, the ultimate load under elastic design is W_e, and under plastic design W_p.

The bending moment under service load is $W_s L^2/8$. At ambient temperatures (20°C) the yield stress reaches a maximum value when $W_e L^2/12 = Z_e f_{y_{20}}$ and the plastic state is reached when $W_p L^2/8 = 2Z_p \cdot f_{y_{20}}$. At high temperatures failure will occur when the yield strength is reduced to f_{yT} such that $W_s L^2/8 = 2Z_p \cdot f_{yT}$.

Consequently the yield strength reduction factor ($\sigma = f_{yT}/f_{y_{20}}$) has different values depending upon the design concept used.

Elastic design:

$$\frac{f_{yT}}{f_{y_{20}}} = \frac{3}{4} \cdot \frac{Z_e}{Z_p} \cdot \frac{W_s}{W_e}, \text{ for I-sections } \frac{Z_p}{Z_e} = 1.15$$

$$\therefore \sigma_s = \frac{f_{yT}}{f_{y_{20}}} = 0.65 \frac{W_s}{W_e}$$

Plastic design:

$$\sigma_s = \frac{f_{yT}}{f_{y_{20}}} = \frac{W_s}{W_p}.$$

The example shows that if the section is plastically designed the reserve at failure is less, and hence there is no gain in fire resistance due to the indeterminate nature of the system. However, if the system has been elastically designed, then the plastic reserve shows a significant gain by raising the

Example 9·4

Calculate the critical temperature for a
simply supported steel beam

Beam size 406mm. x 178.m. x 60 kg.

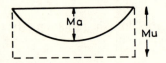

25·5 kN/m

7·4m

Section modules
Elastic Ze = 1058 cm³
Plastic Zp = 1194 cm³
Steel quality - Grade 43
Yield strength fy = 250 N/mm²
Allowable bending stress = 165 N/mm²

Ma

Mu

Service load Ws (dead + live load) = 25·5 kN/m

Bending moment under service load, $M_a = \dfrac{W_s L^2}{8}$

$$= \dfrac{25·5 \times 7·4 \times 7·4}{8} = 174·5 \text{ kNm}$$

Maximum bending stress $= \dfrac{174·5 \times 10^6}{1058 \times 10^3} = 164·9 \text{ N/mm}^2$

It is within allowable limit.

Ultimate moment capacity $M_u = \dfrac{250 \times 1058 \times 10^3}{10^6} = 264·5 \text{ kNm}$

Maximum load to develop M_u, $\quad W_u = \dfrac{395 \times 8}{7·4 \times 7·4} = 38·6 \text{ kN/m}$

If failure is assumed to occur at yield stress f_{yT} at Temperature Ts, the temperature is determined by the ratio between f_{y20} and f_{yT}

$$\sigma_s = \dfrac{164·9}{250} = 0·658$$

Fig.9·1   From figure 9·1 this corresponds to a temperature of 440°C – a value much below that obtained in tests. If failure is considered to occur when a hinge is formed due to plastic strain, then

$$\dfrac{f_{yT}}{f_{y20}} = \dfrac{Z_e}{Z_p} \cdot \dfrac{W_s}{W_u} = \dfrac{2058}{1194} \times \dfrac{25·5}{38·6} = 0·58$$

From figure 9·1, $\sigma_s = 0·58$ at 500°C, the temperature is still on the low side.

If the correction factor 'f' from section 9·5 is used, its value for statically determinate elements is,

$\quad f = 0·77 + 0·15 \times \dfrac{W_s}{W_u} = 0·77 + 0·15 \times 0·66 = 0·89$

then $\sigma_s = 0·89 \times 0·58 = 0·52$

This corresponds to a temperature of 560°C, a value similar to those obtained experimentally.

Example 9·5.   Calculate the critical temperature for
a continuous beam system.

Assuming the same section and
span as in 9·4, the beam design may
use either elastic or plastic
design principles.

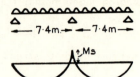

a) Elastic design.
   Moment at middle support, $M_s = \dfrac{W_s L^2}{8}$

   Ultimate moment when the yield strength is reached

   $$\dfrac{W_u L^2}{8} = Z_e . f_{y} 20$$

If the beam is assumed to fail when a plastic hinge
is formed at mid support, under service load W_s
Then the maximum moment at failure $\dfrac{W_s L^2}{11·7} = Z_p . f_{y T}$

   $\therefore$ yield strength reduction factor $\sigma_s = \dfrac{f_{y T}}{f_{y} 20} = \dfrac{8}{11·7} . \dfrac{Z_e}{Z_p} . \dfrac{W_s}{W_u}$

Using values from example 9·4

   $$\sigma_s = \dfrac{8}{11·7} \times \dfrac{1058}{1194} \times \dfrac{25·5}{38·4} = 0·39$$

From figure 9·1 this represents a critical temperature
of 620°C

b) If the beam is plastically designed
   At ambient temperatures $W_u . \dfrac{L^2}{11·7} = Z_p . f_{y} 20$

   Under failure conditions $W_s' = \dfrac{11·7 \times 1194 \times 250}{1·7 \times 7·4 \times 7·4} \times 10^{-3} = 37·52 \text{kN/m}$

   $W_u' = 37·52 \times 1·7 = 63·77 \text{kN/m}$

   $\therefore \sigma_s' = \dfrac{f_{y T}}{f_{y} 20} = \dfrac{W_s'}{W_u'} = \dfrac{37·52}{63·77} = 0·59$

   $$T_s = 500°C$$

critical temperature from 500°C in example 9.4 (before the application of the correction factor) to 620°C.

The calculation of the limit state of steel beams has been based on assuming idealized conditions which do not exist in practice, either in real fires, or in fire tests. Consequently the calculated fire resistance is usually lower than that obtained in tests. Pettersson[7] and Witteveen have identified two main factors which are responsible for these differences.

Material properties are usually assumed to have a characteristic value when determining the test load. However, at the failure point it is the actual value of material strength at high temperature which is critical, and this is related to its actual strength at ambient temperatures. As the quality of materials used in test samples is generally good, the performance is consequently higher. If a grade 43 steel with a characteristic yield strength of 240 N/mm^2 is used, the actual strength for 90% of the samples will be between 240 and 275 N/mm^2. At the upper level the failure temperature under loads based on the characteristic strength can be 70°C higher; at a rate of heating of 10°C/min a difference of 7 minutes can easily occur in fire test results.

In fire resistance tests the temperature of steel members is rarely uniform although an assumption is made in calculations that uniform temperatures exist. In the case of beams, temperature can vary along the length of the beam as well as over the height of a beam. Tests at the laboratories of CECM[8] have shown that the temperature gradient between the bottom and top flanges can be 50 to 70°C midspan and nearly 150°C over supports when testing continuous sections. In the case of columns, a temperature gradient over the height of the section can exist.

It has been suggested that correction factors should be applied when determining fire resistance analytically in order to minimize the difference between fire test data and calculations. An overall correction factor can be applied, depending upon the nature of the construction, to correct the calculated loadbearing capacity under idealized conditions to its true value. As a design procedure this may require an iteration process to align the corrected loadbearing capacity after thermal exposure to the value specified. An alternative method is to use the relationship

$$\frac{W_T}{W_u} \propto \frac{f_{yT}}{f_{y_{20}}}$$

where W_T is the uncorrected loadbearing capacity at T°C as determined in the previous section. Value of the correction factor can be given for various values of W_s/W_u as this is known at the design stage.

The ECCS document[2] has provided a detailed procedure for determining the correction factor. The following is a simplification for practical application when the service load W_s is between 0.2 and $0.85W_u$.

Correction factor for columns: $f = 0.85$

Statically determinate beams: $f = 0.77 + 0.15\dfrac{W_s}{W_u}$

Statically indeterminate beams: $f = 0.25 + 0.77\dfrac{W_s}{W_u}$.

The application of this correction factor has the effect of showing an increase in the residual loadbearing capability of beams and columns; for beams it is related to the design concept as well as the ratio between the actual load and the loadbearing capability at ambient temperatures. If we assume that the load factor is about 1.75, then the values of f for the statically determinate and indeterminate elements are 0.85 and 0.69 respectively.

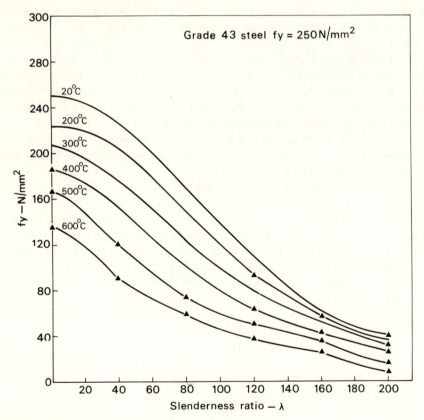

Figures 9.15–9.16   Buckling curves for axially loaded columns.

9.6 Compression members

In the standard fire resistance tests, as explained in Chapter 4, it is the general practice to test columns with the ends restrained and with the test load maintained constant so that a degree of restraint exists, but axially the restraint is less than complete, and expansion of the column is allowed. In a real structure free expansion of columns is rare. The condition may be approached in single-storey structures which have little sub-division within, but in multi-storey framed structures the degree of restraint will be influenced by the stiffness of the surrounding beam members.

The buckling curves for steel columns at high temperatures have a shape similar to that at ambient temperatures when the Euler/Rankine approach is used to establish the collapse conditions. Figures 9.15 and 9.16 show curves

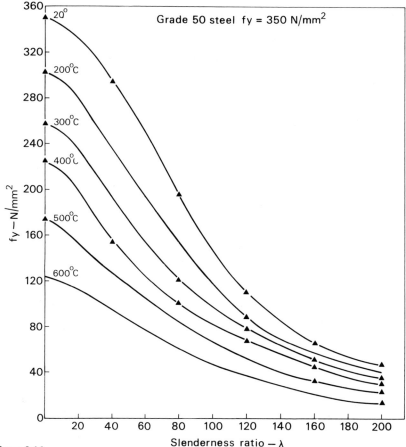

Figure 9.16

for grades 43 and 50 steel relating the axial compressive stress (f_c) to the slenderness ratio (λ). Example 9.6 shows how it may be used to establish the critical temperature. For normal design purposes the effective height is taken to be 0.7L but at failure point the column will behave following the idealized Euler/Rankine concept so that the length of the section between nodes is 0.5L. The example takes a test result on a column and predicts the failure temperature as 500°C. However, this needs to be corrected (for the reasons given in the last section) to 550°C. The actual temperature at the end of the test was 532°C, indicating that the simple method of calculation gives results on the conservative side.

In practice, columns will be subjected to an unpredicted degree of restraint against expansion depending upon the rigidity of the elements to which they are connected, how much fire exposure the other elements suffer and the degree of lateral movement at fixings.

As already noted, in the standard fire resistance test a column is allowed to expand, whilst maintaining a constant load. The net expansion of the column can be determined by considering the reduction in the modulus of elasticity of steel at high temperatures.

Free expansion of the column $= a \cdot T_s \cdot L$ (m)

$$\text{Contraction of the column due to axial force } F = \frac{W_L}{A_s}\left(\frac{1}{E_0} - \frac{1}{E_T}\right) \text{(m)}$$

when a = coefficient of linear expansion (m/°C)
   T_s = steel temperature (°C)
   L = exposed length of column (m)
   E_0 = modulus of elasticity at ambient temperature (kN/mm²)
   E_T = modulus of elasticity at steel temperature T_s (kN/mm²)

Therefore the resultant expansion

$$\delta L = aT_sL - \frac{W_L}{A_s}\left(\frac{1}{E_0} - \frac{1}{E_T}\right) \text{(m)}$$

= DEFLECTION.

The modulus of elasticity at temperature T_s is stated to have some relationship to the ratio between the stress on the section due to load W and the yield stress at ambient temperatures.

9.7 Insulating materials

Insulating materials are placed around the steel when it is shown by calculation that an unprotected section will be raised to a temperature above that considered critical for the given exposure conditions. Designers have a wide choice available to select materials which will provide the necessary

Example 9·6   Calculate the critical load for a steel
              stanchion

Steel section : U.C.203 x 203 mm x 52 kg.
Exposed length = 3 m.
End fixity = Restrained in direction
              at both ends, column
              allowed to expand.
Steel area As = 6640 mm^2
Radius of gyration r $_{x-x}$ =51·6 mm

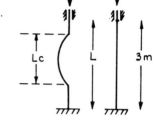

Steel grade - 43
Elastic design for ambient temperature conditions

BS449 Effective length = 0·7L = 2·1m

Slenderness ratio $\lambda = \dfrac{2\cdot1 \times 10^3}{51\cdot6} = 40\cdot7$

BS449 Permissible comprehensive stress pc = 138 N/mm^2
Permissible service load = 138 x 6640 x 10^{-3} = 916 kN
At failure the effective length approaches the
theoretical limit of 0·5L for the specified end conditions.

$\therefore \lambda_T$ at failure = $\dfrac{1\cdot5 \times 10^3}{51\cdot6} = 29$

Fig 9·15 Under comprehensive stress of 138 N/mm^2 and the
slenderness ratio of 29, the buckling temperature
is 500°C (from figure 9·15)
By applying the correction factor f = 0·85 the
corrected temperature corresponds to 138 x 0·85
= 117·3 N/mm^2 and is equal to 550°C from
Figure 9·15 This temperature corresponds to
experimental values.

protection. Some of the products are new developments whilst others have been in existence for a long time.

The insulating materials can be divided into two main categories, those which follow the profile of the section, generally without any gap between the insulation and the steel, and others which provide a hollow box type protection. The first category is generally a wet application and the second usually dry although exceptions are available in both. For a given size of section, the contour protection has a higher P/A value than a box protection and if two materials with identical thermal properties were available, the latter would show an improved performance.

Manufacturers of various products provide data on the protective value of their products for a range of sections for the commonly demanded fire resistance periods. Some have tabulated data whilst others have prepared a series of curves derived empirically from furnace test results. Designers will find such data valuable for making a quick selection. The Association of Fire Protection Contractors and Manufacturers (AFPCM) has published a useful guide listing products available from its members.

It is important for any insulating material to remain in place so that it provides protection to its maximum potential. This characteristic of the protection, best expressed by the term 'retentivity', is not only a feature of the nature of the material but also of the method of its attachment. In the case of directly-applied protective materials following the contour, it depends upon adhesion to the steel section and its capability to withstand any movement or deformation of the section. With hollow or box type protection it is a function of the fastening mechanism provided whether by mechanical means or by adhesives. Sometimes it is necessary to introduce special measures, e.g. reinforcement in plaster coatings, to improve retentivity. It is for this reason that designers need to ensure for themselves that the protective system they select has the necessary retentivity for the period for which protection is required. This requires evidence that the system has been subjected successfully to one or more fire tests for at least the same period in a furnace.

The main types of protective materials or systems which are commonly used for protecting steel are concrete, plaster coatings, sprayed coatings, board materials (mineral fibre boards), slabs and precast shapes. Some of the typical products are described below.

Concrete

Concrete, and brickwork for columns, used to be a common method of protecting steel construction in the early part of the century. Both add a considerable amount of dead load and do not permit full potential of steel to be utilized. Lightweight concrete, density 1600 kg/m^3 as against 2400 kg/m^3

for dense concrete, is preferable, but is still on the heavy side. It is possible however to make use of the structural properties of concrete to add to the stability of the structure. Tests conducted by the author showed that fire resistance of columns can be significantly increased if the cover is at least 50 mm thick and provided with some vertical reinforcement. Concrete encasement to columns has the advantage of withstanding rough treatment in industrial environments—sometimes for instance concrete encasement is provided for the lower part of columns which are exposed to impact damage from vehicles, etc.

Over the last few years a European association of steel tube manufacturers (CIDECT) has been examining the use of concrete-filled steel tubes, of circular as well as rectangular cross-section, to provide fire resistance. Various factors such as the use of reinforcement, level of loading, eccentricity of loading and the end conditions of specimens have been examined. Whilst full design data are not as yet available, it is shown that a reinforced concrete core can significantly improve the performance of hollow section columns. A maximum fire resistance of over two hours has been obtained with a $300 \times 300 \times 7$ mm section, concentrically loaded with 2% reinforcement for the concrete.

Plasters

These provide a hollow encasement by the application of a rendering of cement/sand or gypsum/sand applied to wire mesh wrapped around the section. Both have good retentivity, as the wire reinforcement provides a reliable system. Gypsum plasters are lighter and the endothermic reaction when gypsum releases combined water at around 500°C provides additional benefits in restricting heat flow. Developments have taken place over the recent years in producing lightweight plaster by the use of exfoliated vermiculite/perlite in place of sand. Various premixed grades are available which combine lightweight insulation and a reasonably damage-resistant finish. Cement/vermiculite or gypsum/vermiculite compositions with suitable plasticizers can be sprayed directly onto the steel section to follow the contour and provide a solid encasement. The former has better weathering properties. It is also possible to make both types of products in the form of slabs or shaped sections to go around steel beams or columns. They can be screwed together or held with wire and given a finishing coat of plaster.

The density of plasters varies between 300 and 800 kg/m^3. At the lower end of the range the material is gypsum based with lightweight aggregate. The thermal conductivity varies between 0.17 and 0.21 for the 800 kg material and between 0.10 and 0.15 for the 300 kg material in the temperature range 100 to 900°C.

Sprayed mineral fibres

Sprayed asbestos (i.e. asbestos fibres mixed with a cementitious binder) was a popular method of providing protection to steel, but recent concern with the health hazard of inhalation of asbestos fibres has virtually stopped its use in the UK and some other countries. An alternative product has taken its place, where the asbestos fibres are replaced by other manufactured mineral fibres such as rockwool. Specialized equipment is needed to spray it onto the steel section and the wet material can be pressed and smoothed to the required shape and density. It is applied directly to steel with the binder providing the adhesion, and hence care is needed to ensure that steel is clean and not coated with any incompatible finish. The finished material is soft and easily damaged, therefore its use should be restricted to inaccessible areas. The density of the sprayed material is usually in the range 250–370 kg/m^3 and its thermal conductivity varies between 0.05 and 0.15 W/m °C between 100 and 800°C.

Boards and slabs

Asbestos insulation boards were commonly used for the protection of steel beams and columns until recently, but these have now largely been replaced by asbestos-free boards in which asbestos fibres are substituted by mineral fibres. Lime or cement is used as a binder and some organic materials are mixed to improve fixing characteristics. The boards are cut to size and screwed to each other or to a light angle frame and provide a rigid and hard encasement. The density of the boards varies from 650 to 750 kg/m^3 and the thermal conductivity varies from 0.18 to 0.26 W/m °C.

Vermiculite slabs are made by bonding exfoliated particles with a silicate binder and are available in thicknesses ranging from 25 to 50 mm. They have a density of between 350 and 500 kg/m^3 and the thermal conductivity ranges from 0.09 to 0.17 W/m °C between 100 and 800°C. Mineral wool slabs are lighter and more flexible, with a density around 150 kg/m^3. They can be attached to steel by adhesive or pins but may require some additional method of retention. The thermal conductivity is around 0.035 W/m °C at normal temperatures and increases to 0.32, about ten times, at 800°C due partly to the fusing of the fibres at surface layers.

Intumescent coatings

A new type of protective material which has become popular in the last decade consists of mastics based on epoxy resins which have the property of softening and releasing CO_2 when the temperature exceeds 150°C. This leads to expansion, giving a low density honeycomb with good insulating characteristics. Once the surface layer has intumesced, heat transfer to the interior slows down and further intumescing occurs at a low rate. Beyond 800°C the intumesced material begins to char and decompose and reduction in thickness occurs. The adhesion of the coating at high temperatures to the steel section requires careful consideration. As the material softens there can be a tendency for it to slip. To counteract this, mineral fibre reinforcement is added to the mastic to provide better retentivity. Proprietary products are available to provide protection for up to two hours to steel sections, but only some of these products can withstand prolonged exposure to humid conditions without suffering damage.

9.8 Water cooling

Water cooling of hollow steel sections utilizes the same principle as used in gravity fed water boilers, that is, external heat flow through a water-filled steel tube will raise the water temperature which, due to buoyancy, will rise to the upper level. In a system consisting of hollow steel column connected to a water tank, with a return pipe connection to the base of the column, a circulatory flow will be generated when any part of the column is attacked by fire. A system can be designed[9] so that the temperature of the steel section remains below 200°C and it can withstand fire exposure of unlimited duration provided the flow of water continues and cool water can be injected to the base of columns. Higher temperatures are undesirable, as an appreciable layer of steam between the face of steel and water will limit heat transfer.

A simpler system without provision for replenishment will provide protection only for a limited period of time, probably around 30 minutes. Water cooling of beams is more difficult, and for a beam/column assembly, complex circulation arrangements have to be made. (An ideal solution to this problem has been achieved in Bush Lane House, an office building near Cannon Street Station, London, where a lattice arrangement of diagonal hollow sections with hollow nodes permit water to travel upwards through all members.)

The heat flow pattern through a steel plate of thickness d_s is shown in Figure 9.17. Heat transfer to the exposed surface takes place by convection and radiation as with unprotected steel elements. The temperature of the inner face in contact with the water rises because of heat transfer by conduction. A layer of steam-filled bubbles is formed at the steel/water interface, transferring heat to the mass of water and causing it to rise upwards as its relative density decreases.

Heat transfer to the steel plate:

$$Q = Q_r + Q_c$$

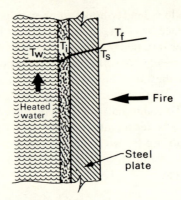

Figure 9.17   Heat transfer through a water-cooled plate.

and to the water:

$$Q = \frac{k_s}{d_s}(T_s^\circ - T_w^\circ)$$

where Q = total heat flow per unit time
        Q_r = heat transfer by radiation
        Q_c = heat transfer by convection
        T_s° = temperature of exposed steel face
        T_w° = temperature of cooled steel face
        k_s = conductivity of steel
        d_s = thickness of steel plate.

If the latent heat of vaporization is taken as 2150 kJ/kg and the specific heat of water as 335 kJ/kg for an 80°C rise in temperature, total heat absorption by the water can be taken as 2485 kJ/kg. This value can be used to calculate the necessary flow rates. Account also needs to be taken of losses due to friction and junctions in the pipework.

Most water-cooled systems have been used for external steel columns expected to be exposed to emerging flames and radiation from the openings. In such cases the rate of heating is likely to be less than indicated above. Depending upon the particular design of the building, an estimation should be made of the rate of heat transfer from the fire.

9.9 External steel

The use of steel sections as part of the structural frame on the exterior facade of a building may require special consideration to determine if it is possible to dispense with protection. The provision of protection may limit the choice to only a few materials such as concrete which can withstand exposure to the elements but can be an undesirable feature architecturally. Water cooling of external columns has been used in a few buildings; the most prominent in the UK is Bush Lane House, mentioned above. In this building the external

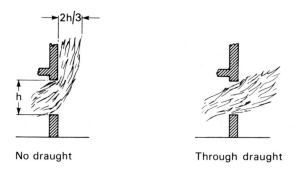

a   Flame shape outside windows

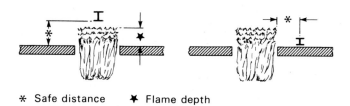

* Safe distance   * Flame depth

b   Plan view showing safe location of steel columns

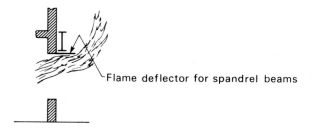

c   Safe location of spandrel beam

Figure 9.18   Exposure of exterior steel structures.

members of hollow circular section form a lattice frame with special connectors at nodes which allow the transfer of stresses as well as the flow of water. This is an expensive solution requiring special sections and the provision of water storage and circulation facilities.

In Chapter 5 when discussing fire severity reference was made to the emission of flames from windows. It has been shown experimentally[10] and theoretically that, due to the fluctuating nature of flames, cooling to the ambient air, and configuration factors, the temperature of steel sections rises at a lower rate than in the compartment in which fire occurs. If the steel sections are not directly in front of the opening or the distance from the opening is sufficient the temperature rise may not be enough to reach the critical value. In that case there is no need to provide any protection. Shielding of the section from direct contact with the flames has a very significant influence and this can be used to advantage for spandrel beams located just above window openings. Figure 9.18 shows the possible flame shapes and various safety principles that can be adopted.

The American Iron and Steel Institute has issued a guide[11] for 'calculating the exposure risk to the external steel sections and the computation of the temperature of the steel elements'. It provides step by step directions for estimating fire intensity, flame characteristics, heat transfer to the steel section and the maximum temperature it is likely to reach. It is shown that for a 20 m wide compartment with a fire load of 50 kg/m^2, if the window height is 2 m a steel column can be located opposite the wall between windows provided the width of the wall is at least 1.2 m. However, if the column is facing the opening, its distance from the opening has to be at least 4 m if 50% of the wall has windows or only 2 m if the openings are 25% of the wall area. This approach is beneficial only if the building has small windows, is not very high, or has storeys separated by fire-resisting floors.

References

1. Pettersson, O. *et al. Fire engineering design of steel structures.* Swedish Institute of Steel Construction, Publication 50, Stockholm, 1976.
2. *European recommendations for the calculation of fire resistance of steel loadbearing elements and steel assemblies exposed to the standard fire.* European Convention for Constructional Steelwork—Committee 3: Fire Safety of Steel Structures.
3. Malhotra, H. L. *The protection of steel from fire.* Paper at the conference organized by the Metals Society, London, and the Cleveland Institute of Engineers, May, 1979.
4. *The Building Regulations*, Schedules 8 Part V, HMSO, London, 1976.
5. Elliott, D. A. *Fire and Steel Construction.* CONSTRADO (Constructional Steel Research and Development Organisation). Croydon, United Kingdom. August, 1974.

6. Read, R. E. H. *et al. Guidelines for the construction of fire resisting structural elements.* Building Research Establishment Report, HMSO, London, 1980.

7. Pettersson, O. and Witteveen, J. *On the fire resistance of structural steel elements derived from standard fire tests or by calculation.* Report reference N 535 to ISO/TC92 Committee, at eleventh plenary meeting, Sydney, September, 1979.

8. Arnault, P. *et al. Resistance au feu de systèmes hyperstatiques en acier (poutres et portiques).* Document CECM 3—74/6F.

9. Bond, G. U. L. *Water cooled hollow columns.* CONSTRADO, Croydon, UK.

10. Law, M. *Design guide for fire safety of bare exterior structural steel.* Ove Arup and Partners, London, January, 1977.

11. *Fire-safe structural steel, a design guide.* American Iron & Steel Institute, Washington, USA, March, 1979.

10 Design of masonry elements

10.1 Introduction

Masonry materials have been used for fire-resisting constructions ever since the need for fire protection in buildings became apparent. Masonry includes bricks and blocks of clay or concrete covering a wide variety of shapes and densities. The main types in common use are listed in Table 10.1.

Solid bricks, i.e. bricks without any indentation or perforation, are not normally used in building construction. Most clay bricks have either a 'frog', a conical depression in one flat face to improve mortar bond, or perforations. BS 3921 considers all bricks with more than 75% material as solid. In the preparation of fire resistance data this definition has been considered to be inadequate, and CP 121[1] has defined solid brick as 'a brick without frogs or with frogs up to 20% of its volume but with no through holes or perforation'. As frogs get filled by a substantial amount by the mortar, this definition allows actual voids of a small amount only. The strength of a brick or block wall is dependent upon the nature of the mortar used, and it is therefore necessary that mortars of the correct quality are employed.

Table 10.1 Main types of masonry units

Type	Material	Shape	Remarks
Brick	Clay	Solid Perforated	BS 3921:1974
	Concrete	Solid	BS 118:1972
Blocks	Clay	Hollow	BS 3921:1974
	Concrete (dense)	Solid Hollow	Density $> 1500\,\text{kg/m}^3$
	Concrete (lightweight)	Solid Hollow	Density $< 1500\,\text{kg/m}^3$
	Concrete (aerated)	Solid	Density $< 625\,\text{kg/m}^3$

Clay bricks are made by the firing of the clay at high temperatures. This imparts to the brick an ability to withstand exposure to fire conditions without suffering much physical or chemical damage—they can be considered to be virtually inert at high temperatures. Failure of brick walls in fires has resulted when the construction could not withstand thermal movement because of its large size and lack of provision for stability and expansion, or when there was movement of other parts of the construction. Perforated clay bricks with small holes behave as well as solid bricks but have lower heat capacity; as the size of the perforations increases the performance is affected, and bricks with a cellular construction and thin webs or walls can perform adversely if the webs are unable to resist high thermal stresses at the junctions. The exposed layers can also disintegrate in such cases.

One of the important developments in the clay brick area has been the introduction of the 'Calculon' brick which is larger than the standard brick, but is perforated and so has a similar weight and handling characteristics. Its use dispenses with the provision of a cavity and allows the whole of the construction to bear loads, whereas in a normal cavity wall, the two leaves have to be tied together to improve stability and the load is mainly carried by one leaf.

The behaviour of solid concrete blocks is similar to that of concrete walls as the material properties are similar, but the presence of mortar joints allows improved capacity to compensate for unequal expansion of the section when one face is exposed to heating. Hollow block walls have better insulation but the loss of the solid material necessitates increase in section thickness to support similar loads. Both solid and hollow block walls are not susceptible to damage by spalling. Aerated concrete blocks, owing to the thermal properties of the product, provide good fire resistance as loadbearing and non-loadbearing systems. Low elastic properties result in little thermal movement when the walls are heated.

Some typical properties of bricks and blocks are shown in Table 10.2.

Table 10.2 Properties of bricks and blocks

Type	Density (kg/m^3)	Compressive strength (N/m^2)
Clay bricks		
solid	1450	4–180
perforated	1800	35
Concrete blocks		
dense	> 1500	3.5–35
lightweight	< 1500 > 625	2.8–7.0
aerated	< 625	2.8

10.2 Fire resistance

In a fire resistance test, a loadbearing masonry wall is subjected to heating on one side, and transfer of heat to the interior of the section is gradual, depending upon the thermal diffusivity of the system. Unequal temperature conditions on the two wall faces cause buckling to occur with the heated face bulging towards the source of heat (Figure 10.1). As long as the amount of buckling is less than the thickness of the wall, the resulting eccentricity, whilst imposing higher compressive stresses on the heated face, is unlikely to promote failure. As soon as the load line is outside the wall thickness, the eccentricity increases deformation and causes tensile stresses to be developed on the exposed face, leading to collapse of the wall. The slenderness ratio of most walls is such that failure in compression is uncommon.

Ingberg[2] has reported over 80 tests on brick walls of clay and concrete, solid and hollow, in thicknesses ranging from a 100 mm single leaf wall to 300 mm cavity wall. Tests were conducted on loadbearing and non-load-bearing constructions, with and without plaster finish and with and without a hose stream test after the heat exposure. Residual strength of walls was determined by cutting small sections from the test specimens and comparing data with similar specimens before heating. It was found that the average reduction in strength was 40 % whereas the design stresses were around 25 % of the compressive strength. His results are briefly summarized in Table 10.3.

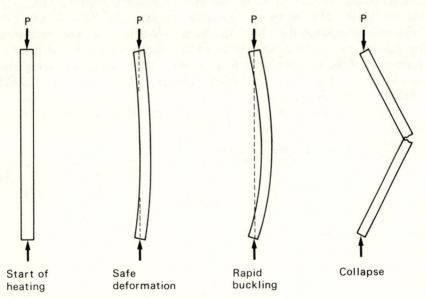

| Start of heating | Safe deformation | Rapid buckling | Collapse |

Figure 10.1   Different stages in the collapse of a masonry wall.

Table 10.3   Ingberg's fire tests on loadbearing brick walls

Type	Thickness	Fire resistance
Clay brick	100 mm	75 min
„	200 mm	300 min
„	300 mm	450 min
Concrete brick	200 mm	360 min
„	300 mm	720 min

Davey and Ashton[3] examined the fire resistance of a few typical brick and block walls, and the author has collected these and other data together in the Fire Note No. 6,[4] and prepared a notional table of fire resistance gradings for such walls. These were used in the tables given in the earlier codes on brickworks and walls of blocks and slabs and have been consolidated in CP 121: Part 1.[5] Walls are divided into four categories: loadbearing single leaf, non-loadbearing single leaf, loadbearing cavity walls and non-loadbearing cavity walls. The data do not show the minimum thickness in absolute terms but the minimum thickness brick or block available for the stated fire resistance. It is for this reason that identical thicknesses are shown for a number of fire resistance times.

The behaviour of a new type of perforated brick developed at the Building Research Station has also been examined by the author.[5] These bricks have rectangular through cavities, with cavity walls 8–10 mm in thickness. Unplastered walls were found to be susceptible to severe damage by cracking of webs and spalling of face layers, but with plaster finish fire resistance of up to four hours was possible. The higher periods of fire resistance required the use of lightweight plasters.

Harmarthy[6] has studied the fire resistance of concrete block walls, primarily to develop a mathematical model for predicting heat transfer. A number of wall constructions of dense and lightweight concrete blocks were examined, their thermal properties determined and numerical relationships evolved to express the flow of heat from one side to the other. One of the most useful developments was the concept of 'layered thicknesses' (Figure 10.2) which allows a hollow block of different shapes to be reduced to a corresponding layered arrangement for predicting heat transmission. The application of the technique to practical situations has been explained by Allen and Harmarthy.[7] On the basis of thermal data the time for the temperature on the unexposed face to reach the limiting value is calculated for a solid wall of the same thickness and then for a two-layer configuration. An equivalent time is then computed depending upon the ratio between the solid and the hollow parts of the block. The calculations are based on dry materials

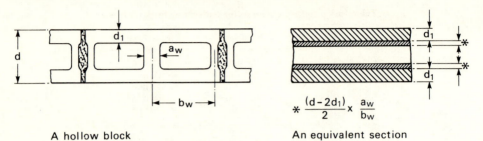

A hollow block   An equivalent section

Figure 10.2   Layered transformation of hollow blocks.

and the effect of moisture can be included by adjusting the value obtained to allow for the increased heat capacity of the section.

This technique does not give any indication of the loadbearing capacity of walls after heating. It has been assumed that in practice walls fail to meet the insulation criterion before they become structurally unstable, and this may be the case with walls made from blocks which are more than 150 mm in thickness.

Byrne[8] has reported results of tests in Australia in which the effect of load and slenderness ratio were examined on walls made of $290 \times 90 \times 90$ mm clay bricks. By constructing walls of 2.1, 2.4, 2.7 and 3.0 m height it was possible to alter the slenderness ratio between 17.5 and 25.0. Loads varying from 12.5% to 125% of values permitted by the design codes were used with 2.4 m high walls and from 17.5% to 125% for the 3.0 m walls. Fourteen samples were tested to failure in times varying from 27 to 220 minutes. Figure 10.3 shows the effect of slenderness ratio and Figure 10.4 that of test load variation.

The 90 mm brick walls in Figure 10.3 were all tested at loads equal to 50% of the permissible load. Walls with a larger slenderness ratio have a smaller permissible load, but despite this the slenderness ratio is a critical factor in determining the collapse time. Slenderness ratios of 20 or more lead to a virtually linear reduction in fire resistance, and at lower values there is a disproportionate increase. Slender walls will be more prone to buckling and consequently reach the critical stage earlier.

The effect of loading on the fire resistance of 90 mm walls appears to be more complex. With high slenderness ratio, failure occurs within a narrow band of time irrespective of the load. With lower slenderness ratios the minimum fire resistance was obtained with 50% load, but at other loads the fire resistance bore no direct relationship to the value of the load. It would seem that loads higher than 50% may have had a beneficial effect by providing a restraining effect on the buckling of the wall. No data are available for other thicknesses and hence it is not possible to predict if similar behaviour is likely to be expected from thicker walls.

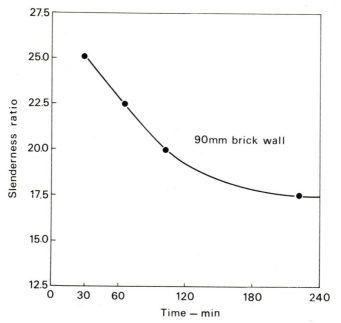

Figure 10.3   Effect of slenderness ratio on fire resistance.

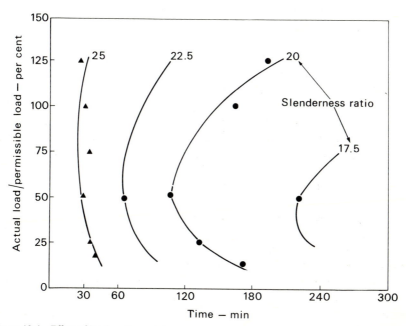

Figure 10.4   Effect of load on fire resistance.

Fisher[9] has reported a number of fire resistance tests on walls made with the currently available British bricks, viz. flettons, calculon and perforated. Flettons and perforated bricks were 105 mm wide, one of the perforated bricks with three holes had 90% solid material, flettons were 85% solid and the other perforated ones about 80% solid. One of the bricks had rectangular slots and the rest round holes of varying sizes. The calculon bricks were

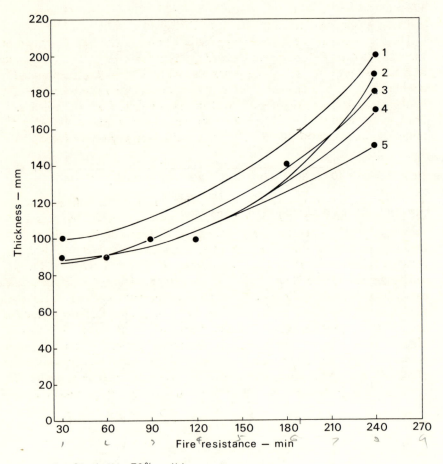

1   Claybrick 70% solid
2   Solid dense concrete bricks/blocks
3   Aerated concrete blocks
4   Claybrick solid
5   Lightweight concrete solid blocks

Figure 10.5   Fire resistance of masonry walls.

Table 10.4   Fire resistance of brick walls

Type	Width	Fire resistance
Fletton	105 mm	120 min
Calculon	178 mm	360 min
Perforated	105 mm	120 min

178 mm wide, 86 % solid with a double frog in the central part. Loads on the walls were calculated in accordance with CP 111.[10]

The tests were not performed to the failure point in all cases. Only two of the walls collapsed during heating, and in other cases tests were terminated at predetermined times. In some cases, the walls were loaded to failure after cooling, and in such cases the failure loads were at least five times the test loads, indicating a virtual recovery of initial strength. Only the perforated brick with rectangular slot did not perform as well as others—it failed at 65 minutes. Fire resistance obtained by other walls were as given in Table 10.4.

10.3 Design

The brief description of research on masonry constructions indicates that as yet no calculation methods have been developed to predict their structural stability at high temperatures. Most designers make use of the tabulated data in codes or regulations to ensure that walls will be acceptable for fire resistance. Data used are of the type included in CP 121: Part 1: 1973 which separate single leaf solid walls, walls made with hollow bricks or blocks and cavity walls. Figure 10.5 gives an indication of the relationship between wall thickness and fire resistance for walls up to 3 m in height. For low periods of fire resistance there is little difference between various types of bricks or blocks but for three or four hours' fire resistance lightweight concrete offers advantages. Data on hollow block walls are not extensive. In all cases the use of plaster finish increases fire resistance: the maximum benefit is gained by the application of a lightweight plaster finish based on vermiculite or perlite

Table 10.5   Thermal properties of dry masonry materials

Material	Density kg/m³	Conductivity W/m °C	Specific heat J/kg °C	Diffusivity m²/h
Siliceous concrete	2080	1.47	879	0.0029
Calcareous concrete	2080	1.45	837	0.003
Expanded slag concrete	1460	0.50	837	0.0015
Expanded clay concrete	1400	0.50	921	0.0013
Clay brick	1450	1.15	1080	0.0026
Aerated concrete	620	0.30	800	0.0022

aggregate. It is important to ensure the compatibility of the plaster with the wall material. A 13 mm coating of lightweight plaster is likely to increase the fire resistance by up to two hours.

One calculation method available at present allows the thermal insulation of the wall to be determined. To use the method it is necessary to have a knowledge of the thermal properties of the wall material as shown in Table 10.5. Allan[7] describes the method for determining the 'critical time', i.e. the time when the temperature of the unexposed face is likely to exceed the limit permitted by the standard fire test criteria.

References

1. CP 121: Part 1: 1973. *Code of Practice for Walling, Part 1: Brick and block masonry.* British Standards Institution, London, 1973.
2. Ingberg, S. H. *Fire tests of brick walls.* Building materials and structures report 143, National Bureau of Standards, United States Department of Commerce, Washington D.C., 1954.
3. Davey, N. L. and Ashton, L. A. *Investigations on building fires, Part V. Fire tests on structural elements.* National Building Studies Research Paper No. 12, HMSO, London, 1953.
4. Malhotra, H. L. *Fire resistance of brick and block walls.* Fire Note No. 6. Ministry of Technology and Fire Offices' Committee Joint Fire Research Organization, HMSO, London, 1966.
5. Malhotra, H. L. Fire resistance of perforated brick walls. *The Builder,* March 9, 1962.
6. Harmathy, T. Z. *Thermal performances of concrete masonry walls in fire. Symposium on fire test performance.* ASTM Technical Publication 464, American Society for Testing & Materials, Philadelphia, USA, 1970.
7. Allan, L. W. and Harmathy, T. Z. Fire endurance of selected concrete masonry walls. *American Concrete Institute Journal,* September, 1972.
8. Byrne, S. M. Fire resistance of loadbearing masonry walls. *Fire Technology.*
9. Fisher, K. *The performance of brickwork in fire resistance tests.* Loadbearing Brickwork Symposium, British Ceramic Society, London, 1980.
10. CP 111: Part 2: 1970. *Structural recommendations for loadbearing walls.* British Standards Institution, London, 1970.
11. Harmathy, T. Z. *Effect of moisture on the fire endurance of building elements. Moisture of materials in relation to fire tests.* STP 385, American Society for Testing and Materials, Philadelphia, 1965.

11   Design of timber elements

11.1 General

Timber is a non-homogeneous material—its exact nature and properties are governed by factors related to its growth and species. A piece of timber may contain faults and discontinuities in its structure, and hence its use will be influenced by the degree to which these affect its structural properties. To assist in quantifying these properties, procedures such as stress grading have been developed. Solid sections of common structural timbers can be used for beams of widths up to 100 mm or for columns up to 150 mm square. For larger sizes the use of laminated sections allows timber to be used to best advantage, as these have more predictable structural properties and can be fabricated to a given length or span. It is therefore common to find solid timber sections employed in the construction of beams for floors, columns and framed walls for use in domestic buildings, offices, schools etc. With few exceptions, for these constructions timber sections are used in conjunction with various lining materials. Timber floors and timber stud walls are therefore examples of composite constructions in which the combined behaviour of timber and the associated materials determines structural behaviour in a fire.

The laminated elements are capable of being used in such a way that they may be directly exposed to fire, hence their behaviour when unprotected is of interest to a design engineer. Such constructions can be assessed on the basis of principles applicable to flexural and compression members of concrete and steel.

As shown in Chapter 6, timber differs in a significant way from the other constructional materials in its response to high temperature. As it is exposed to fire and the surface temperature increases it begins to decompose.[2] However, the charring is progressive, and for many practical situations it is possible to use a specified rate of charring. The thermal conductivity of timber is low, therefore the charred and the uncharred sections are distinctly separated. There is some increase in the temperature of the uncharred section

179

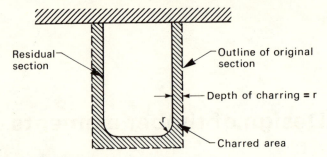

Figure 11.1   Charring of a beam.

leading to a strength reduction of the order of 10%. Consequently one method of determining the fire resistance of a structural timber element is to estimate the amount of charring that will occur, and to compute the ability of the uncharred section to support the imposed loads. If the laminated sections are made by the use of thermosetting resorcinol, phenolic or urea-based adhesives and the laminations are 15 mm or more in thickness, delamination of the section is prevented and it behaves like a solid section. However, the notional rate of charring may have to be increased to allow for slight differences in the charring pattern in the two principle directions, i.e. parallel to, and at right angles to, the laminations. A study on laminated timber columns[1] has shown that each lamination tends to become rounded at exposed edges (Figures 11.1 and 11.2) so that in comparison with a solid section a slightly higher rate may be experienced. In the column tests the charring rates measured in the two directions were 0.76 and 0.65 mm per min.

Box sections using plywood sides, or beams with plywood webs, are unable to withstand the effects of fire for long as the plywood sections are more quickly destroyed. A 6 mm web will burn through in 5 minutes or in a lesser time if attacked from both sides. To prevent premature destruction of the uncharred section due to shrinkage or splintering it is suggested that the exposed sections should have a minimum thickness of 50 mm and sections protected by sheeting materials or other protective materials should not be less than 25 mm in thickness.

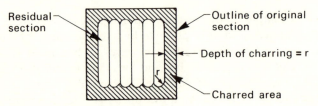

Figure 11.2   Charring of a laminated column.

Table 11.1 Notional rates of charring

Species	Rate of charring per min*	Charring in 30 min	Charring in 60 min
	mm	mm	mm
(a) All structural species listed in Table 1 of CP 112: Part 2: 1971, except those in (b) and (c)	0.66	20	40
(b) Western red cedar	0.83	25	50
(c) Hardwoods as oak, utile, keruing, teak, greenback, jarrah	0.50	15	20

* These rates are appropriate for periods between 15 and 90 minutes and apply to sections not less than 25 mm in thickness.

11.2 Rate of charring

Chapter 6 has already described investigations on the rate of charring of timber. For practical design purposes the Code of Practice[2] on the structural use of timber has proposed charring rates for various species of timber by dividing them into three categories on the basis of their density as shown in Table 11.1. The amount of charring undergone at corners is slightly greater and leads to the corners becoming rounded (Figure 11.1). The shape can be idealized as the sector of a circle with radius $r =$ depth of charring. Hence the additional area lost due to rounding $= 0.215r^2$. Where the residual section is at least 50 mm thick and the exposure does not exceed 30 min the additional loss of timber due to rounding is not significant and can be ignored. With built-up sections all exposed arrises suffer the rounding phenomenon and can acquire the appearance shown in Figure 11.2.

When determining the loss of timber due to charring, account should be taken of protection provided by other parts of the construction. For example, a column partly built into a wall will suffer damage on faces directly exposed or inadequately protected. In a partition with protective skins, charring of studs is at a reduced rate and may be negligible as long as the facings remain intact; the damage is at an increased rate as soon as the facing is destroyed. Figure 11.3 shows some typical examples of the extent of damage that may be caused by charring to various timber elements.

11.3 Flexural members

The performance of simply supported flexural members is computed on the assumption that the uncharred section has to support the service load without reaching the ultimate state of instability. Two approaches are possible depending on the design procedure to be adopted. If fire resistance

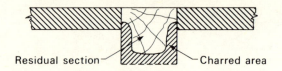

Column built into a fire resisting wall

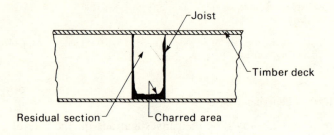

Timber floor with a ceiling

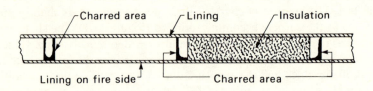

Timber stud wall with one side exposed to fire

Figure 11.3   Damage to timber sections in different situations.

for a certain period is needed, the critical section should be determined and to it added the necessary amount of 'sacrificial' timber which will be consumed by charring. Alternatively, the fire resistance of a given section can be established by determining the amount of timber available for charring and computing the time it will take for it to be consumed.

BS 5268: Part 4: Section 4.1[3] specifies (Clause 5.1.2) that the ultimate state is reached when the tensile stress is 2.25 times the permissible long-term dry stress. If the initial width of the beam is less than 70 mm, a lower critical level of 2.00 times the permissible stress is specified to allow for some reduction in the strength of the uncharred section due to slight rise in its temperature. Example 11.1 shows the application of the principle to a simply supported beam.

Calculations   *Reference*

Example 11.1   Determine the fire resistance of a simply
supported beam of European Redwood spanning 3 m
and supporting a uniformly distributed load of 3 kN/m.

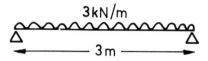

CP 112:
Part 2:
1971
Table 11

European Redwood is species group S2, assume grade 50
timber
Dry stresses (moisture content $\not> 18\%$)
Bending and tension parallel to grain $= f_p = 6.2$ N/mm^2
Max. bending moment under specified load

$$M_a = \frac{3 \times 3 \times 3}{8} = 3.375 \text{ kNm}$$

$$= f_p \times \frac{bd^2}{6}$$

$$\therefore bd^2 = \frac{3.375 \times 6}{6.2} \times 10^6$$

$$= 3\,266\,125 \text{ mm}^3$$

If $b = 75$ mm, $d = 208$ mm
Take $d = 225$ mm

$$f_p = \frac{3.375 \times 6}{75 \times 225 \times 225} \times 10^6 = 5.33 \text{ N/mm}^2$$

Maximum permissible stress $f_p = 6.2 \times 2.25 = 13.95$ N/mm^2

(a) Charring of wood after 30 min exposure $= 20$ mm for each exposed face
.˙. uncharred section $= 205 \times 35$ mm

$$\text{Stress} f_p = \frac{3.375 \times 6 \times 10^6}{35 \times 205 \times 205} = 13.76 \text{ N/mm}^2$$

the beam will provide fire resistance for 30 min.

(b) Alternatively the critical stress $= 13.95$ N/mm^2

$$bd^2 \text{ for the critical section} = \frac{3.375 \times 6 \times 10^6}{13.95}$$

$$= 1.4516129 \times 10^6 \text{ mm}^3$$

By trial and error, reducing d by 5 mm and b by 10 mm steps

when $b = 35$ and $d = 205$ $bd^2 = 1\,470\,875$ mm^3

          $b = 33$ and $d = 204$ $bd^2 = 1\,373\,328$ mm^3

the critical section is $b = 35$ and $d = 205$.

Depth of charring $= 20$ mm, time of charring $= 30.3$ min
As the depth to breadth ratio is 3, the beam ends need to be stiffened, for example by end strutting.

    A number of authors have used the early work on charring of wood and developed empirical relationships to express the fire resistance of rectangular beams. One such relationship has been expressed by Ödeen[4] and Lie[5] for beams exposed on all sides as

$$\frac{U}{\sigma} = \frac{\dfrac{B}{D}}{\dfrac{d}{D} - \left(1 - \dfrac{B}{D}\right)} = \frac{d^2}{D} \tag{11.1}$$

where B and D are the width and the depth of the beam
       d is the critical depth, i.e. the minimum dimension
       σ is the reduction factor for the compressive strength and modulus of elasticity in the uncharred section, and
       U is the ratio between the service load and the collapse load for the original beam $(B \times D)$.

$$t_f = \frac{D - d}{2\beta} \tag{11.2}$$

where t_f is the fire resistance in min, and
       β is the rate of charring in mm/min.

For beams exposed on 3 sides, i.e. with a floor on top, the Equations 11.1 and 11.2 are modified as below:

$$\frac{U}{\sigma} = \frac{\dfrac{B}{D}}{\dfrac{B}{D} - 2\left(1 - \dfrac{d}{D}\right)} = \frac{d^2}{D} \tag{11.3}$$

$$t_f = \frac{D - d}{\beta} \tag{11.4}$$

Graphical or numerical methods are needed to solve these equations, as d, the critical depth, appears as an implicit variable. Lie has developed more approximate formulae, which take into account the rate of charring and depletion of the strength characteristics of uncharred wood due to its temperature rise, and compensate for the loss of additional wood from corners. This relationship can be expressed as follows:

$$\text{four-sided exposure}: t_f = 0.033 \times \frac{\sigma}{\beta} \times U \times B\,(4 - 2B/D) \qquad (11.5)$$

$$\text{three-sided exposure}: t_f = 0.033 \times \frac{\sigma}{\beta} \times U \times B\,(4 - B/D) \qquad (11.6)$$

To allow for the situations where the service loads are considerably less than the loads which develop the allowable bending stresses, the value of the factor U can be increased by 30% if the service load is half that needed to develop the maximum dry stresses in bending according to Table 11 of CP 112.

The increase is proportionately less for loads between 50% and 100%. If $\sigma = 0.87$, $\beta = 0.66$ mm/min, and $U = 2.25$, then applying Equation 11.6 to the beam in Example 11.1, we get

$$t_f = \frac{0.033 \times 0.87 \times 2.25 \times 75}{0.66}\,(4 - 75/225)$$

$$= \frac{0.33 \times 0.87 \times 2.25 \times 75 \times 3.66}{0.66} = 28.5 \text{ min.}$$

This value is slightly lower than that obtained in Example 11.1, where σ was assumed to be 1.0.

11.4 Compression members

A compression member if fully exposed on all four sides can suffer charring at a slightly higher rate. Rogowski[6] analysed the data from a series of tests on laminated timber columns made with different species of wood and various types of glues, and showed that charring was at a greater rate perpendicular to the laminations than in the parallel direction. The mean charring rates in the two directions were found to be 0.68 and 0.76 mm/min, giving an average charring rate of 0.70 mm/min.

The charring of wood from the outer surface not only decreases the size of the section capable of supporting the applied load but also increases the slenderness ratio thereby increasing the buckling stresses. Whether a column will fail in buckling or compression depends upon its original slenderness ratio and the duration of testing.

If the Euler relationship is applied, the buckling load is given by the expression

$$F_e = \frac{\pi^2 E \cdot A_w}{\lambda^2} \qquad (11.7)$$

where E is the modulus of elasticity, A_w the cross-section of the timber column and λ the slenderness ratio. If the effective length of the column is l, the radius of gyration r and the minimum width D, then

$$\lambda = \frac{l}{r} = \frac{l}{D\sqrt{12}} = \frac{3.464l}{D} \qquad (11.8)$$

If the effective length l represents the theoretical buckling length, the formula can be applied to different end conditions. With fixed end conditions $l = 0.5L$ where L is the actual length, and with pin-ended elements $l = L$.

The Euler relationship, as mentioned in Chapter 7, does not provide an accurate prediction for columns with low slenderness ratios, where the buckling loads indicated are higher than the capability of materials. The relationship can be corrected by the application of the Rankine correction to allow for compressive stresses. For timber columns the relationship can be expressed as

$$F = \frac{A_w \cdot f_c}{1 + a\lambda^2} \qquad (11.9)$$

where f is the load, A_w the area of the column and a the Rankine Constant. The value of a has to be established experimentally for different species of timber. When applying this formula to fire-exposed wood columns it is also necessary to use the value of λ which represents charred section, and f_c should take into account any strength reduction of the uncharred timber.

Lie[5] developed an empirical relationship for laminated timber columns based on their size, loading and the possibility of buckling failure

$$\frac{U}{\sigma_w} \cdot \frac{\dfrac{B}{D}}{\dfrac{d}{D}\left(1 - \dfrac{B}{D}\right)} = \left(\frac{d}{D}\right)^n \qquad (11.10)$$

where U is the relationship between the applied and ultimate loads (i.e. the load factor), σ_w is the reduction in the compressive strength of the uncharred section, B and D are the width and depth of the original section and d is reduced (or critical) depth of the section. n has a value between 1 and 3 depending upon the slenderness ratio: it is equal to 1 for short and 3 for long columns. A simplified relationship has also been developed,

$$t_f = 100fD\,(3 - D/B) \qquad (11.11)$$

t_f is the time at which failure is expected, and f depends upon the level of loading and the slenderness ratio, $f = 1.0$ for columns carrying more than 75% of the permissible load with slenderness ratio of more than 10. Between 50% and 25% loading its value is 1.3 for short (i.e. $\lambda < 10$) and 1.1 for long columns.

Example 11.2 To analyse the performance of four laminated timber columns reported in reference 1.

Column material: European redwood, laminated with casein glue.
Column height $L = 2974$ mm
Effective length $l = 0.5L = 1487$ mm
Permissible dry stress $= 11.00$ N/mm^2 (CP 112: Table 4)
Column design and performance:

Section mm	Slenderness ratio	Stress correction factor	Maximum axial load	Fire resistance
1. 150×150	47.3	0.88	202.3 kN	40 min
2. 230×230	31.5	0.935	492.2 kN	54 min
3. 300×300	23.7	0.95	896.7 kN	67 min
4. 380×380	18.9	0.96	1424.8 kN	77 min

Section properties after fire tests, rate of charring 0.7 mm/min:

Section mm	Area mm^2	Slenderness ratio
1. 94×94	8 836	54.8
2. 154×154	23 716	33.4
3. 206×206	42 436	35.0
4. 272×272	73 984	18.9

According to Euler's buckling formula

$$F_e = \frac{\pi^2 E A_w}{\lambda^2}$$

CP 112 gives the modulus of elasticity at minimum as 4500 N/mm^2. Using this the following buckling loads are obtained in comparison with the actual failure loads.

Specimen no.	Estimated failure load kN	Actual failure kN
1	130	202
2	348	492
3	624	897
4	1088	1425

It is obvious that the failure loads are being underestimated. The Rankine constant

$$a = \frac{f_c}{\pi^2 E}$$

CP 112 suggests that the failure compressive stresses can be taken to be equal to twice the design stresses; this gives the value of f_c as $11.03 \times 2 = 22.06 \, \text{N/mm}^2$. If it is assumed that the strength of the uncharred timber section is reduced by 10% the new value of $f_c = 19.85 \, \text{N/mm}^2$.

$$a = \frac{19.85}{9.89 \times 4500} = 4.46 \times 10^{-4}$$

$$F = \frac{A_w \times f_c}{1 + a\lambda^2}$$

Specimen no.	λ^2	$1 + a\lambda^2$	$A_w \cdot f_c$	F (kN)
1	3025	1.84	175.4	95
2	1156	1.32	470.7	356
3	625	1.17	842.3	719
4	361	1.10	1468.5	1335

With the exception of specimen no. 1, the other estimated loads are higher than shown by assuming the failure in buckling alone. The fire resistance of the columns can also be obtained by using the relationship in Equation 11.11.

$$t_f = 100f \cdot D \, (3 - D/B)$$

as $D = B$ (dimensions in metres)

$$t_f = 200f \cdot D$$

$f = 1.0$ for column with $\lambda > 10$ and carrying more than 75% of the permissible load.

Specimen no.	Section size mm	Test duration	t_f
1	150×150	40 min	30 min
2	230×230	54 min	46 min
3	300×300	67 min	60 min
4	380×380	77 min	76 min

Table 11.2 compares the computed results with those obtained experimentally. All methods underestimate considerably the performance of the smallest section but the simple Euler formula even for the largest section gave values 24% below the experimental data. Rankine's correction improves the

Table 11.2 Comparisons of experimental and estimated data

Experimental failure load kN	Experimental failure load min	Euler		Rankine		Lie	
		Estimate	Error	Estimate	Error	Estimate	Error
202	40	130	-36%	95	-53%	30	-25%
492	54	348	-30%	356	-28%	46	-15%
897	67	824	-30%	719	-20%	60	-11%
1425	77	1088	-24%	1335	-6%	76	-1%

performance of larger section to acceptable variability, but the prediction of the smallest section column underestimates the performance by 50%. Lie's relationship, which is empirically derived, has given the best estimates.

Some data have also been obtained to show the effect of shape and reduction in the service load. Figure 11.4 shows the modification factor which can be used for loads varying between 100% and 25% of the maximum permissible and for rectangular shapes having B/D ratios between 1 and 4. Figure 11.5 shows the application of the load factor to columns varying in size between 100 and 400 mm square. It is suggested that the fire resistance of wood columns in this range can be estimated by the use of the empirical relationships in Equations 11.5 or 11.6 and by the appropriate application of the modification factor from Figure 11.4.

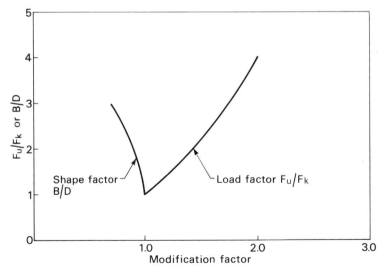

Figure 11.4 Modification factor for different loads and shapes.

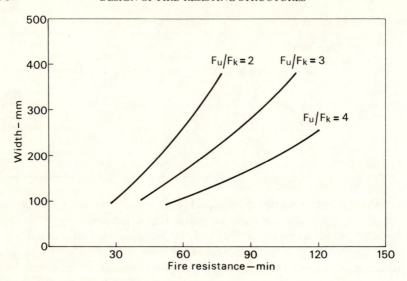

Figure 11.5   Fire resistance of laminated timber columns.

11.5 Timber floors

No computational techniques have been developed so far to predict the behaviour of timber floors which are covered with a deck and protected by a ceiling underneath. In the simple case of floor without a ceiling the performance of the joists can be calculated as shown in Example 11.1. However it is also necessary to ensure that adequate resistance to fire penetration is provided by the decking and this can be estimated by the use of the data on the rate of charring in Table 11.1 provided at least 10 mm of undamaged section is retained at the end of the heating period. However with timber decking the weak area is the joint between adjacent panels, which if of plane edge type will provide little resistance to fire penetration. Tongued and grooved joints are superior but still do not have the same resistance to flame penetration as solid wood. For example, a well-made tongued and grooved joint in a 30 mm deck will allow flame penetration to occur in 10 to 15 minutes. The weakness can be overcome by using a deck of two layers spanning in opposite direction so that the joints in the two layers do not coincide.

Floor constructions with a ceiling give improved performance and a well-designed ceiling can allow a timber floor of normal design to provide a fire resistance for 1 hour, and with special provisions for up to 2 hours. The stability of the floor depends upon the size of the joists and the quality of the ceiling whereas its integrity is a function of the ceiling type and the decking.

Two types of ceilings are commonly used, those which are capable of staying in place, such as sodium silicate boards or mineral fibre tiles, and others which have a predictable life, after which they break up, for example, plasterboard. The protection a ceiling provides is a function of the type of material, its thickness, the system of erection and additional protection if any.

Table 11.3   Timber floors—fire resistance

Fire resistance 30 min (modified)

Joists	Flooring	Ceiling
37 mm wide	15 to 21 mm plain edge or t & g	15 mm plaster on timber batten
		12.7 mm plasterboard
		9.5 mm plasterboard plug 5 mm plaster finish (13 mm with p.e. boarding)

Fire resistance 30 min

Joists	Flooring	Ceiling
37 mm wide	21 mm boarding t & g	12.7 mm plasterboard
		9.5 mm plasterboard plus 13 mm sanded or light weight plaster
		9 mm asbestos insulation board
	15 mm boarding t & g	22 mm plasterboard
		9.5 mm plasterboard plus 15 mm sanded plaster or 13 mm lightweight plaster
		9 mm asbestos insulation board

Fire resistance 60 min

Joists	Flooring	Ceiling
27 mm	15/21 mm t & g	Metal lath with 13 mm lightweight plaster
		12 mm asbestos insulation board plus 25 mm mineral fibre insulation
50 mm	15/21 mm t & g	31 mm plasterboard in two layers

Fire resistance 120 min

Joists	Flooring	Ceiling
37/50 mm	15/21 mm t & g	Metal lath with 25 mm lightweight plaster as a suspended ceiling

Table 11.4   Timber walls—fire resistance

Internal, fire resistance 30 min

Stud width mm	Facing	Fixing	Cavity insulation	Surface finish
37	9.5 mm plasterboard	nails at 150 mm	none	10 mm lightweight plaster
	10 mm lightweight plaster	metal lath	none	none
	18 mm plywood or chipboard	nails at 300 mm	none	none
44	9.5 mm plasterboard	nails at 150 mm	none	13 mm gypsum plaster
	12.7 mm plasterboard	nails at 150 mm	none	none
	12 mm asbestos insulating board	nails at 400 mm	none	none

Internal, fire resistance 60 min

37	22 mm gypsum plaster	metal lath	none	none
44	25 mm plasterboard in two or three layers	nails at 150 mm	none	none
	12.7 mm plasterboard	nails at 150 mm	none	13 mm lightweight plaster
	13 mm lightweight plaster	metal lath	none	none

External, fire resistance 30 min

Stud width mm	Internal lining	Fixing	Surface finish
37	12.7 mm plasterboard	nails at 150 mm	10 mm gypsum plastic
	13 mm gypsum plaster	metal lath	none
	10 mm lightweight plaster	metal lath	none
	12 mm asbestos insulating board	nails through 9 mm asbestos fillets	none

External, fire resistance 60 min

37	31 mm multilayer plasterboard	nails at 150 mm	none
	12.9 mm plasterboard	nails at 150 mm	13 mm lightweight plaster
44	9.5 mm plasterboard	nails at 150 mm	13 mm lightweight plaster
	22 mm plywood	nails at 300 mm	none

Timber floors are commonly used in domestic buildings and others where the fire resistance requirements do not exceed 60 minutes. The UK building regulations allow a relaxation on the integrity requirements for floors in one- or two-storey houses, and for a 30-minute fire-resisting floor the integrity criterion need be complied with for only 20 minutes. This is termed a 'modified $\frac{1}{2}$ hour fire resistance'. Table 11.3 gives some typical examples of timber floor constructions which are considered capable of providing 30- and 60-minute fire resistance. Attention needs to be paid to the method of fixing the ceiling, and most manufacturers provide guidance on acceptable techniques.

11.6 Timber walls

Loadbearing timber walls are usually to be found in low rise buildings intended for domestic or office accommodation. Consequently the fire resistance requirements are for 30 or 60 minutes depending upon the use of the wall. Such walls are an essential component of timber-framed housing which though a recent innovation in the UK has been used in North America for many years with great success. The walls consist essentially of a timber stud framework of storey height, 2.8 m or so, in which the uprights are held in place by timber plates at the top and bottom with one or more intermediate stiffeners or noggings. Two common sizes for the studs are 37 mm or 44 mm finished thickness and a depth of at least 100 mm. The spacing is usually 600 mm although sometimes spacing of 450 mm may be employed with the thinner studs.

The loadbearing capacity of such walls is calculated following the recommendations in CP 112.[2] Empirical tables have been drawn up by manufacturers and others to show the fire resistance of various combinations of facing materials and stud sizes. Some typical examples are shown in Table 11.4 of the forms of construction which are commonly employed to provide fire resistance for 30 or 60 minutes. It is assumed that the construction will be exposed to the heating conditions from one side only; in the case of external walls it is the inside face.

The exposed skin or lining, if of suitable material, prevents studs from suffering damage, and if it is capable of remaining in place the charring of wood is by conducted heat and usually limited in extent. Once the facing material is seriously damaged or destroyed timber studs are more directly exposed and will suffer charring at the rates given in Table 11.1. However if the cavity fill of mineral fibres is properly applied, the charring will occur predominantly on one face and thereby prolong the useful life of the construction. For design purposes the essential considerations are the minimum stud dimensions needed to withstand failure, the protection provided by the lining, and the insulation, when present. The fixing of linings in a satisfactory manner is an important consideration and recommendations of manufacturers should be followed. As most internal surfaces of buildings are given a decorative or protective finish, the use of a suitable plaster can enable a substantial improvement to be made in the fire resistance of walls, as Table 11.4 shows.

References

1. Malhotra, H. L. and Rogowski, B. W. F. Fire resistance of laminated timber columns. Symposium No. 3. *Fire and structural use of timber in buildings.* HMSO, London, 1967.
2. *The structural use of timber.* British Standard Code of Practice CP 112: Part 2: 1971. British Standards Institution, London.
3. *The structural use of timber. Part 4: Fire resistance of timber structures. Section 4.1. Method of calculating fire resistance of timber members.* BS 52G8: Part 4: Section 4.1: 1978. BSI, London.
4. Ödeen, K. Fire resistance of glued, laminated timber structure. Symposium No. 3. Ibid.
5. Lie, T. T. *A method for assessing the fire resistance of laminated timber based columns.* DBR Paper No. 718, Division of Building Research, National Research Council of Canada, Ottawa, 1977.
6. Rogowski, B. W. F. Paper No. 4. Charring of timber in fire tests. Symposium No. 3. Ibid.
7. Read, R. E. H. *et al. Guidelines for the construction of fire resisting structural elements.* Building Research Establishment Report, HMSO, 1980.

12 Fire resistance of assemblies

12.1 Introduction

The description given so far of the fire resistance requirements and the method of testing indicates that elements of building construction are treated individually and not as forming part of a composite structural system. This is not due to a considered approach on the part of the specifying and testing authorities but represents the development of the fire resistance test procedure since its early days. In a building various elements are customarily tied together and consequently the structure responds as a composite construction to any external loading condition, transmitting stresses and strains to adjoining members. Such interactions also occur under fire conditions and in general have a beneficial influence on the behaviour of structures in fires. This may be one of the reasons why structural collapse is not a frequent occurrence in building fires which manage to spread and involve large parts of the building. A few severe fires have occurred in reinforced concrete buildings in South America[1] in which fires virtually burnt themselves out as firefighting was quite impossible. The structures withstood the attack with local damage and have since been repaired and re-used.

There are exceptions to this behaviour pattern where structural interactions are unable to develop. The Ronan Point[2] disaster was a good example of this, where the precast elements were inadequately tied together and the failure of one element resulted in progressive collapse of a large part of the multi-storey building.

However, the topic has not been studied in any depth so far in connection with fire behaviour of structures; consequently no precise rules have been developed and only limited concession is made to allow for the interaction of elements in a building. In some simple cases it is possible to demonstrate the beneficial effects and obtain a more economical design.

12.2 Flexural members

Reference has been made in Chapter 7 to the effect of continuity and restraint on the behaviour of flexural members. In a building with *in situ* construction,

195

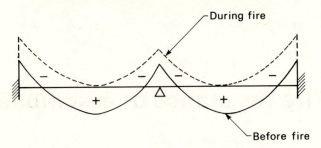

Figure 12.1   Effect of fire on moment distribution in restrained beams.

precast concrete elements tied together, steel sections bolted or welded together the moment diagram (Figure 12.1) shows that the central part of the element is under positive moment but negative moments exist over the supports. When the elements are heated the central span is restrained by the adjacent elements from deflecting, thereby generating an additional negative moment which reduces the mid-span positive moment but increases the moment over the support. This has a beneficial effect as the moment capacity over the support decreases at a lower rate than that at mid-span. Thus the ability of the beams to withstand fire exposure is improved. It should be noted that the shift in the point of contraflexure necessitates that concrete elements have adequate reinforcement in this region.

   Further heating can lead to the formation of a plastic hinge at mid-span. However, if the degree of restraint provided by the adjacent elements is adequate the beam can be transformed into two cantilevers, thereby allowing it to resist collapse as long as moment capacity over the support remains sufficient for the loads. It is also possible for the beam to develop a catenary action so that the whole section is subject to horizontal stresses. With concrete beams of a reasonable depth an arch action can also develop, in which case the role of any reinforcement become less significant. The arch action requires adequate fixity at the supports to other elements having sufficient rigidity to resist lateral thrusts. The development of the arch action is facilitated by the thermal stresses developed when the expansion of the beam is resisted by the supports.

   The thermal stresses are not uniform over the cross-section (Figure 12.2) as the lower parts are heated to higher temperatures, resulting in a negative moment at the centre of the span. It should be noted that thermally induced moments are present when the specimen is hot and restrained, and will reduce in value when the modulus of elasticity is reduced and disappear as the specimen cools down. It is also worth noting that if 100% restraint is provided the thermal stresses may reach dangerously high values. Selvaggio[3]

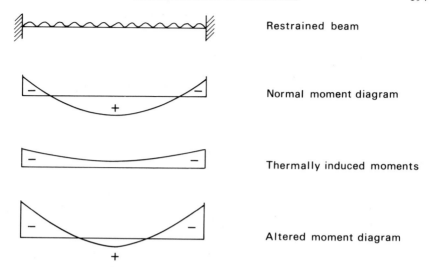

Restrained beam

Normal moment diagram

Thermally induced moments

Altered moment diagram

Figure 12.2   Effect of thermal restraint on moment distribution.

found that with prestressed concrete T-beams restraints between 20% and 80% gave the best results.

The behavioural mode outlined above assumes the heated span is surrounded by unheated spans. If all the spans are heated or if the heated span is the end span the degree of restraint may be considerably reduced. A similar behaviour pattern is expected from concrete slabs, particularly if a heated part is surrounded by cooler parts of equal rigidity. Radial stresses will be generated at the corners, leading to the development of cracks (Figure 12.3) and it will be essential to provide reinforcement in the upper zone to prevent collapse. Partly heated slabs can develop high compressive stresses in the soffit and with certain types of concretes this may lead to damage by spalling.

12.3 Compression members

In a building, the compression members may consist of columns or walls; columns are usual with steel construction and with framed concrete systems. Compression members do not benefit from the existence of restraint as the flexural members do. In a simple system this leads to increase of compressive stresses and a decrease in their fire resistance. With a steel section the temperature distribution over the section is virtually uniform, but in a concrete column the outer layers will be hotter compared to the interior of the section. Consequently the hotter outer layers are subjected to considerably higher compressive stresses compared to the cooler central core. As soon as

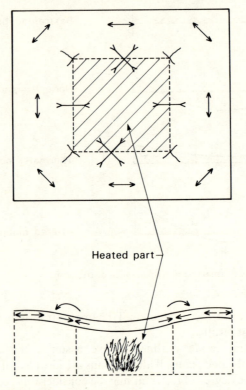

Figure 12.3   Partial heating of a concrete slab.

the material weakens, or cracks are formed, transference of load to the central core takes place. If the degree of vertical restraint is not excessive some relaxation of thermal stresses may occur due to creep effects, thereby preventing the premature failure of the column.

Few columns are subject to pure compression in practice and often in framed constructions the expansion of the horizontal member will generate bending moments in the column. The shape of the moment diagram will depend upon the fixity at the ends. Very few columns in use have pin-jointed ends, and most in practice are able to develop some moment resistance at the base.

12.4 Composite system

The simplest form of a composite system is a beam and column assembly. If the beam is simply supported, it is able to deform without any constraint, and its behaviour will be as predicted in Chapter 8 or 9 depending upon the

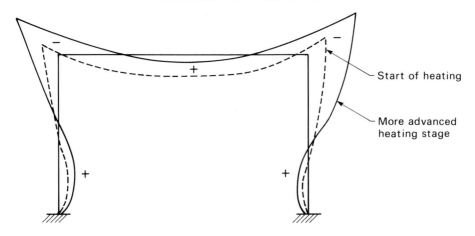

Figure 12.4   Effect of heating on moment distribution in a beam/column assembly.

material of construction. In practice it is rare to find a complete lack of interaction; even frictional resistance at supports and the closeness of adjacent elements can develop restraining forces. In tests on a steel framed roofing system where the beams had been bolted to column tops as means of retention and designed as simply supported elements, it was found that sufficient interaction was developed to increase the temperature at which collapse occurred from the nominal 550°C to about 800°C.

Figure 12.4 shows the effect of restraint provided by the column on the moment distribution in the beam and the bending moment induced in the column. The column section has therefore to be designed to be able to resist such bending moments. A special case of this system occurs with steel portal frames. These have been studied and it is suggested[4] that with properly fixed bases, progressive collapse of the rafter can occur without dislodging the columns even when the rafter is not protected, providing the fire attack is not too severe. Initially, the expansion of the rafter will cause a slight outward movement of the uprights. As soon as the first hinges are formed (Figure 12.5) the rafter will behave like a 2- or 3-pinned arch and will begin to collapse, deflecting downwards. As it loses stiffness it will sag and behave like a catenary. The columns move to the vertical position, and if protected retain the major part of their rigidity. With fixed-base systems, the rafters can collapse completely without causing damage to the columns. With pin-ended columns collapse is possible, but if a degree of fixity exists, an equilibrium stage may be reached when the columns have deflected inwards by a slight amount.

An analytical model has been developed to calculate the overturning

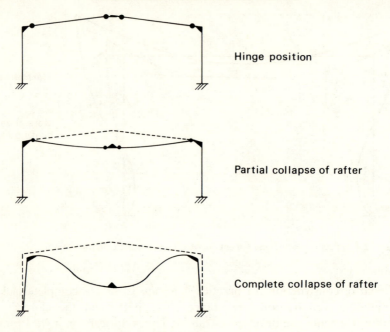

Figure 12.5   Collapse pattern for a steel portal frame.

moment, M_B, at the base of the column. If it is assumed that hinges have been formed in the middle of the rafter and close to the haunches, then

$$M_B = H \cdot Y + W_1 X_1 + W_2 X_2 + M_1$$

M_B is the turning moment at the base
$H \cdot Y$ is a moment due to horizontal thrust at the top of column
$W_1 X_1 / W_2 X_2$ are moments caused by the roof loading, and
M_1 is the moment on the hinge near the haunch.

Most portals are used for single-storey industrial buildings having a light roof construction which is not designed to resist collapse in case of a fire. As the roofing fails, the fire is vented leading to lowering of temperature in the building and a reduction of load on the rafter. The variation of the overturning moment with time is shown in Figure 12.6, indicating that the maximum moment occurs when the hinges are formed and decreases with the sagging and weakening of the rafters.

Portal frames of reinforced concrete will also behave well in a fire. The rafters are unlikely to suffer damage to the same extent as the steel section, and therefore induce higher bending moment in the columns. Adequate reinforcement is needed on the outside face to resist the bending moment

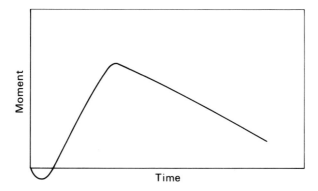

Figure 12.6   Overturning moment in a portal frame column.

induced by the expansion of the rafter. In the case of wood portals, the additional moments in the columns will be nominal, the columns are likely to remain upright and collapse of the rafter section is unlikely to bring down the columns.

Columns may be supporting slabs in a building and can be subjected to severe horizontal stresses if the expansion allowances are inadequate. In a four-storey concrete building in the United States[5] fire in the upper floor led to the shear failure of columns. The slab was about 220 m long (Figure 12.7) without an expansion joint, and expanded nearly 1 m in the course of the fire. This induced large horizontal thrusts at the top of columns leading to the collapse of the column heads near the ends of the slab. Shear failure of columns has also been reported in other fires[6] where no allowance has been made for the expansion of the floor slabs. Masonry walls also suffer in fires when either floor slabs or beams or frames butt tightly against them and have no expansion allowance. It has been suggested that concrete floor slabs should be provided with expansion joint equal to $l/600$, where l is the distance between expansion joints or the slab end and the expansion joint. It is also important the joints are not too large, otherwise fire can penetrate through gaps with inadequate sealing. It is suggested that the maximum width of each joint is not more than 25 mm, i.e. joints are provided at intervals not exceeding 15 m.

12.5 Multi-storey frames

In a multi-storey building a fire is likely to attack only a part of the structure, particularly where good compartmentation is provided. Sullivan[7] has carried out an analytical study of a seven-storey building with five bays on each floor,

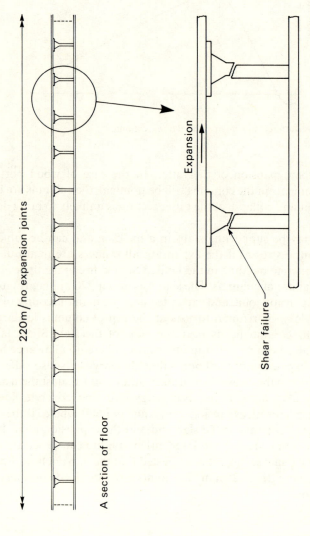

Figure 12.7 Expansion of slab causes shear failure of columns.

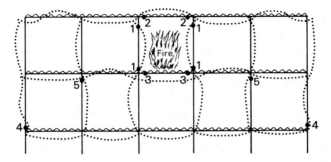

1···5 sequences of hinge formation

Figure 12.8 Deformation and hinge formation in a frame structure.

assuming fire to attack a specified compartment. Figure 12.8 shows the sequences of plastic hinges being formed, initially in the columns, followed by the floors forming the boundaries of the fire compartment. However, the next hinge (no. 4) was not formed in the adjacent compartment, but at the boundary of the building, followed by others in another nearby column. This assumption has been confirmed in fires where cracking of elements well removed from the initial seat of the fire has been observed.

The deformation pattern of beams and columns depends upon the stiffness of the members and the rigidity of joints. Figure 12.9 shows if the beams are

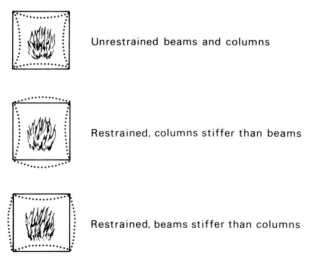

Unrestrained beams and columns

Restrained, columns stiffer than beams

Restrained, beams stiffer than columns

Figure 12.9 Effect of stiffness on deformation.

simply supported, beams and columns will deform towards the fire. With rigid joints and columns stiffer than beams, the less stiff beams deform away from the fire. This is reversed when the columns are less stiff than the beams, and as a result they deform away from the fire. This illustrates that standard fire tests will not necessarily reproduce the deformation pattern that may occur in a building on fire. However, fire test data can be used in an analytical model of the actual building. The need for research activity in this area has been recognized by many institutes and studies are in hand to provide data on which to base a realistic approach for predicting the behaviour of a complete building in case of a fire.

References

1. Malhotra, H. L. *Some noteworthy fires in concrete structures.* Proceedings of the Eighth Congress, Fédération Internationale de la Préconstrainte, London, May, 1978. Cement and Concrete Association, Slough, England.
2. *Report of the inquiry into the collapse of flats at Ronan Point.* Ministry of Housing and Local Government, HMSO, London, 1968.
3. Selvaggis, S. L. and Carlson, C. C. *Restraint in fire tests of concrete floors and roofs.* ASTM STP 422. American Society of Testing and Materials, Philadelphia, USA.
4. *The behaviour of steel portal frames in boundary conditions.* CONSTRADO (The Constructional Steel Research and Development Organization, Croydon CR9 3H), London, April, 1980.
5. Bressler, B. *Fire protection of modern buildings. Engineering response to new problems.* Department of Civil Engineering, North Carolina State University, Raleigh, North Carolina, USA, April, 1976.
6. *Fire resistance of concrete structures.* Report of the joint committee of the Institution of Structural Engineers and the Concrete Society, August, 1975, Institution of Structural Engineers, London.
7. Sullivan, P. J. E. Computer model of a fire in building structures. *Fire Prevention Science and Technology* No. 7, November, 1973.

13 Repairability of fire-damaged structures

13.1 Introduction

There has been a tendency in the past to replace structures damaged in fires, particularly in buildings where the insurance cover would enable such reconstruction to be financed. An exception to this attitude occurred during and following the 1940–45 period when the wartime shortage of building materials and manpower necessitated maximum use of material resources. The Building Research Station issued a number of technical notes[1-4] giving guidance on the assessment of damage and repair techniques for concrete and steel structural elements. These wartime studies were based on early work on the properties of material at the Building Research Station and an examination of damaged buildings. As soon as the supply of building materials again became plentiful, interest in repairability diminished and it was not until the early part of 1970 that there was renewed interest in the subject. An impetus was provided by the concern of building owners in the commercial section over delays in the erection of replacement structures. An example of a concrete-framed building used as a department store has been quoted by Green[5] who showed that reinstatement was preferable to demolition and rebuilding owing to the reduced capital cost and savings resulting from earlier occupation of the building. In 1969 a technical committee was set up by the Concrete Society to examine ways and means of assessing fire damage and repairing damaged concrete buildings. Its report[6] dealt in detail with the assessment of damage after a fire and provided data on repair using gunite. It intends to examine other repair techniques as well. More recently the British Steel Corporation has also entered the field and provided data[7] to assist engineers in the repair of steel-framed buildings. Similar data have not so far been provided for wood or masonry structures but some of the general principles can be used when considering structures made of these materials.

The first impression when visiting a scene of fire is usually not very favourable. The debris, smoke, smell, and water dripping from various areas can evoke the subjective reaction that the building is beyond repair. However, it is necessary to make a thorough appraisal as soon as it is possible to get into the building and examine various materials and structural elements. Attempts should be made to find if design details for the building are available, preferably before inspecting the damaged structure. This is frequently not the case and some assumptions may have to be made of the design principles used, based on the age of the building.

The main steps to be taken when considering the suitability of a building for repair after a fire are

(1) assessment of fire severity
(2) assessment of damage
(3) feasibility of repair, and
(4) the repair technique.

If it is decided to carry out the repair, it will then be necessary for the designer to plan a scheme for reconstruction. It is necessary to remember that both the local authority and the insurance company will require assurance that the repaired building possesses the necessary fire resistance and is able to satisfy other requirements as if it was a new structure built for the same purpose.

13.2 Assessment of fire severity

If the first inspection shows that the building is not totally damaged or has suffered serious damage in one part only, an assessment needs to be made of the fire severity so that the amount of damage can be quantified. One of the main differences between standard fire resistance tests and fires in buildings is that real fires do not have a uniform intensity throughout the building and may have reached different peaks in different parts. It may therefore be necessary to divide the building into zones, horizontally as well as vertically, and make a fire severity assessment for each zone.

Three approaches are feasible for making such assessments. Firstly, the fire reports, usually prepared by the brigade, will indicate the times of start and finish, the effort required to control the fire and any other problems experienced. Whilst this does not enable a quantified assessment to be made, it allows a qualitative judgement as to whether the fire was small or large, more or less damaging, of long or short duration and whether particular areas had higher temperatures than others.

The second, complementary, approach is to examine the debris to study damage to different types of materials. This will allow a judgement to be made on the maximum temperatures achieved in different parts, and with some

Table 13.1 Melting and softening temperature of some common metals

Material	Characteristic	Temperature (°C)
Lead	Melting	300–350
Glass	Softening	600
	Melting	850
Aluminium	Melting	660
Brass	Melting	800–900
Copper	Melting	1080
Mild steel	Melting	1400

materials an idea of equivalent fire severity can be obtained. Buildings usually contain a range of metallic and non-metallic materials, each of which has a different temperature at which it suffers physical or chemical damage. Table 13.1 shows the softening and melting temperatures of some common materials to be found in buildings. Softening and melting of metals is a reliable indicator that certain temperatures have been exceeded. However, if a particular metal is found to be present in molten form it only means that temperatures capable of causing it to melt were exceeded: there is no direct indication as to how high the actual temperatures were and for how long they persisted.

One of the most useful materials for estimating equivalent fire severity is wood. As explained in Chapter 6, for all practical purposes wood can be assumed to char at a consistent rate in the standard furnace tests. If it is possible to find a reasonably substantial piece of wood, 50 mm or more in thickness, which has been exposed to the fire without being shielded or damaged by the falling debris, the depth of charring should be measured at one or more points. From the average depth of charring it will be possible to establish the equivalent fire severity, i.e. the duration of exposure in the furnace test which would have led to a similar degree of damage. Attention should be paid to the species of wood and the nature of the fire load (see Chapter 6). Care is also needed to ensure that the samples were present in a typical position; those at higher levels in a room for instance would have been exposed to more severe conditions compared to ones near the floor.

The third method available is based on the technique for determining equivalent fire resistance described in Chapter 5. If data are available on the nature of the building and the fire load it is then possible to calculate the fire severity assuming an uninterrupted burning regime. Estimations have to be made for each and every compartment or floor, depending upon the layout of the building. The following information is needed in order to make such estimations:

(1) *Size of the compartment*—i.e. floor area and height in order to calculate the total exposed surfaces.

(2) *Size of openings*—this generally means window size and any doors which may have let the air into the fire zone.

(3) The *fire load*, i.e. the total amount of combustible materials, although such information is unlikely to be available with any degree of accuracy. If the description of contents is available, an assumption can be made on fire load density. If no information is available at all, an assumption can be made on the basis of the use to which the building was being put.

(4) The *nature of the construction*, i.e. the compartment boundaries, if Equation 5.3 from Chapter 5 is being used for calculating fire severity.

The author has used this method in examining the behaviour of a few selected concrete buildings in fire.[8] Some of the incidents considered had occurred in other countries, some years previously, and consequently difficulty was experienced in obtaining reliable data on the fire load. Assumptions had to be made on the reported usage of buildings, e.g. office type accommodation or a manufacturing plant etc. However, if a building can be examined soon after the incident it should be possible to obtain more reliable data on the fire load from the owners or occupiers of the building.

In practice it will be found that the assessment of fire severity requires the use of all three approaches to obtain confirmation.

13.3 Assessment of damage

After data have been obtained to allow an assessment to be made of fire severity, assessment of damage can be started. The building should be cleared of debris so that it is possible to inspect the structure closely. Buildings may be divided into three categories, which will be useful particularly when dealing with large or multi-storey constructions: (a) damaged beyond repair, (b) repairable damage, and (c) no damage. Decision on parts of the structure irreparably damaged is not difficult to arrive at. Collapse or excessive deformation is apparent and the construction, if not collapsed, has an unstable appearance. Concrete beams or slabs will be sagging badly and might be seriously cracked, and the columns might have buckled or show shear cracks. Steel columns and beams will be twisted, and with wood constructions cracking or splitting may have developed, and some of the sections may have charred right through.

Similarly, decision concerning part of the structure *not* damaged is also relatively easy. Smoke marking may need to be cleared to see if any cracking has developed. If the structure has deformation within limits permitted by the codes for normal design, and is free of cracking, spalling or other damage, it can be assumed to be undamaged. In case of doubt, loading tests can be carried out and deformation measured to check if this is within predictable limits for the design of the structure.

Assessment of repairable damage is comparatively more difficult and requires close examination of each structural element. Data are needed on the residual properties of materials involved. Some of these have already been discussed in Chapter 6, some will be described in this section. It is often necessary to check the residual material properties by taking samples or by non-destructive means where this is feasible.

13.4 Concrete

The initial visual inspection of a concrete structure should try to establish the occurrence of spalling and its seriousness. Corners of beams and columns are particularly prone but often the soffits of floors also suffer damage by spalling. Its effects are not significant if the damage is restricted to arrises without exposure of the main reinforcement. The exposure of links or supplementary reinforcement in the concrete cover is less serious, or if only a few surface patches have blown off the soffit of a floor. If extensive spalling has taken place and fire has continued for some time before being brought under control the elements need to be carefully examined for weakened reinforcement or relaxation of prestress.

Together with spalling, note should be made of any cracking in slabs, beams or columns. Fire cracks in the tensile zone are not critical but transverse cracks on top of slabs, horizontal cracks in beams or shear cracks in columns indicate a reduction of loadbearing capacity even if no collapse has occurred.

It is necessary to establish the residual strength of concrete and reinforcement, and for this purpose a number of techniques are available. One method consists of establishing the temperature rise within the section and the associated residual strength. Bessey[9] noted that when concrete is heated a change in colour occurs which is irreversible and allows an estimation to be made of the temperature to which it has been heated. The normal grey colour of ordinary Portland cement concrete changes to light pink at around 300°C, and the colour darkens attaining maximum intensity at about 600°C when it begins to lighten, becoming whitish grey by 800°C. The colour change is caused by the transformation of ferric compounds, present in sand as impurities, to ferric oxide. The intensity of colour depends upon the level of impurity and colour changes have been noticed even with limestone aggregate concrete when river sand is used as the fine aggregate. The Concrete Society report[6] has used this as the main basis for establishing the suitability of concrete for re-use by suggesting that if no colour change occurs (Figure 13.1), the residual strength is not significantly reduced. The loss in

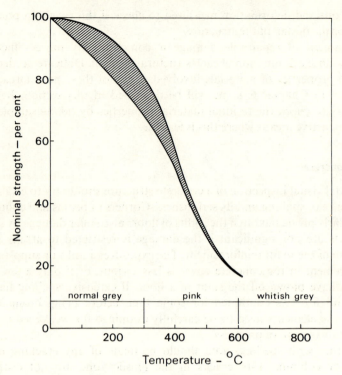

Figure 13.1   Strength vs. colour changes for a typical dense concrete.

strength is expressed as a 'fire damage factor'; at 300°C the value of the factor is between 0.7 and 0.8, i.e. 70% to 80% of the initial strength is retained. To determine whether any colour change has occurred a piece of concrete from the damaged section should be removed, including the exposed surface, to establish the spectrum of colour changes. The furthest depth at which pink colour can be seen may be taken as the boundary for the 300°C isotherm. This can also be used as an indirect method of determining equivalent fire severity. With a slab, a beam or a column it should be possible to use the temperature curves in Figures 8.3 and 8.4 in Chapter 8 to determine the duration of heating in a furnace which would have led to the 300°C isotherm occurring at that depth.

With beams and slabs, concrete in the tensile zone is likely to suffer first, and even when this is weakened, concrete in the compression zone is likely to retain most of its strength. However, with continuous constructions the compression zone is directly exposed and needs to be examined carefully. In a similar way concrete on the outside of a column suffers more damage and so reduces the compressive strength of the column. The residual strength of concrete in slabs, sometimes in beams and columns as well, can also be determined by cutting cores. These will also provide a means of checking colour changes.

Non-destructive techniques using ultrasonic wave transmitters have been tried but find a limited application. The main problem with such devices is that at best they provide comparative data and some knowledge of the original material is needed as a reference. Ultrasonic methods examine the whole thickness of the concrete element and therefore assess the average properties. Another technique which is being investigated consists of subjecting a small sample of the cement mortar to thermoluminescence examination. It is claimed that silica undergoes progressive changes in its structure at high temperatures and these can be detected and the temperature established.

The next step is to determine the condition of reinforcement in beams and slabs. Figure 6.26 in Chapter 6 showed that reinforcing bars of mild steel and high strength alloy steels regain almost all of their original strength even when heated to 600°C. The cold worked deformed bars suffer some loss of strength at this temperature. If steel has been raised to higher temperatures, additional reinforcement in the repaired structure will need to be provided.

With prestressing wires or tendons, two important differences have to be taken into account: firstly, the greater loss of strength (Figure 6.26), and secondly the relaxation of prestressing wires leading to permanent deformation and loss of prestress. Hence temperature estimation for prestressing wires and tendons is more important and an estimation of residual ultimate strength and proportionality limit is necessary to judge the re-usability of the structure.

There is no simple method of estimating the strength of reinforcement or prestressing steel if an assessment of its maximum temperature is not possible. In case of doubt, it would be necessary to remove a small sample and subject it to mechanical tests.

The Concrete Society report[6] suggests that each element should have a damage classification[1] on the basis of assessment. Four classes are suggested:

Class 1—superficial damage, no serious repair needed
Class 2—some surface damage without affecting structural strength
Class 3—substantial damage, repair and partial replacement needed
Class 4—serious damage, replacement or considerable repair essential.

Available repair techniques include making good any slight loss of concrete (for Class 1 and 2 damage) by the use of plaster or spray materials such as gunite. In case of more serious damage (Class 3) all damaged concrete has to be removed and some reinforcement added, and then either new concrete applied, or, in some cases, guniting used. In either case care is needed to ensure that the old and the new materials provide a composite construction.

With Class 4, construction elements either have to be replaced or reconstructed *in situ*, or in some cases duplicate elements provided beside the damaged ones to take over their function.

13.5 Steel

There are two types of steel structures which an engineer may be asked to consider for repair. One is the single-storey factory type construction comprising a framework in which the roof members may be unprotected and the stanchion may be shielded or provided with partial protection. The other is a steel-frame multi-storey building, which may include concrete and steel members acting together, e.g. concrete floor slabs or steel decks with concrete topping. Such constructions are usually fully protected with steel sections provided with individual insulation or other protection to allow a specified fire resistance to be provided.

After a fire the single-storey factory type construction usually gives the appearance of severe damage. The roof may be damaged, unprotected purlins badly twisted, and often the rafters may have become dislodged. In a severe fire the whole framework would have suffered distortion. Such constructions have however been used for schools and assembly buildings where protective ceiling constructions when applied properly protect the framework so that the damage is negligible. Multi-storey framed constructions are also capable of successfully resisting fire damage provided the protection remains in place and is effective.

In the construction of steel-framed buildings mild steel rolled sections were customarily used, but nowadays a choice is available between mild steel (Grade 43A) and alloy steel (Grade 50B) materials. Smith *et al.*[7] have examined the properties of these steels and shown that when heated up to 500°C the reduced strength is not less than the applied stress, and the modulus of elasticity is unlikely to decrease by more than up to 600°C. Consequently if steel sections have been protected such that their temperature is not expected to exceed 550°C, failure of the structure is unlikely. Tests on protected steel beams of Grade 43A and 50B material have shown that at collapse the lower flange temperature may be as high as 700°C, whereas with unprotected steel temperature reaches about 650°C before collapse. The lower failure temperature of unprotected steel is probably due to a more rapid rate of heating, as shown in Chapter 6. Residual strength tests have shown that in both cases if no collapse or instability has occurred, on cooling to ambient conditions the structure will regain most of its original strength (Figure 13.2). Some old buildings may contain cast iron columns. Tests have shown that its strength is reduced by 50% at about 600°C, after which the strength loss is more rapid than that of mild steel.

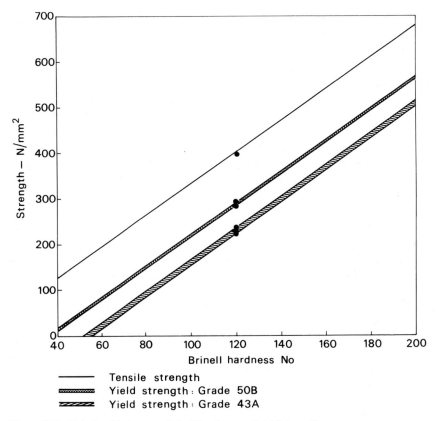

Figure 13.2   Relationship between Brinell hardness and steel strength.

Smith[7] has also examined steel sections from buildings involved in fires and obtained the data shown in Table 13.2.

It is clear from these examples that in many cases, little if any permanent loss of strength would be expected from steel structures which have not collapsed in the fire. Rigidity of the structure will have a significant influence on its deformation during a fire. If a steel section is completely restrained,

Table 13.2   Residual strength (N/mm^2) of mild steel

Reference	Actual strength		Specified strength	
	Yield	Tensile	Yield	Tensile
Fire A	242–307	444–469	247	432–510
Fire B	235–258	359–422	247	432–510
Fire test	262–382	396–478	255	430–510

expansion resulting from a temperature rise of 100°C can lead to high enough stresses for the section to yield. However, in practice structures have a great deal of flexibility and even where end fixity is provided it may exert no more than 50–60% restraint. Deformation of the section will also lead to a reduction in thermally induced stresses.

There is no visual method of determining if a fire-exposed steel section has lost any strength. A simple non-destructive method is available using an indentation technique customarily employed for determining hardness. Portable apparatus is available to establish the Brinell hardness number which is directly related to the tensile strength of steel (Figure 13.2). There is also a direct relationship between the tensile strength and yield strength for each type of steel so that it is possible to determine yield strength from the hardness number.

Bolts and riveted connections are likely to be subjected to additional stresses generated by the expansion of the sections. In most cases the fixings are subjected to shear stresses, though in some cases tensile stresses may also be imposed. Mild steel bolts have been progressively replaced with friction grip devices. As these are heavily stressed, they are likely to have lower reserves of strength and can therefore suffer plastic deformation.

After the fire a visual examination of the structure should be carried out. If all the steel is badly twisted and distorted, the structure is beyond repair. If the structure is not obviously deformed, and (if protected) the protection though damaged has stayed in place, then either the structure is not at all damaged or only slightly affected. Hardness tests on exposed and unexposed sections will show if any permanent loss in strength has occurred. In case of doubt it is possible to take small samples and subject them to mechanical tests. All bolted and riveted connections should be examined to see if any distortion has occurred, and in case of doubt these should be replaced. Weakening of welded junctions will be shown by the formation of cracks.

Structures where partial damage has occurred require a more careful examination as a decision has to be taken whether the individual elements can be retained or need to be replaced. If an element is distorted, provided the distortion is not significant (e.g. in the range up to $\frac{1}{360}$ of the span for beams) it can be re-used. If the deflection is greater than this limit it may be still possible to straighten the elements. Next, the temperature to which the sections were raised should be estimated, using the approaches previously described. If the temperature has not exceeded 600°C, it may be assumed that no significant loss in strength has occurred. With suitably insulated elements, if the insulation has been retained in position it is unlikely that steel temperatures would have exceeded 600°C.

Where it is not possible to estimate the steel temperature it will become necessary to carry out the mechanical test. Either the hardness test with a portable instrument may be undertaken or alternatively a small section cut for tests in the laboratory. If the strength is within permissible limits, the section should be re-used; if not, consideration should be given to providing additional reinforcement. In all cases it is desirable to replace all bolts, particularly those of the friction grip type. With protected sections which have not suffered deterioration necessitating replacement, the protection should be completely replaced to ensure that the sections are fully protected to the required level.

13.6 Masonry

The most common use of masonry is in the construction of walls, of factories, storage buildings, offices and high rise blocks. It can be used in conjunction with concrete, steel or wood structures. Masonry constructions are usually able to withstand exposure to fires without much distress. However, problems arise when other elements, particularly beams and slabs, undergo expansion. A steel beam over a span of 20 m can expand as much as 150 mm when its temperature is raised by 500°C. This can cause deformation of a masonry wall against which it may be bearing, and as a consequence a hole may be punched in the wall or it may be pushed out. Similar behaviour patterns can occur also with concrete elements; there are examples of concrete frames toppling gable walls in industrial buildings during the course of a fire. Where timber elements are present such problems do not occur.

If a masonry wall has not collapsed in a fire, shows no pronounced deformation, and has little cracking, it can be considered for re-use. Where the wall has seriously deformed or badly cracked there is no alternative but to demolish and replace it. If the wall has been provided with piers it may be necessary to replace only the damaged parts between piers.

With cavity construction it may be that only one leaf suffers serious damage, in which case, provided the ties are still in good condition, the damaged leaf may be replaced. Plastic ties are likely to be suspect if they have softened. Similarly, if plastic foam has been used as a cavity fill for insulation purposes, it will be necessary to examine if the foam has been destroyed. Cavity temperatures in excess of 200°C would affect most plastic foam materials. Walls which have a plastic finish will usually suffer minimal heat damage although the plaster finish may have to be replaced.

Aerated concrete blocks and those made with limestone aggregate can suffer damage which makes the blocks friable on the exposed face. Such damage can be easily established by a pointed tool. If the wall is non-structural and the damage is not too deep, the friable material may be rendered and a coating of lightweight plaster applied.

Walls of monolithic concrete or precast panels will be susceptible to the same type of damage as the concrete material of which they are constructed. If no serious spalling has occurred, and the pink coloration is near the surface only, the wall can be considered for re-use. Where cracking has occurred it will be safer to replace the wall. No data are available on the residual strength of clay bricks but observations in fire tests, and data on relevant tests[10] show that very little permanent loss in the strength of materials occurs after it has cooled down to ambient temperatures. If the brick walls are otherwise satisfactory their loadbearing capability can be assumed to be satisfactory.

13.7 Timber

Timber is used for the construction of floors in domestic type buildings, as well as for partitions and walls. Its use in industrial buildings is limited to members made from laminated sections as this is the only reliable way to obtain large sections with well-defined structural properties. Laminated beams, columns and arches are used in industrial buildings with spans of 50 m or more. For purposes of repairability two types of situations have to be considered:

(1) solid timber joisted floors, timber faced walls and timber roof trusses used in domestic type buildings in association with board facings such as plasterboard; and
(2) industrial use of larger sections, often without any protection.

As pointed out in Chapter 6, the charred section of timber has no strength and the uncharred part can be assumed to retain at least 90% of its initial properties. Hence the first objective when examining a timber construction is to establish how much of the section is uncharred. Charred material can be scraped off and the dimensions of the uncharred section established. Where elements have board facings or ceilings and these are not completely destroyed they should be carefully removed to see if the timber behind is damaged. If no damage can be seen, the element is re-usable after the facing material is replaced.

Where partial damage has occurred, it is possible to build up the section to the required size by glueing or nailing additional timber sections to achieve the initial structural capability, although often it will be more economical to replace the damaged parts completely rather than spend time in attaching additional timber.

With large elements, beams or arches, serious damage is likely to occur with sections having thin webs. Tenning[11] has reported a fire in an aircraft hangar structure with arches of 54 m span, 1.4 m deep, webs 70 mm thick and flanges 112 mm thick. Due to failure of the web the arches collapsed prematurely. In a case like this repairability is not a possibility, but where laminated sections have been used, and the fire has not been very severe, repair may be possible.

With prefabricated timber elements, metallic fixings or connectors are often used and these could be affected more seriously than the timber section, as they would transmit more heat to the interior and cause localized charring adjacent to the metallic parts. This can weaken the fixing provided by sheet metal connectors and loosen the fixity of bolted joints.

It is more than likely that in practice only the lightly affected timber elements will be re-used. If the damage is more than slight it may be economically preferable to replace the damaged elements by new ones.

References

1. Building Research, Repair of damaged buildings, Note No. 2: *Repair of structural steelwork damaged by fire.* Issued by the Building Research Station, Department of Scientific and Industrial Research, Garston, Watford, 1944.
2. Ibid, Note No. 18. *Reinforced concrete columns damaged by fire.*
3. Ibid, Note No. 19. *The repair of solid concrete and hollow-tile floors damaged by fire.*
4. Ibid, Note No. 24. *Repair of damaged buildings: reinforced concrete beams damaged by fire.*
5. Green, J. K. Technical study: reinstatement of concrete structures after fire. *The Architects' Journal,* Vol. 141, No. 2, 14 July, 1971, pp. 93–99; No. 3, 21 July, 1971, pp. 151–155.
6. *Assessment of fire-damaged concrete structures and repair by gunite.* Concrete Society Technical Report No. 15, Concrete Society, London, 1978.
7. Smith, C. I. *et al. The reinstatement of fire-damaged steel-framed structures.* Report No. T/RS/1195/15/80/C. Teesside Laboratories. British Steel Corporation, March, 1980.
8. Malhotra, H. L. *Some noteworthy fires in concrete structures.* Proceedings of the Eighth Congress, Fédération Internationale de la Préconstrainte. London, May, 1978. Cement and Concrete Association, Slough, England.
9. Bessey, G. E. *Investigations on building fires: Part 2. The visible changes in concrete or mortar exposed to high temperatures.* National Building Studies Technical Paper No. 4, HMSO, London, 1950.
10. Fisher, K. *The performance of brickwork in fire resistance tests.* Loadbearing Brickwork Symposium, British Ceramic Society, London, November, 1980.
11. Tenning, K. *Glued laminated timber beams, fire tests and experience in practice.* Symposium No. 3: Fire and structural use of timber in buildings, Joint Fire Research Organization, HMSO, London, 1967.

14 Future developments

The book has dealt with the basis of structural fire protection and the design of structural elements to provide the fire resistance which is demanded of buildings by the controlling authorities. It has been shown that the subject is far from fully developed, that more work needs to be carried out by research institutes to advance the design of structures to the same level as the structural design under normal use conditions. The subject has intentionally been treated in a simple manner to provide an introduction for those who have no previous knowledge of the topic. There are more advanced papers available but these have not as yet reached the stage where they could be regarded as acceptable techniques by the designers as well as controlling authorities. Future developments in this field are expected to follow a number of parallel routes to lead to the universal applications of designing for fire resistance.

Research on the behaviour of structural elements of composite nature is in progress in a number of institutes in different countries. The main purpose is to study the behaviour pattern of complex systems present in buildings and to establish mathematical models of the structure as it undergoes exposure to high temperatures. This is considered to be an essential step towards predicting the behaviour of a complete structure or a building when it is subjected to a fire. Fire resistance requirements should apply to complete buildings and whilst the performance of individual elements is an important consideration for this purpose it cannot be regarded as the sole objective of design or control. Moreover the controlling authorities would need to have sufficient confidence in any model of behaviour proposed for this purpose before agreeing to its acceptability.

An important input into this work concerns data on appropriate material properties. Chapter 6 showed how the existing knowledge is based primarily on properties investigated using the classical steady state approach. Its direct application to fire problems has been questioned, and the need established for obtaining data under transient conditions similar to those experienced in fires. RILEM is particularly active in this field and is collecting data from various international sources for the use of engineering and design organizations. It expects to examine the possibility of standardizing test procedures for this purpose.

The fire resistance test procedure also needs some improvements, particularly to enable the test data to be used for computational purposes. The sole purpose of fire tests should not be to allow products or systems to be classified. It should also provide information which enables the use of that construction in a variety of different ways in buildings. The first need in this connection is to develop appropriate techniques for interpolation and extrapolation of data from tests. A committee of the International Standards Organization is actively engaged on this task. Work is also in hand to improve the test procedure to enable the use of techniques with better repeatability. An important new development will concern the measurement of heat flux received by the construction under test. The main advantage of such data is to enable an accurate assessment to be made of heat transfer through the construction. At present, only an estimate is possible of the actual surface temperature on the heated side of a construction. With heat flux measurements the data will more reliably indicate the surface temperature. In the long run, this approach will improve uniformity in the method of controlling exposure conditions for different constructions.

The level of protection required for different buildings, and consequently the fire resistance needs, are generally arbitrarily determined or relationships are used which are not always capable of analysis. It is apparent that requirements should be related to the expected risk of fire in the building and the consequential hazard to the structure. This needs to take into account not only a more realistic assessment of the fire load, but also the probability of it becoming involved and creating predictable hazardous conditions. The use of a probabilistic approach in defining fire hazard is receiving attention at present and the use of limit state concepts is being investigated. This should allow a truer assessment to be made of the fire which might occur in a building and permit the designers to provide optimum design solutions. An optimum solution should combine economy with acceptable level of reliability. The present systems, followed in most countries, have an 'overkill' approach with certain types of occupancies and yet can allow hazardous conditions to exist in others. The final system would need to be simple enough to be included in the normal building codes and regulations.

It is essential that future requirements for structural fire protection and the methods of compliance attach due importance to various components of the system and provide a facility for interaction amongst these as well as with other parts of the fire protection system. A systems approach is needed to develop a technically sound scheme for this purpose, and it may be useful to consider the use of a decision to 'calibrate' the scheme. The two essential aspects are the needs or requirements, and the methods of compliance.

The needs should be based on a study of the following:

1. An assessment of risk
2. Fire load and other features which influence fire severity
3. Estimation of fire severity
4. Level of protection necessary for life safety
5. Level of protection necessary for property protection.

The methods of compliance should consider interaction amongst the following:

1. Fire resistance of building structure
2. Fire detection and warning systems
3. Provision of sprinklers
4. Fire fighting and control facilities.

The provision of fire resistance of the building structure should allow alternative approaches to the designer:

1. Standard tests where appropriate
2. Use of tabulated data or empirical relationships
3. Computation of fire resistance on the basis of test data or from a knowledge of material properties, structural design and heat exposure conditions.

For such a scheme to operate in a sound manner, it will be necessary to introduce reliability concepts into the analytical procedures.

With the advent of computing machines in design offices and their use for normal design purposes, it is inevitable that similar techniques should be considered for fire design. The analytical approach of the type suggested in this book forms an essential step towards such a system. The development of analytical programmes for different components of structural fire protection should be a real possibility in the next decade or two. This would enable both the controlling authorities and the designers to arrive at solutions which represent the optimum level of protection commensurate with the risk, but this position is likely to have to be gradually achieved.

Additional bibliography

Chapter 2

British Standard 4422: Part 2: 1971. *The glossary of terms associated with fire.* Part 2—*Building material and structures.* British Standards Institution, London, 1971.

Ingberg, S. H. *NFPA Quarterly*, Vol. 22 (1928). National Fire Protection Association, USA, 1928.

Harmathy, T. Z. Relationship between fire resistance and fire tolerance. *Fire and Materials*, Vol. 2, No. 4, 1978.

Malhotra, H. L. *Fire resistance versus fire behaviour.* CIB Symposium on systems approach to fire safety in buildings, Tsukuba, Japan, August, 1979.

Chapter 3

Fire grading of buildings. Part 1. General principles and structural precautions. Ministry of Works, Post-War Building Studies, No. 20, HMSO, London, 1946.

Ingberg, S. H. Tests of the severity of building fires. *NFPA Quarterly*, Vol. 22 (1), 43–61, 1928.

Malhotra, H. L. *Determination of flame spread and fire resistance.* Current Paper CP 72/74, Building Research Establishment, Fire Research Institute, Borehamwood, Herts, July, 1974.

Rules of the Fire Officers' Committee for the Construction of Buildings, Grades 1 and 2. Fire Officers' Committee, London, January, 1978.

Chapter 4

Fang, J. B. and Scott, J. T. *Heat transfer in furnaces for CIB cooperative program and heat balance analysis of wall furnace.* National Bureau of Standards, US Department of Commerce, NBS Report IR 75-794, November, 1975.

Paulson, O. *On heat transfer in fire test furnaces.* Laboratoriet for Varne ag Klimateknik, Denmarks Tekniske Højskola, Copenhagen, 1975.

Chapter 5

Harmathy, T. Z. Relationship between fire resistance and fire tolerance. *Fire and Materials*, Vol. 2, No. 4, 154–162, 1978.

Harmathy, T. Z. The possibility of characterising the severity of fires by a single parameter. *Fire and Materials*, Vol. 4, No. 2, 71–76, 1980.

Chapter 6

FIP/CEB report on methods of assessment of the fire resistance of concrete structural members. Cement and Concrete Association, Slough, 1978.

Meyer-Ottens, C. *The behaviour of concrete structural elements in fires—spalling of normal concrete elements under fire stress, causes and preventive measures.* Library Translation No. 2058, Building Research Establishment, Garston, Herts, 1978.

Schneider, U. *et al.* Strength losses of concrete at high temperatures, cause and effects. *Mitteilungsblatt für die amtliche Materialprüfung Niede-sodren*, Jahrg. 18/19, Claustral-Zellerfeld, 1979.

221

Appendix 1

List of standards for fire resistance tests

1. International   ISO 834 (1975). *Fire resistance tests, elements of building construction.*
2. Australia   AS 1530. *Methods of fire tests on building materials and structures. Part 4. Fire resistance test of structures.*
3. Belgium   NBN 713-020. *Fire resistance of building components.*
4. Canada   ULC-S101-1977. *Standard methods of fire endurance tests of building construction and materials.*
5. Denmark   DS 1051. *Fire resistance tests of structures.*
6. France   Arrêté du Janvier 1959—*Determining the fire resistance of elements of structure.*
7. Germany   DIN 4102—Part 2. *Definitions, requirements and testing of structures.*
8. Italy   Circ. Min. Interno del 14 Settembre 1961 n. 91. *Safety standard for protection against fire in steel buildings.*
9. Netherlands   NEN 1076—Chapter D. *Fire resistance.*
10. Sweden   SIS 02 48 20/2. *Fire tests on structures and components.*
11. Scandinavia   NT FIRE 005. *Fire tests on structures and components.*
12. UK   BS 476: Part 8. *Test methods and criteria for the fire resistance of elements of building construction.*
13. USA   ASTM—E119 and UL-263. *Fire tests of building construction and materials.*

Appendix 2

Reference to publications on the design of structural elements for fire resistance

1. *Design and detailing of concrete structures for fire resistance.* The Institution of Structural Engineers, Belgrave Street, London SW1.
2. Code of Practice for the structural use of timber: BS 5268: Part 4: Section 4.1: 1978. *Method of calculating fire resistance of timber members.* British Standards Institution, London.
3. *Guidelines for the construction of fire resisting structural elements.* R. E. H. Read, F. C. Adams and G. M. E. Cooke, HMSO, 1980.
4. *Méthode de prévision par la calcul du comportement au feu des structures en béton.* Document Technique Unifié (DTU) No. 208, April, 1980. Centre Scientifique et Technique du Bâtiment, Paris.
5. Méthode de prévision par la calcul du comportement au feu des structures en acier. Construction Metallique Nr 4, Dec 1976. Centre Technique Industriel de la Construction Metallique, Paris.
6. *Fire engineering design of steel structures.* O. Pettersson, S.-E. Magnusson and J. Thor. Swedish Institute of Steel Construction, Stockholm, 1976.
7. *European recommendations for the calculation of fire resistance of loadbearing steel elements and structural assemblies exposed to fire.* European Convention for Structural Steelwork.
8. Guide for determining the fire endurance of concrete elements: Report of ACI Committee 216. *Concrete International*, February, 1981.

Index